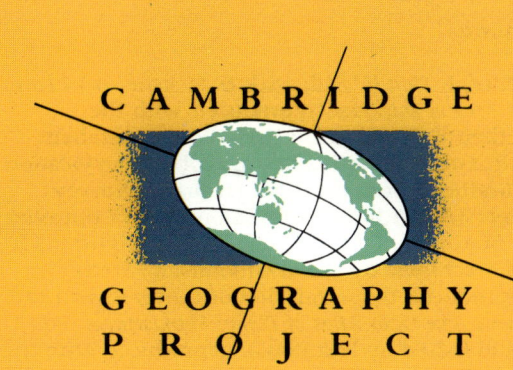

GREEN PIECES

David Lambert

Lecturer in Geography, Institute of Education, University of London

Published by the Press Syndicate of the University of Cambridge
The Pitt Building, Trumpington Street, Cambridge CB2 1RP
40 West 20th Street, New York, NY 10011–4211, USA
10 Stamford Road, Oakleigh, Victoria 3166, Australia

© Cambridge University Press 1992

First published 1992

Printed in Great Britain at the University Press, Cambridge

A catalogue record for this book is available from the British Library.

ISBN 0 521 40991 8

Designed and produced by The Pen and Ink Book Company Limited, Huntingdon, Cambridgeshire

Illustrated by Harvey Brazier, David Graham, Maureen and Gordon Gray, Andrew Greenwood, David Parkins, Rodney Sutton and John York.

Cover artwork by Jane Smith

Acknowledgements

p.8 from Bob Geldof, *Is That It?* Sidgwick & Jackson; p.17 from V.S. Naipaul, *An Area of Darkness,* reproduced with the permission of Aitken & Stone Ltd; pp.65–67 from Graham Swift, *Waterland,* © Graham Swift 1983, available from Picador; Map on p.74 reproduced from the 1990 Ordnance Survey 1:50 000 map sheet 180 with the permission of the Controller of Her Majesty's Stationery Office © Crown Copyright; p.130 'The Marriage of Machines' by Stella Gibbons, © Stella Gibbons 1933 reproduced by permission of Curtis Brown Ltd, London; p.146 from *The Gaia Atlas of Planet Management,* ed. Norman Myers, published by Pan Books, reproduced with the permission of Gaia Books.

Photographs:

J. Allan Cash: p.5, p.30, p.48 Figs.3.5, 3.6, p.57 Fig.3.19, p.58, p.67, p.70, p.78 Figs.4.23 a, b, p.84, p.88 Fig.5.12, p.102 Fig.6.2, p.103 Figs.6.3, 6.4, p.105 Fig.6.8, p.106 Fig.6.9, p.118 Figs.7.2 a, b, c, p.120, p.121, p.123, p.125, p.142, p.143, p.157; Science Photo Library: – Claude Nuridsany and Marie Perennou p.7; – NSIDC p.52 Fig.3.14; – Dr Morley Read p.57 Fig.3.20; – Sinclair Stammers p.78 Fig.4.24; – John Mead p.85 Fig.5.6; – Tom McHugh p.117 bottom left; – Peter Menzel p.89, p.117 bottom right; – Simon Fraser p.149; p.153 (Bitterfeld); Zefa: p.8 Fig.1.4, p.45, p.88 Fig.5.13, p.93, p.110 bottom right, p.117 top, p.137; Steve Scoble: p.8 Fig.1.5, p.9, p.10, p.12, p.13, p.14, p.15; copyright details from The British Library p.14; Susan Griggs Agency: – Mike Andrews p.17; – Nathan Benn p.64; – Nik Wheeler p.106 Fig.6.11; – Andreas Heumann p.110 bottom left and middle; – Leo Touchet p.129 Fig.7.19a; – Martin Rogers p.131; – Victor Englebert p.153 (Yanomami); Sainsburys p.23 Fig.2.1 background, p.26; Impact: – Penny Tweedie p.23 foreground; – Ben Edwards p.59, p.151; – James Fraser p.81 top; – Paul O'Driscoll p.85 Fig.5.8; – Victoria Ivleva p.107; – Piers Cavendish p.146; David Lambert: p.27, p.65, p.73, p.75, p.77, p.79 left; Network: – Silvester Rapho p.28; – Lewis p.101; Betty McAskie: p.38, p.40; Mansell Collection: p.43, p.63; Andy Buck: p.44; Barnaby's Picture Library: p.45, p.48 Fig.3.7, p.92; R.K. Pilsbury: p.52 Fig.3.13; Crown: p.53; The Independent: – Herbie Knott p.61; – Nicholas Turpin p.148; Paul Marriott: p.66, p.79 right; Bruce Coleman: p.81, p.92, p.129 Fig.7.19b; Jeremy Hartley/ WaterAid: p.83; Frank Spooner Pictures: – Saussier p.98; John Massey Stewart: p.105 Fig.6.6; Chris Fairclough: p.106 Fig.6.10, p.118 Fig.7.2d; Jet Propulsion Laboratory: p.145; Press Association: p.153 (Aberfan); British Antarctic Survey: – C.J. Gilbert p.158.

Every effort has been made to reach the copyright holders; the publishers would be pleased to hear from anyone whose rights they have unknowingly infringed.

CONTENTS

UNIT 1
People Working with the Land
Steve Scoble
5

UNIT 2
The Food Business
Betty McAskie and David Lambert
23

UNIT 3
What's the Weather Like Today?
Andy Beaumont
43

UNIT 4
Water Shapes the Land
David Lambert
61

UNIT 5
Water: a Scarce Resource?
Paul Dowgill
81

UNIT 6
Industry and the Environment
Jane Herrington
101

UNIT 7
Disaster Strikes!
Al Tenquist
117

UNIT 8
Consuming the Earth's Resources
David Lambert
137

To the pupils

This book contains eight units. Each one is different. This is because the *themes* change from unit to unit and the *places studied* also change.

The themes and the places are also different from those we meet in Books 1 and 3. For example, in Book 1 Britain, Europe and Africa were featured. In this book there is more emphasis on North America, parts of the old Soviet Union, and India.

As in the other books, each unit is divided up into three Key Questions. In order to answer each one there are plenty of exercises and activities which we hope you enjoy doing. Also, there is much in these books to read on your own, especially under the sections headed 'Setting the scene'.

Why *Green Pieces*?

In this book, the main aim is to investigate how *environments* are used — and sometimes abused — by people. We need to understand from the start that most environments in which people live are *created by themselves*. There is no place left on Earth that is not affected by human action: traces of pesticide are now found even in the ice of Antarctica.

In Units 1 and 2 we examine how we use environments to provide food. Units 3, 4 and 5 then ask questions about parts of the physical environment: the atmosphere, the hydrosphere and landforms. But we never wander too far from the ability of people to change these things — sometimes with disastrous results.

Finally, in Units 6, 7 and 8 we look at the risks we are taking with our environment, as some parts of the world become more and more 'wealthy' as a result of people's industry and technology.

Do we have choices? What does the future hold? What kind of a future do we *want*?

Many people know that a 'green' future is possible, but only if environments are protected and conserved, not exploited and destroyed. This idea is the main theme of this book — and it is why we have called it *Green Pieces*.

David Lambert

People Working with the Land

UNIT 1

1·1 *The magnificent rice terraces of Benaue in the Philippines show clearly how people have carved out land from the mountainside for farming.*

UNIT 1

What do you know?

What was your first reaction when you saw the photograph on page 5? Do you think all the terraces are natural, or were they made by people? Are they recent or very old?

Of course, the mountains were formed by natural forces, but the terraces were cut into the steep slopes nearly 5,000 years ago by the Ifuago people. Their way of farming has remained unchanged to the present day.

You can see the differences in the landscape before and after the terraces were built in the diagrams below.

Benaue

Location:	Benaue, Luzon Island, Philippines
Height:	200–2,900 metres
Climate:	25°C during the year, heavy rainfall for 11 months (more than 50 millimetres)
Vegetation:	Originally tropical forest
Relief:	Mountainous, steep slopes, little flat land

1·2 *The landscape at Benaue before and after terraces were made for farming.*

1 Study the diagrams on this page, and write down the changes that took place when the area was used for farming.

2 Imagine that you lived in Benaue 5,000 years ago. To make the changes that you have just listed you would have to consider the following questions:
▸ Why do I need to farm in this area?
▸ What land can I use for farming?
▸ Why can't all the land be used for growing crops?
▸ What problems might there be living and farming in this area?

As a group, discuss these questions and write down all the answers that your group members give for each one. Keep a record of your answers. Look at them again when you have worked through this unit, to see if you still give the same answers to these questions.

Setting the scene

It will be useful to have an atlas handy as you read this section.

Since prehistoric times people have tried to conquer or work with nature. The main reason for doing this has been to farm the land to provide food for people.

Only 11 per cent of the world's land surface can be used to grow crops or raise animals. To continue to feed the world's population, two things must happen: farms must produce more food, or more land must be used for farming. Sometimes the results of doing either of these things are good, but sometimes they are bad.

The Ifuago people of the Philippines have shown that it is possible to farm successfully even in very difficult environments. One recent traveller to the Philippines described a journey to Benaue as one of the most beautiful but terrifying experiences.

There is a point over halfway through this journey where your breath will be taken away. The bus rounds a bend high up in the mountains, and there below you, stretching away 20 miles into the distance, is the deep jade green of the Chico river valley. The river has cut its way deep into the mountains, and man has carved out of the mountains 'the eighth wonder of the world' – massive rice terraces, dyked with stone, a god-like staircase climbing sometimes 2,000 feet to the peaks and the heavens above. These astonishing terraces, many of them believed to be up to 5,000 years old, have their own natural water supply, but just how the system works is something of a mystery. It is also a mystery how the people of the region have managed to maintain their terraces so perfectly to this day, especially if you consider that if all the terraces were placed side by side they would stretch one-quarter of the way around the world.

Although this is a very effective way of farming in this part of the Philippines, there are some drawbacks, as the writer goes on to explain.

Every available inch of mountainside for miles around has been turned into a giant garden where beans, potatoes, carrots, cabbages and other vegetables are grown and supplied to markets all over Luzon. It is back-breaking work. One family's fields may step down 1,500 feet of near-vertical mountainside.

from 'A Hard Road to Paradise', Quest Magazine, 1990

▶ **Can you suggest some of the difficulties that these families might face?**

However, these are minor problems compared with those faced by some farmers in other parts of the world. Certain types of natural hazard can make farming impossible, such as plant diseases and insects.

1·3 *Plant diseases and insect pests can be a disaster for the farmer. It has been estimated that ½ million locusts can eat as much in one day as 10 elephants, or 2,500 people! A single swarm can contain 40 million locusts . . .*

If the balance of nature is disrupted, there may be severe problems. For example, one of the reasons why famine has struck Africa so many times since the 1970s is that farmers have sometimes misused the land. Bob Geldof, who raised millions of pounds for famine relief through Live Aid, saw this during a trip to Africa.

> The sands of the Sahara are sweeping southwards at the rate of 20 miles a year. Elsewhere, the land is turning to desert through overgrazing and other bad land uses. In Niger we pushed north into the Sahara to examine the lot of a few of the millions of destitute nomads throughout the Sahel where goats and cattle died long ago in a drought so severe that in many places even the camels have been wiped out!
>
> B. Geldof, Is that it? 1986

So events such as droughts – long periods of dry weather – can add to farming problems. But it is mainly the way the land is used that will decide the success or failure of growing crops or raising animals.

1·4 *Overgrazing and erosion have ruined this land in Niger.*

This unit is all about how and why land is used for different types of farming. It also examines how changes in farming take place and how the changes affect people and the natural environment. Finally, we look at the problems of soil erosion and how they might be solved in the future.

The three key questions in this unit are:

▶ How do people in rural south India make a living?

▶ Are farming changes for the best in rural south India?

▶ Should we treat soil like dirt?

▶ How do people in rural south India make a living?

Why do farming types vary in south India?

Southern India is made up of the three states of Karnataka, Tamil Nadu and Kerala. Most of this area has a moist tropical climate and before the area was farmed it had a covering of tropical forest.

This part of India has a monsoon climate, which means that between June and September there is a lot of rain but the rest of the year is dry. Between March and May is the hottest time of the year.

1·5 *Lush tropical forest in Kerala State, where there is plenty of rain and high temperatures.*

The differences in rainfall and temperature and the relief of the land mean that there are different types of farming in different places. There are two main types of farming here:
- *Commercial*: the farmer grows crops for sale, and uses little of what is grown.
- *Subsistence*: the farmer grows most of the food for his or her family to eat.

On some farms, both types of farming are practised.

A wide range of crops can be grown in south India because of the hot, wet climate. Some of the commercial crops were first brought here by European settlers who used the land to grow food. Tea, pepper, rubber and coffee were needed in Europe.

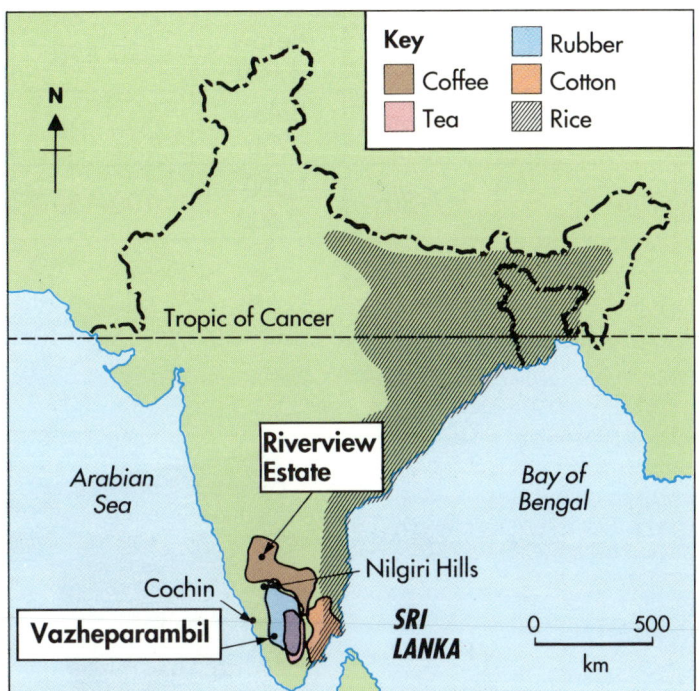

1·6 The main types of farming in south India.

1·7 A young woman picks the tender leaf-tips from a tea bush in the Nilgiri Hills, Kerala State.

Annual rainfall (mm)	400 mm	250 mm	150 mm	100 mm	90 mm
Temperature range (°C)	24–32°C	21–32°C	15–33°C	10–30°C	21–32°C
	A	B	C	D	E

1·8 Cross-section of the states of Kerala and Tamil Nadu, with rainfall, temperature and relief features.

UNIT 1

1 What are **a** subsistence and **b** commercial crops?

2 What do you think are the advantages and disadvantages for a farmer in rural India growing only commercial crops? Write two lists, one headed *advantages*, the other *disadvantages*.

3 Look at the list of crops in the table on the right. Which are **a** commercial crops and **b** subsistence crops?

4 Make a copy of the cross-section on page 9. Look again at the information in the table, and decide which crops are grown in areas A, B, C, D and E of the diagram.

5 Describe the changes in climate and farming from west to east in the cross-section.

The growing conditions needed for different crops.

Name of crop	Growing temp. (°C)	Growing height (m)	Rainfall needed (mm)
Rubber	21–35	Below 200	175–300
Coffee	15–30	300–1,800	100–200
Cotton	21–32	Below 1,000	80–120
Rice	24–32	Below 200	Over 150
Tea	7–30	1,000–2,500	100–150

The tale of two farms – Riverview Estate and Vazheparambil

Farm 1: Riverview Estate

Location: Madapura village, Kodagu District, Karnataka State
Owner: Mr T. Mathews

Mr Mathews.

It's 22 years since I first grew coffee here. My estate covers 80 acres of land and it is mainly planted with arabica coffee bushes in 49 rows. I had to replant them in 1982 at a cost of £5,000, and for three years I earned nothing while they were growing. Now I produce three lorryloads per year. That's about 18 tonnes, and I earn £18,000 per tonne. In New York where they buy and sell coffee the price is £72,000. It's not me who makes the money!

To start with, the coffee bushes are raised in seed beds in the nursery, and after four years they produce ripe red berries along the stem. Most berries are picked between February and June after they have fully ripened in the sun. Too much sun is bad for them, so shade trees protect them from the fierce temperatures. These rosewood trees are so valuable that they are owned by the Indian government.

1·9 *The estate house where Mr Mathews lives. Coffee bushes and shade trees grow on the slopes opposite the house.*

Copy and complete the diagram (right) to show the sequence (stages) of coffee-growing on Mr Mathews' estate. Use the phrases that are underlined in Mr Mathews' statements, and place each one in the correct box.

After being picked the <u>berries are dried for 6–8 days, then put in sacks</u>. The lorry takes the beans to an old English coffee company called Aspinalls and Co. where <u>the beans are blended and then sent overseas</u> from the port of Cochin.

I am not just responsible for coffee, though! I have <u>eight families living on the estate</u>. The men work entirely for me and in return I pay them and provide them with housing. They work from 7.30 am to 4.00 pm and I pay them 15.05 rupees (about 60 pence) for their day's work. During the picking season I need more labour so I <u>hire about 80 casual workers</u>.

STAGE 1	What does Mr Mathews need?
	• shade trees • • • •

STAGE 2	How is the coffee produced?
	• coffee bushes are raised in seed beds in the nursery • • •

STAGE 3	What are the results of growing coffee?
	• three lorryloads per year •

Farm 2: Vazheparambil, 'The land of the plantain trees'

Location: Mallapally village, Kottayam District, Kerala State
Owner: Mr Kuruvilla

My farm has been in the family for over 200 years. I was born here and although it is only a smallholding of 1.2 hectares it is enough to support my family.

My main source of money is from the rubber trees. I have 100 of them and I pay someone 8 rupees (about 25 pence) to 'tap' them each morning. He cuts a channel into the bark and latex runs down the tree and collects in a coconut shell. These are emptied into a clean bucket 2–3 hours after tapping and an acid turns the latex into a rubbery mass. After one hour the rubber is pressed into sheets, then dried on a line outside the house for two days.

There is a saying that you can tell how rich a man is by the number of rubber sheets on his line!

After drying, the rubber is collected and sold to a rubber trader. I produce five sheets of rubber a day. That's 2½ kg. For this I get paid 25 rupees a kilogram. It may not seem a large sum of money, but we save money in other ways.

We produce nearly all the food that we eat. We keep chickens for eggs and meat and cows for milk. We get our water from the local well. Wood for burning, and bananas, mangoes, coconuts, tapioca and pepper are all grown on the farm. I have a young boy – Pushparaja – who comes from the village to help out with the farm work.

Also, my son-in-law works in the Middle East and sends money home. This way we can afford to buy more luxury goods.

UNIT 1

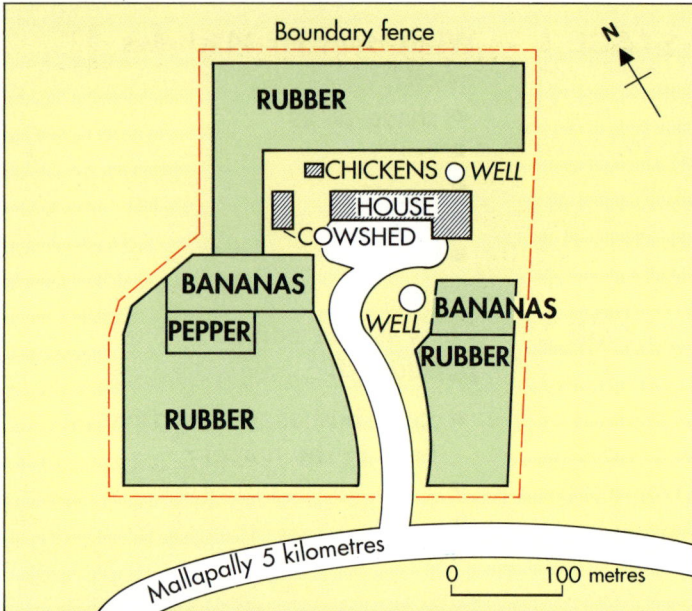

1·10 *Plan of Vazheparambil.*

1·11 *Pushparaja tapping a rubber tree.*

1·12 *Mr Kuruvilla with his grandchildren. Rubber sheets are hanging out to dry on a line. Plantains, sweet potatoes and coconuts ripen in the sun.*

Class activity

Study the information on pages 10–12. Then complete these activities in pairs.

1 Imagine one of you is Mr Mathews and one of you is Mr Kuruvilla.

a If you are Mr Mathews answer these questions:
- Do you think your coffee pickers are paid well for their work?
- What would you say to one of your workers if he or she complained that your wages were too low?
- What are your main problems in growing coffee?
- Who benefits most from the coffee you grow on your estate?

b If you are Mr Kuruvilla, answer these questions:
- What does the name of your farm mean?
- Could you describe how your farm is laid out?
- How do you get rubber from your rubber trees?

2 Contrast the two farms in a table like the one set out below.

Feature	Riverview Estate	Vazheparambil
Size		
Crops		
Labour used		
Income		

3 Who do you think is the 'richer' of the two farmers? Give reasons for your answer.

4 Which farm would you like to live on most? Why?

Are farming changes for the best in rural south India?

To find out about a rural area of south India in more detail we can study Madapura and its surroundings. Madapura is a village in the Kodagu District of Karnataka State. It is in the mountainous area of the Western Ghats.

The area is a picturesque highland of valleys, ravines, peaks and fast-flowing streams. Rising up to 1,900 metres (6,000 ft) on the eastern side of the Ghats, the land is clothed with the lush greenery of forests and coffee estates. The forest cover is broken only by a few cultivated valleys.

This small district alone produces 25 per cent of India's coffee and it is also famous for its oranges, peppers, and a spice called cardamom.

1·14 *The main street of Madapura village. Bicycles are the main form of transport here.*

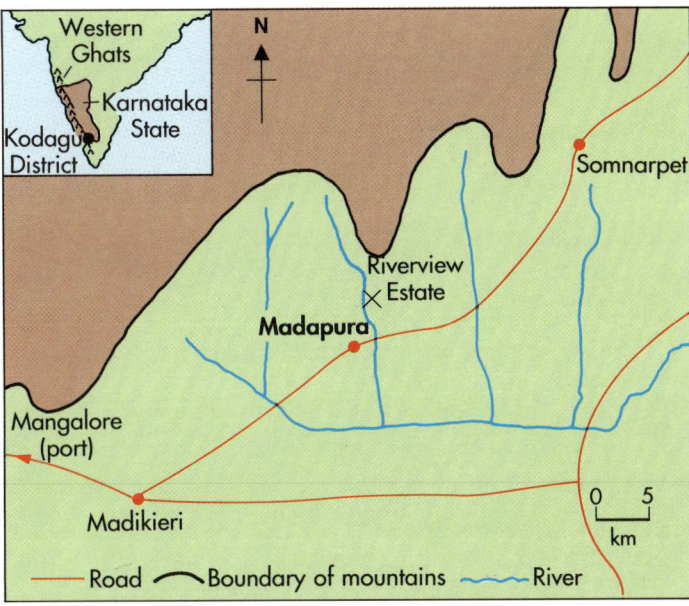

1·13 *The location of Madapura in southern India.*

Look at the map on page 14 of part of the Kodagu District.
1 How can you tell that this area has
a high, steep slopes,
b high rainfall?
2 What types of buildings can be found in and around Madapura (spelt 'Madapur' on the map)?
3 How many coffee estates can you find in the area of the map?

Madapura village, Kodagu District, Karnataka State

Population:	2,738 (male 1,437; female 1,301)	Communications:	post office with phone *pucca* (tarmac) road bus service
Growth rate:	2.2% per year [UK 1%]		
Number of households:	603	Health services:	hospital
Average number of people per household:	4.5 [UK 2.1]	Types of jobs: Farmers:	4%
Water supply:	wells, river and handpumps	Labourers: Industry:	11% 0.5%
Electricity:	for agricultural use only	Farm estate workers: Services:	70% 14.5%
Education:	2 primary schools	Average income:	£86 [UK £6,000]
Literacy:	male: 57% [UK 97%] female: 36% [UK 93%]	Scheduled 'castes' (the poorest class of people) = 19% of population	

Source: Census of India, 1981

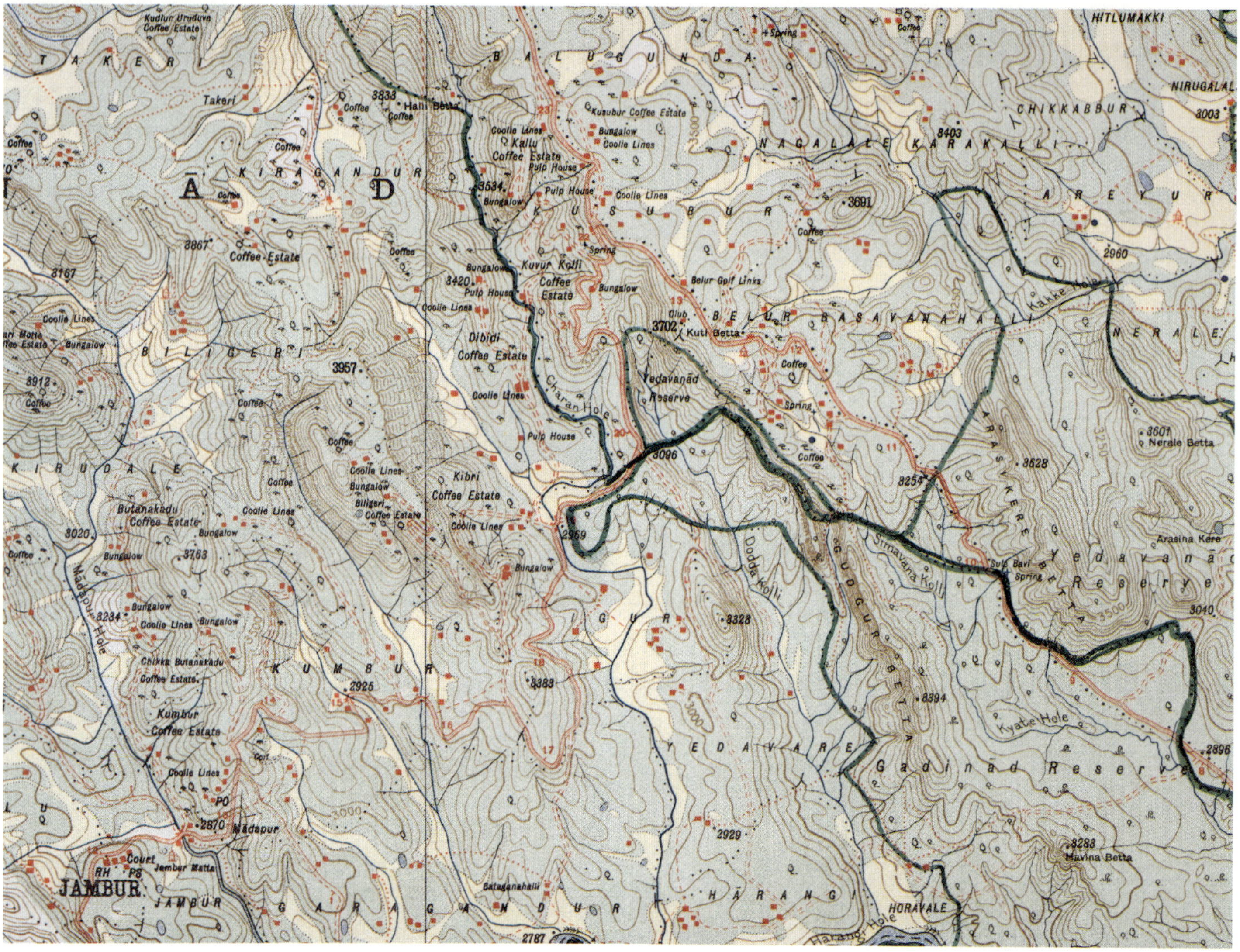

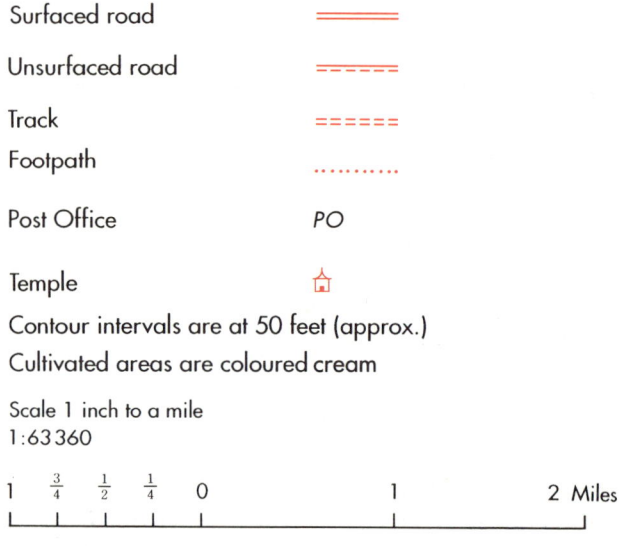

Surfaced road

Unsurfaced road

Track

Footpath

Post Office PO

Temple

Contour intervals are at 50 feet (approx.)

Cultivated areas are coloured cream

Scale 1 inch to a mile
1:63360

1 $\frac{3}{4}$ $\frac{1}{2}$ $\frac{1}{4}$ 0 1 2 Miles

1·15 *Indian Survey map of part of the Kodagu District.*

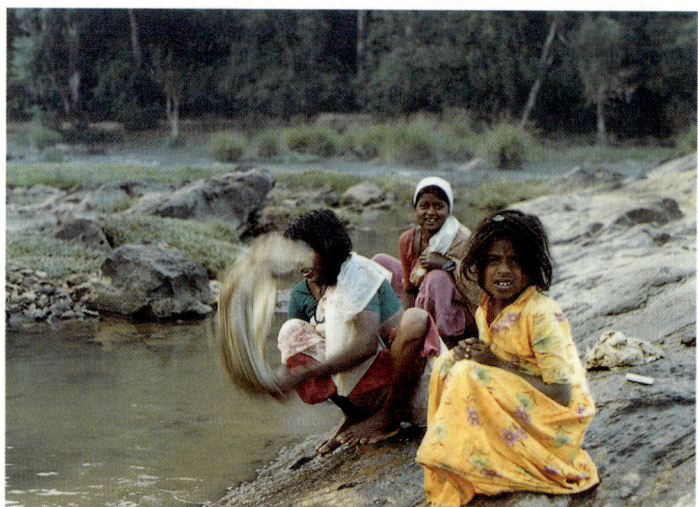

1·16 *Doxie Ferrau gets up at 6 am to help her mother wash clothes in the Madapura river. Later, she goes to the primary school in Madapura.*

1 Draw a copy of the map on page 13.

2 Refer to an atlas, and describe in your own words where Madapura is **a** within India, **b** within Kodagu District.

3 Give two reasons why Madapura is a good place to site a village.

4 Use the descriptions of Kodagu District on page 13 and the map on page 14 to help you draw a picture of the landscape in the area.

5 Look at the photograph of Madapura on page 13 and write a paragraph about the main street. How would you describe the buildings and road? What are the people doing?

6 Use the information in the box on Madapura on page 13, and refer to the photographs, then answer the following:
▸ How are clothes washed in Madapura?
▸ Why do people rely on water from the river?
▸ Draw *either* a bar graph *or* a pie graph to show the types of jobs people do in Madapura.
▸ Which figure tells you that coffee growing is important in Madapura?
▸ Find three pieces of information which show that Madapura is 'economically developing'. (*Remind yourself*: What is an economically developing country?)
▸ A growth rate of 2.2 per cent means that in ten years Madapura's population will be 3,400. What effect will that have on the following:
• water supply
• education
• health
• jobs?

7 If you visited Madapura, what questions would you ask Doxie Ferrau to find out about her way of life? (See the photograph on page 14.)

8 Write a travel article about Madapura village, its people and surroundings, for a young people's magazine or newspaper.

How has farming changed in Madapura?

You have seen that the most important type of activity in the Madapura area is farming. Most workers in the village are coffee-pickers. Why is this? The climate and soil make it suitable to grow coffee, but how did it all start?

In 1854 an English army officer planted the first coffee estate near Madikieri. Soon, more estates were planted with coffee by local farmers and by the Europeans who introduced this new system of farming. The local Kodagu Raja (king) gave permission for the land to be used for coffee cultivation. By 1856, an area of 28,000 hectares was covered by this cash (commercial) crop.

The main food crop of this area is rice, which needs to be grown where there is plenty of water. The fields are rainfed and produce only one crop a year. Not enough rice is produced locally to feed the growing population, so it must be bought from other areas. Clearly, people must rely on growing and selling coffee for wages to pay for their needs.

1·17 *Rich pickings on the coffee estates – but should the natural environment be sacrificed for profit, or protected for the future?*

The new system of farming brought many changes. People moved into the area because there was work here, and the people who originally lived here, and their agricultural methods of farming, have almost disappeared.

Where the land was particularly well suited to coffee growing, areas of forest were removed. Large areas of the natural habitat vanished. The trees provided good cover for tigers, panthers, wild bears, deer, monkeys and elephants. The rugged country, plentiful water and fast-growing vegetation encourage these forest animals, but now they are in danger.

To protect the forest from disappearing altogether, there is now a National Forest Policy. This is designed to preserve the ecological balance, and to stop the soil washing away, which can happen when the forest is removed. It is now illegal to cut timber without permission. Forest reserves have been set up to protect the natural forest area of 138 square kilometres. These are now some of the richest and most valuable natural areas of India.

Gadinale Forest Reserve: A decision-making exercise

Until quite recently coffee growing was in decline in the Madapura area. Imported Brazilian coffee caused prices to fall, and a disease killed thousands of bushes. But in 1945 the Indian Coffee Board raised the prices for coffee, and the number and size of estates grew. Coffee growers started to demand more land. The pie graph shows how the land is used in Kodagu.

Some of the land that the estate owners want to use is forested. The Gadinale Forest Reserve is one such area. Look back to the Indian Survey map on page 14 and see if you can find the reserve (spelt 'Gadinad' on the map). Should it remain a natural tropical forest, or be used for coffee growing?

1 How long has coffee been grown in Kodagu?

2 Give three reasons why it is a good area to grow coffee.

3 Suggest why the local ruler, the Kodagu Raja, allowed the British to grow coffee.

4 How would planting coffee estates change the area?

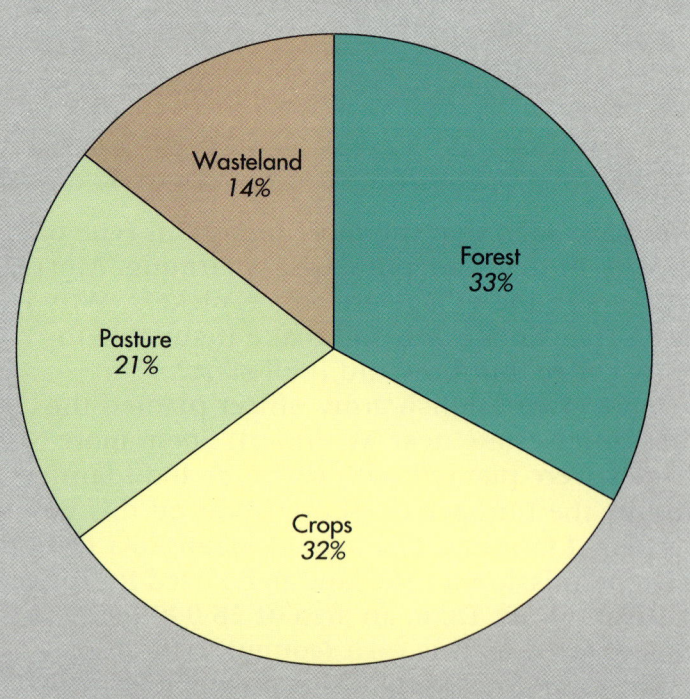

Source: Census of India, 1981

1·18 *How the land is used in Kodagu.*

Should we treat soil like dirt?

In other parts of India there are different problems for farmers. One of these was described by the writer V.S. Naipaul when he visited India for the first time. Farming the soil looked difficult and risky.

It takes between 100 and 400 years to form one centimetre of soil. To build enough soil to form productive land takes 3,000 to 12,000 years. Soil is a country's most valuable possession, but once it is destroyed by *soil erosion* it is gone for ever.

Most soil erosion is caused by the action of rain, running water and wind on bare land. If the soil is unprotected by vegetation and the binding effects of plant roots, raindrops first loosen then wash away soil particles. Dry, unprotected soil can simply blow away.

> When you drive through parts of western and central India you wonder about the teeming millions; settlements are so few and the brown land looks so unfruitful and abandoned. Here wonder was of another sort. The land was flat. The sky was high, blue and utterly without drama; below it everything was diminished. Wherever you looked there was a village, low, dust-blurred, part of the earth and barely rising out of it. Every turbulence of dust betrayed a peasant; and the land was nowhere still.
>
> V. S. Naipaul, An Area of Darkness, 1964

Types of soil erosion

* Water erosion, the commonest type of soil erosion.
* Wind erosion.
* Salinity – salts collect in the soil, forming a hard crust and poisoning all plants.

Causes of soil erosion

* Steep land that is badly farmed – soil is washed away in gullies or sheets.
* Overgrazing by cattle, sheep, goats and camels in semi-arid areas – grass is eaten and trampled and the wind blows the soil away.
* Poorly drained land which is irrigated in tropical countries; salts accumulate.

1·19 *Severe soil erosion in Ethiopia means that the land here can no longer be used for farming.*

Soil erosion: a world problem

Each year 25,000 million tonnes of soil are wasted on planet Earth. This soil ends up in rivers and the oceans. Economically developing countries face the worst problems because their populations depend directly on farmland. They are also short of money and equipment to stop it happening.

1·20 *Areas of the world with severe water and wind erosion.*

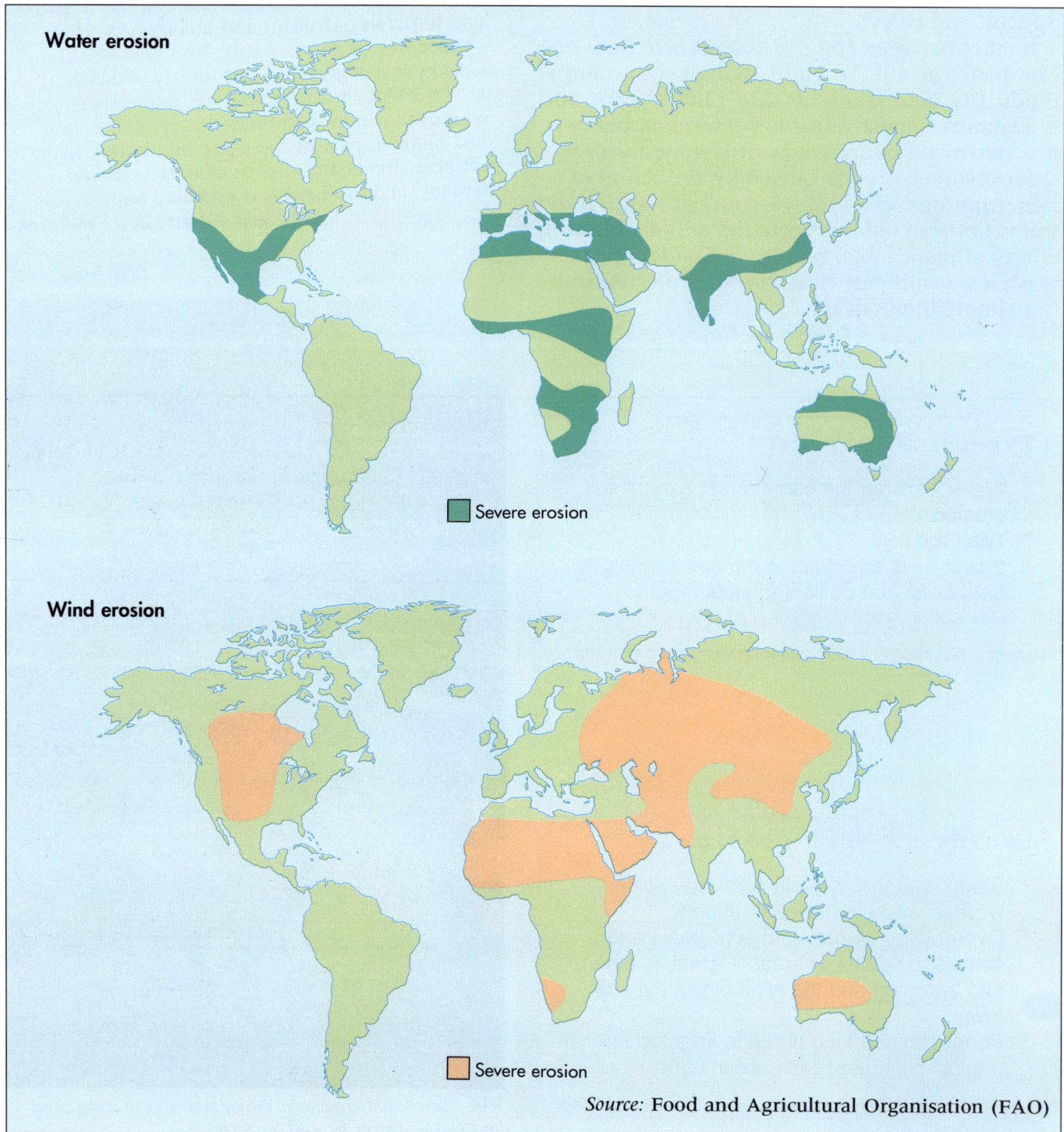

Source: Food and Agricultural Organisation (FAO)

UNIT 1

1a Read the piece by V. S. Naipaul on page 17 and draw a picture of the scene described by the writer.
b How does this part of India differ from Kodagu?

2 What type of soil erosion would be caused by the following:
a farming on steep slopes
b keeping large numbers of cattle
c increasing the amount of water used on crops, without putting in drains?

3 What type of soil erosion is shown in the photograph on page 17? How was the soil eroded?

4 On a copy of a world map, draw in the areas affected by **a** water erosion, **b** wind erosion.

5 From your map, estimate the percentage of land affected by soil erosion in
a Africa
b Asia
c North America
d Australia.*

6 Name one country in Africa and one in Asia which seems entirely affected by soil erosion.

7 Referring to the diagram below, complete the table to show the percentage of land affected by soil erosion in India, the Near East and Africa.

Type of soil erosion	Near East	India	Africa
% water erosion			
% wind erosion			
% salinity			
% total land eroded			

*Note Estimates of area must be treated with caution, especially if your map is not drawn on an equal area projection.

Soil erosion limits the amount of land that can be used for farming. In India 90 million hectares are at risk from water erosion alone. But it is not just a problem for economically developing countries. For example, the USA has lost one-third of its soil since farming began.

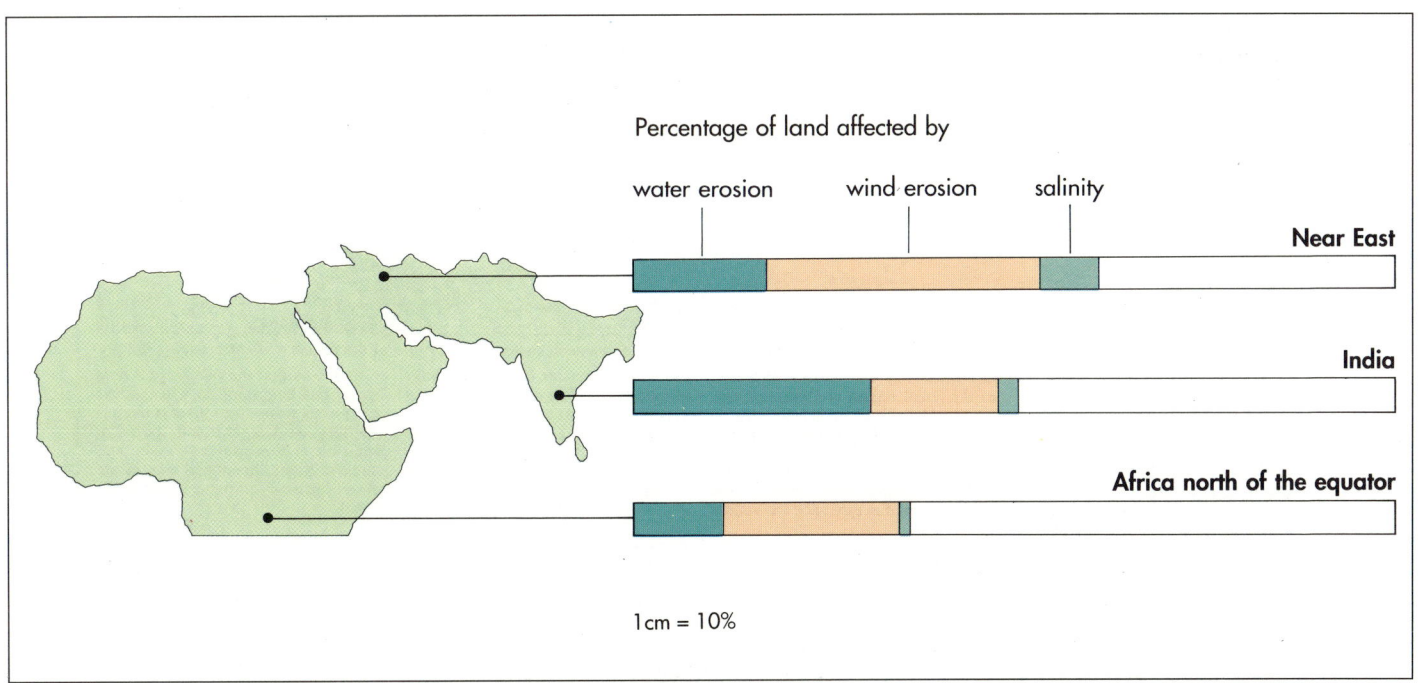

1·21 *The seriousness of soil erosion in the Near East, India and Africa north of the Equator.*

However, vanishing soil is a greater problem in countries with growing populations. Between 1980 and the year 2000 the population of the economically developing world will increase by 50 per cent to 4,874 million! How will the world's people be fed, and will there be enough land to support them?

One way is to use more of the land that is not presently used for farming. Some continents like South America and Africa are using only a small amount of the farming land that is available. But it would be pointless to use more if soil erosion continues at the present rate, because at the same time as new land is farmed the same amount will be wasted!

So what can be done? The newspaper article below shows one way in which soil erosion can be stopped to improve farming.

YOUNG NEWSPAPER PUBLISHING LTD

Beating back the Sahara

People of the Sahel region of Burkino Faso build low walls to stop the advance of the desert *Photo: Jeremy Hartley*

THE GRADUAL advance of the desert, reducing once-fertile land to dust, may be one ecological problem that is on its way to being solved. And the really good news is that the solution requires no expensive technology. All that's needed is a spade and a few rocks - you build a wall.

The growth of deserts, or desertification, occurs due to overuse of farm land in semi-arid areas. This causes the soil to weaken and the death of grasses and plants previously able to protect the soil from wind. Once exposed, the desert creeps up and eventually makes the land useless.

The raindrop of hope for the future has fallen onto the parched landscape of the Sahel region of Burkina Faso, the world's third-poorest country. It lies perilously close to the ever growing Sahara.

A report for the British charity, Oxfam, by Robin Sharp outlines how Sahel managed to turn back the yellow tide of sand.

The idea is to construct low walls which help channel rain-water and stop wind erosion. Another experiment was to dig U-shaped earth walls to catch rain-water for the tree seedlings planted inside. This created a barrier of vegetation against the desert.

As a result of the initiatives, crop yields doubled within a single year.

The news of such local achievements spread from village to village. Three years after the project was organised, the area has been transformed from semi-desert to productive arable land.

The last two years have seen record harvests in Burkina Faso.

It seems that the people of Africa are at last beginning to win the war against desertification. What is more is that they are doing this with the aid of such basic weapons as stones and ditches. Every threatened area of the planet can easily learn the lesson of the Sahel.

Bob Kelsey

Burkino Faso. New life for the Sahel? by Robin Sharp published by Oxfam Books, £3.95

1·22 *An article in 'The Indy', 6 December 1990.*

1   Read the newspaper article 'Beating back the Sahara'.
a   What type of soil erosion affects Burkina Faso?
b   How does the Sahara Desert move southwards?
c   Describe what the people of the Sahel region are doing to stop the advancing desert.

2   Now look carefully at the diagram below. Imagine you are trying to explain to a younger person the different ways to stop soil erosion. For one or more of the methods, draw a cartoon to show how it works. An example of a simple cartoon is given here to help you.

1·23   *'Hey, you! Which needs cover the most – you, or the soil?'*

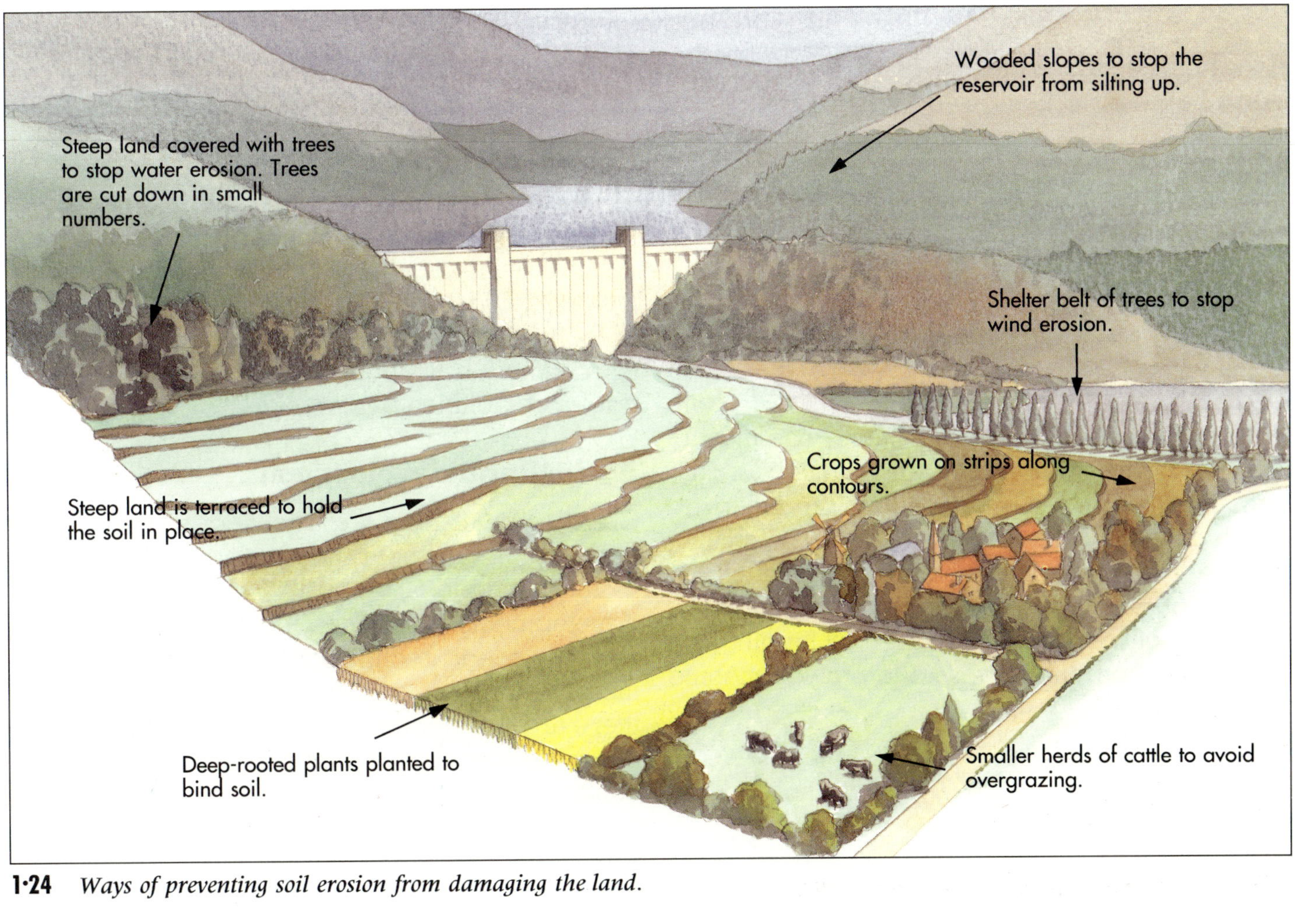

1·24   *Ways of preventing soil erosion from damaging the land.*

- Wooded slopes to stop the reservoir from silting up.
- Steep land covered with trees to stop water erosion. Trees are cut down in small numbers.
- Shelter belt of trees to stop wind erosion.
- Steep land is terraced to hold the soil in place.
- Crops grown on strips along contours.
- Deep-rooted plants planted to bind soil.
- Smaller herds of cattle to avoid overgrazing.

In this unit we have seen how people in one part of India make a living from the land. These people know that to continue to make a living, they must care for the land: they must *work with* the land, and *not against* it. We came across other key points too.

A natural environment – is there such a thing?

There are small patches of forest – even in the UK – which have evolved unaffected by people over thousands of years. Are these areas more 'natural' than most of the Earth's surface which has been modified (changed) by people, for example farmers?

Subsistence and commercial farming

When a farmer and his or her family use most of what the farm produces, the farm is a *subsistence* farm. A small surplus is sometimes produced which can be sold at a local market. The small income from this is spent on things the family needs but which the farm cannot produce: tools, books, electrical goods. *Commercial* farming is a business: all products are sold to provide income to the farmer.

Farming patterns

Different *kinds* of farming, like subsistence and commercial farming, take place in different areas. Different areas also produce different farm products. These differences can be mapped and the map shows a *pattern*. (Use an atlas to find examples.) It is usually possible to find *reasons* for the patterns.

Factors affecting farming

These are the reasons behind farming patterns. Usually the reasons for a pattern of farming are a mixture of *physical* and *human* factors. Physical factors include rainfall, temperature, relief (shape of the land) and soil. Human factors include level of economic development or wealth, and transport facilities to markets.

Agricultural development

Changes in farming are usually designed to increase the amount of food grown to bring in more income to farmers. These are agricultural developments, which can include changes in crops or seeds, technology or machinery, or increasing the amount of land farmed. When there are developments, not everyone benefits in the same way. Developments often lead to conflicts between different groups of people.

The Food Business

UNIT 2

2·1 Food, like access to clean water or the availability of shelter, is a vital requirement for living. The world produces more than enough food to feed everyone, and it could grow even more. But worldwide, 750 million people suffer from hunger. The photos above show that people in some parts of the world are spoilt for choice, while in other areas people are dying of starvation.

UNIT 2

Brainstorm: What do you know about farming and food?

Work through these activities in pairs.

1 Food

a Individually, list on a piece of paper all the different types of food you have consumed over the last week. You need only name each type of food once, although you may eat it often (bread, for example).

b Compare your lists and combine them into one list.

c Re-write your combined list under two separate headings:

▶ Food which cannot be grown in Britain
▶ Food which can be grown in Britain.

Divide up the list under the first heading again: food which can be grown in Europe, and food which cannot be grown in Europe. You could organise these lists like this:

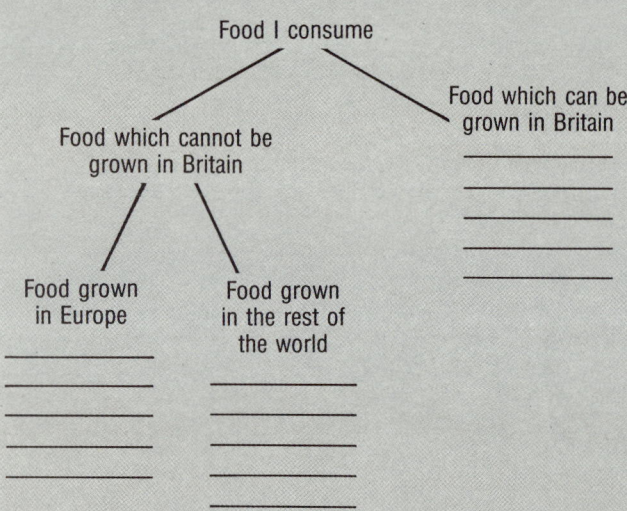

To do this properly you will need to do some finding out. For example, look at food labels to see where different types of food come from.

d For each item of food in your lists, write down the farm product (or products) which go to make it. For some, the food and the product are the same: for example, oranges. For others they are not: for example, bread (food) comes from wheat (product). Remember that some foods will be made from more than one farm product.

2 Farms

Your work for the previous activity showed that farms produce a lot of different foods! Let us think more about the farms which produce all this food. In your pairs:

a Write out a list of all the different British farm products. Check with another pair that your list is as complete as you can make it.

b Now try to separate your list under the following headings, which show the main types of farming:

Arable farming	Farms which specialise in growing large quantities of crops such as wheat, oilseed rape, sugar beet, beans. These farms are usually quite large.
Market gardening	The name given to small farms that specialise in growing fruit and vegetables which will fetch a good price when sold fresh. These farms often have huge greenhouses.
Hill farming	The kind of farming found in the hilly west and north of Britain. The main products of hill farms are animals, especially sheep. This kind of farming is sometimes called *livestock farming*.
Dairy farming	The kind of farming that specialises in milk products (such as cream, butter, cheese). Some crops such as grass are grown, mainly for the cows.
Factory farming	The animals, for example chickens, are given a certain amount of space, a special scientifically calculated diet, and a carefully controlled environment in order to grow quickly.

Setting the scene

Food, glorious food!

How long can you go without any food? A few hours? Maybe a day or so? People can *survive* without food for several weeks, but *not* in good health. People without food feel tired and lack strength and energy. How important it is to have enough food!

Deficiency diseases are found mostly among people living in countries in the economically developing world, or in 'the South'. Countries of 'the North' (sometimes called 'developed countries') are rich and are able to buy all the food they need.

Common deficiency diseases

Name	Cause	Effect
• Kwashiorkor	Lack of protein	Swollen stomach, emaciation, reduced growth
• Rickets	Lack of vitamin D	Bones grow soft and bend under the weight of the body
• Beriberi	Lack of vitamin B1	Reduced stamina, depression, lack of concentration, increased tiredness and eventually paralysis
• Scurvy	Lack of vitamin C	Bleeding gums, poor endurance, reduced ability to combat infectious diseases

But it is wrong to think that *all* people in the North have a healthy diet. Many people here are persuaded by advertisements to spend their money on more expensive processed foods. It is not healthy to eat these all the time. For example, some brands of baked beans contain sugar, and it is not easy to know how much just by looking at the tin. The beans are healthy but the sugar is not. Too much sugar can lead to rotten teeth, becoming overweight and even to heart disease. From 1992 all European Community countries are to use the same food labelling methods, which will make it easier for shoppers to see what they are buying.

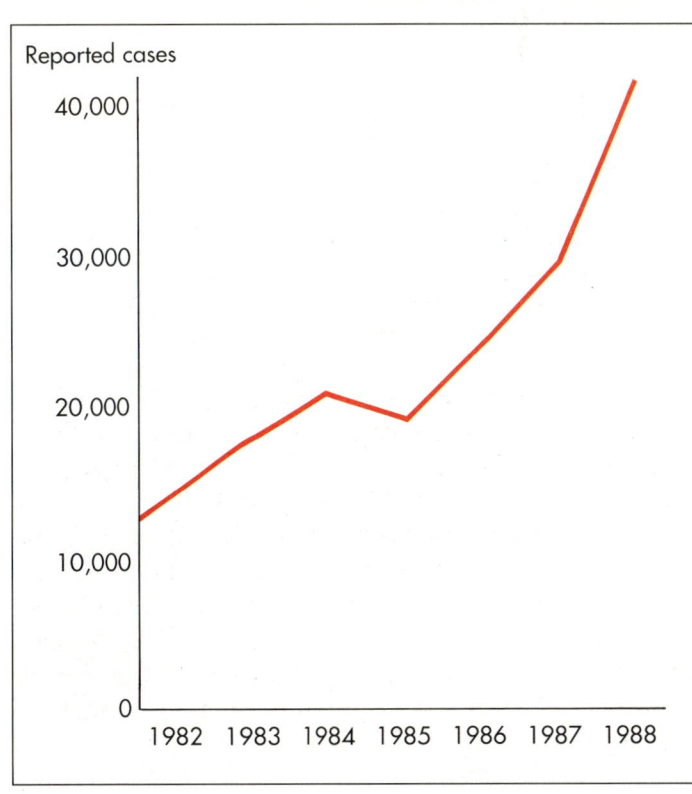

2·2 *Food poisoning in the UK, 1982–88. This graph shows cases of food poisoning going up rapidly. This may be because victims now report it to their doctors, rather than suffering in silence. But many food experts think that the way some foods are processed and then stored in shops leads to contamination by bacteria like* **listeria** *and* **salmonella**.

From where do we obtain our food?

In 1961 there were 150,000 grocery shops in the UK. This means that there was one shop for every 350 people in the country. Now, there are about 40,000 (or one 'shop' for every 1,400 people). In other words, we now buy from a smaller number of shops which are larger than before. This comparison is even more interesting if we think of the ownership of these shops. In 1961 most of the grocery shops were small family businesses. Now, just six firms own about 70 per cent of grocery trade.

UK grocers' share of the market in 1990

Company	Share of grocery trade (%)
Sainsbury	12.6
Tesco	12.3
Co-op	9.6
Argyll (Presto/Safeway)	8.4
Asda	8.1
Gateway (Fine Fare)	5.4
Marks & Spencer Food	3.8
Others	39.8

2·3 *The changing face of our food shopping: a grocer's shop in the early 1900s (left), and a modern supermarket (right). Ask your grandparents how food shopping has changed since* **they** *were children. Today's very large supermarkets are called 'hypermarkets'. They sell all kinds of food, from all over the world, and they sell lots of other things too, from electrical goods to clothes.*

Class activity

Conduct a class survey, which your teacher will help you to organise.

1 Each person should say where his or her family obtains the following foods, and how often.

bread	butter/margarine	rice
milk	coffee/tea	tinned food
cheese	vegetables/fruits	frozen food
meat	flour	sweets
biscuits	pasta	drinks

2 Either in small groups, or as part of a whole class discussion, answer the following questions:
- How many different shops are used by families in your class?
- Does one shop dominate? Why?
- What other kinds of shops are used? *Why* are these shops used instead of the main shop(s)?
- How often are smaller shops used?
- How often are larger shops used?
- Can you think of a reason for any differences you observe between your answers to the last two questions?

Where does the food in our shops come from?

The food we buy in the supermarkets comes from two main sources. In 1989,
- about 56 per cent of all the food consumed was grown on UK farms, and
- about 44 per cent was imported from overseas countries.

Quite a lot of the food we eat cannot be grown in Britain. The climate is not suitable for growing tropical foods like bananas. If we take away food that we are unable to grow in Britain, the figures look like this:
- about 75 per cent is grown on UK farms, and
- about 25 per cent is imported from overseas countries.

These figures show the *success* of British farming. In times gone by it was a different story.

For example, in the nineteenth century Britain was a very powerful industrial country and was known as 'the workshop of the world'. Many people at this time believed that Britain should make things in the many factories here, and sell to the rest of the world. In return, cheap food would be imported. It seemed like a good idea. But British farms were left to rot. On some farms it simply was not worth the back-breaking work needed to grow crops, because imported foreign food was so cheap.

Also, in the 1930s many people did not have enough food or the right kinds of food for a healthy diet. And the Second World War (1939–45) gave the British a real scare: if enemy submarines stopped ships from importing food, would the British just starve to death?

In 1947 the Agriculture Act was passed by Parliament. From now on farmers would be paid to produce more and more food. Never again would Britain be dependent upon imports. Farmers were encouraged to buy new machines, drain the land, use new fertilisers and pesticides (weedkillers and insect killers) and use new, specialised varieties of seeds.

In other parts of Europe, too, similar efforts were made. The European Economic Community was set up in 1957. One of its main aims was to help farmers produce more food so that starvation would never be seen again. It did this a few years later by setting up the Common Agriculture Policy (CAP). This guarantees farmers high prices for the crops they grow.

2·4 *A sign of success? Expensive heavy machinery is used to plough huge fields, and helps to produce, from each hectare, three times more grain than 50 years ago. These machines can plough five times faster than tractors could at the end of the Second World War.*

UNIT 2

Quantity not quality?

The Common Agriculture Policy was designed to increase the quantity of food. Farms in Britain and in Europe now produce more food per hectare than ever before. But now many people are asking questions about the quality of food (which may contain traces of pesticides and fertilisers), and the quality of the landscape (which has fewer hedgerows and less wildlife than before). The three items which follow illustrate the kinds of problems that concern people now.

▸ **What concerns do *you* have about the food business?**

(This could be the topic for an interesting class discussion.)

In this unit you will find activities and information which will help you think about these issues. To do this we have three key questions:

▷ Why are there food surpluses and food shortages?

▷ How does a farmer decide what to grow?

▷ What kinds of farming might we see in the future?

Dear Sir

As your recent 'Contaminated Land' report shows, the risk of soil pollution should be taken very seriously.

Only recently has soil been seen to be at risk. People usually see soil as being able to absorb all sorts of wastes such as farm manure or, in the past, 'town wastes'. But the nature of wastes, from both farms and towns, has changed, and some soils are being poisoned.

Soil is a vital resource upon which we depend for our food. The time has come when the UK should have a policy of soil protection.

Professor Dee Erder, University of Wales

2·5 *A letter to a national newspaper, February 1990.*

Now, the nothing tomato

A few years ago, the huge companies which control much of the agriculture here decided that the cost of human labour in gathering tomatoes was too great. So they went to the boffins at the University. These superbrains came up with the automatic tomato harvester, costing £80,000 a piece.

There was a problem, though. The steel 'hands' of the machine were too rough for the tomatoes, and the result was a sticky goo.

So a new variety of tomato was developed. It is red, lustrous and firm, perfect to the eye. More, it has a tough skin and suits the harvester perfectly. And it tastes of nothing. Perhaps the superbrains will come up with a spray to give these fruits the right smell and taste.

Alternatively, you can grow your own knobbly, uneven, peculiar-looking objects. They may look like nothing – but they *taste* like tomatoes.

2·6 *A piece translated from an article in a local paper in the Netherlands.*

Going green down on the farm?

THE fate of Europe's countryside depends on the policy of its farmers, a leading environment group has said. And now it wants measures introduced to encourage farmers to 'go green'.

The Royal Society for the Protection of Birds [RSPB] has called for a huge rethink of the basis of farming throughout the European Community. Europe's countryside has developed over centuries and much of it, says the group, is 'man-made'.

Farming in particular is a key factor in deciding the fate of about 312 million acres of rural land across Europe. It plays a vital part in looking after large areas of land which are important for the future of Europe's wildlife.

But, says the RSPB, farming practices can also lead to the destruction of wildlife, a drop in landscape quality, soil erosion and pollution.

A particular worry is the move towards intensive farming, with larger fields and fewer hedges.

Now the RSPB wants farmers who use environment-friendly methods to be rewarded, and aid for farmers who want to divert land-use to new wildlife and leisure uses.

"Agriculture [farming] and the environment are inseparable," says Jim Dixon, spokesman for the RSPB. "In the past 30 years they have diverged and come into conflict. Now is the time to make agricultural policy more sensitive to the environment."

2·7 *From the 'Early Times', 6–12 December 1990.*

▷ Why are there food surpluses and food shortages?

The world produces more than enough food to feed the entire population. But while some parts of the world produce surpluses which are either left to rot, or stored – often in huge refrigerated buildings at colossal expense – other parts of the world are suffering severe famine.

Even in a single country there can be extremes. For example, during the great Ethiopian famine of 1986, when several million people there were in danger of starving to death, Ethiopia was still exporting strawberries to Europe! And a huge country such as the former Soviet Union has difficulty in transporting its home-grown food to other parts of the country that need it.

Such problems are not new. This is what a newspaper journalist, George Dawson, reported about 150 years ago when he went to Ireland to find out about the great famine of 1845–49.

> There is no want of food in this neighbourhood; but it is at such a price as makes it impossible for a poor man to support his family. There is corn, there is meat and there is milk, much of which will be set out on the shelves of markets across the Irish Sea.
>
> The humble person's food is the potato. This is what he grows and this is what he must eat. But there are no potatoes after the blight and the poor man and his family are starving.

Half a million people died, and more than one million emigrated.

2·8 'Mountains' of food, like these heaps of apples in France, were to be found in many parts of the European Community in the 1970s and 1980s. Much surplus food was stored in butter and beef 'mountains' and in wine 'lakes'.

Soviets make desperate worldwide plea for food aid

Hungry for help

by Nick Fox

PRESIDENT Mikhail Gorbachev of the Soviet Union has found this week that his country can send a rocket into space — but just can't feed its own people.

Despite a bumper harvest this year men, women and children throughout the vast Soviet empire are starving because there isn't enough food to go around.

Most of the major cities in the country have been forced to introduce rationing in a bid to make the dwindling supplies go around. But still the Soviet people are facing endless queues outside the state-owned food stores.

The crisis is the result of panic buying by Soviets after government warnings to expect the worst this winter. Although the food is in the country, the transport system in the Soviet Union is so old and badly run that the harvest is left rotting in remote railway sidings.

Things have been made worse by the growing black market system, with short-supply foods being sold at very high prices for personal profit rather than through the state.

Now the huge Red Army is being employed to combat the food problem. Soldiers nationwide are being used to transport food and to support a crackdown on black marketeers.

Mr Gorbachev last week cancelled a visit to Norway to receive the Nobel Peace Prize. Instead the state of emergency forced him to stay in Moscow to coordinate plans to counter the desperate situation.

At the same time, children's homes and hospitals were receiving emergency food and medical aid from the West [mainly from Germany]. European Community leaders are expected to approve more than £1 billion worth of food aid to the country when they meet in Rome next week.

Soviet Ambassador Levgenny Zamyatin said: "The dire situation is a price the Soviet Union is paying for the difficult transition to a market-oriented economy."

2·9 From the 'Early Times', 6–12 December 1990.

UNIT 2

World Hunger Week has been organised by several aid agencies with two aims:
1 To raise money to help people in need of food.
2 To help people in the UK to have a better understanding of the problem of hunger.

Either imagine you have been asked to design a *symbol* and a *slogan* to advertise World Hunger Week, *or* imagine you are a journalist for a local newspaper and you have to write an article about World Hunger Week. Prepare a piece for next week's paper. It will help you to think of these key words:

*surplus   shortage
distribution* (transport)   *poverty*

You should use all the information in this section. It might also help you to re-read 'Setting the scene' on page 25.

Factfile

- Developing countries are caught in a trap. In 1963, 3 tonnes of West African bananas raised enough money to buy one tractor. In 1990 a tractor cost 20 tonnes of bananas. This is why some developing countries now produce less food for their own people.

- Between 1973 and 1983 the areas of food crops grown in the developing countries of the South increased by 8 per cent.

- In the same period the areas of cash crops like coffee, cocoa and cotton (all sold abroad) increased by 48 per cent.

Are surpluses and shortages linked?

Jan Gatt, an expert on world trade, thinks that the farming policy (CAP) in the European Community has encouraged the production of huge surpluses of food such as wheat. These surpluses, she says, must be stopped because they *cause shortages in other parts of the world.*

2·10 *Farming communities like this one in Nigeria are being undermined by policies such as the CAP of Europe. This community now has few farmers and is less able to feed itself than 20 years ago.*

The rich, over-producing nations have for 20 years 'dumped' their surplus food on the Third World. For countries producing surpluses in Europe, for example, the African countries south of the Sahara are places to deposit the leftovers. It is much cheaper to do this than to store ever-increasing mountains of food. Now at first glance this cheap food in countries desperate to feed their people seems to be a very good idea. Just the job!

But no. What it does is to undercut the local farmer. Local farmers have less money from the sale of their grain to improve their farms with. The land suffers. It is often deserted completely when people give up, and try their luck in the cities.

Read the newspaper article below, and then answer the questions that follow.

YOUNG NEWSPAPER PUBLISHING LTD

Photo: Glynn Griffiths

Dennis Long on the Norfolk farm that the European Community pays to be unproductive

Paid £80 an acre not to farm

Old American farming joke: "Last year I didn't grow tomatoes. This year I'm not going to grow corn. There's more money in not growing corn than in not growing tomatoes."

DENNIS LONG has more than 200 acres in Norfolk. For the last two years they have been set aside. That means he grows nothing on that land. The Ministry of Agriculture pays him £80 per acre per year to leave it fallow for five years. So he receives an income of over £16,000 per annum.

In Britain, 134,000 acres were set aside in 1988, and another 136,000 in 1989. Across the European Community the figure is 1.23 million acres.

Set-Aside has a bad reputation – farmers getting paid to do absolutely nothing – but Mr Long says the popular judgement is unfair in his case. His idea is to rest the land to build up some fertility.

This all goes against his deeply-embedded instinct to produce food, but he believes he is doing the right thing for his farm. He used to produce cereals but it was just not making enough money. Profits had been going down since 1984 as EC policy changed. The policy of guaranteed EC prices to encourage high production made the fall inevitable.

"We [grain farmers] had been doing very well in cloud cuckoo land," he says. "Eventually it had to have repercussions." After a long period of intervention, Europe's grain stores were full. Mr Long has planted his set-aside land with nitrogen-enriching clover, and grass seed, because his aim is to improve the land so when the set-aside period ends it will be better land than before.

The whole post-war period, when the message from British governments was to improve productivity, also went against Mr Long's instincts. Land was used for the wrong crops too many years running. "I was unhappy about the uses of chemicals – not that I'm saying it did any damage – we just don't know."

In global terms, Mr Long believes Set-Aside will remain illogical while there are people starving. "There isn't a *world* surplus of grain," he says.

Stephen Ward

2·11   *From 'The Indy', 24–30 August 1990.*

1 What is 'Set-Aside'?

2 Why has Set-Aside been introduced to Europe?

3 In what ways does Mr Long think it will benefit his farm?

4 In what ways does Mr Long believe Set-Aside is a bad idea?

5 Imagine Mr Dennis Long and Ms Jan Gatt meeting at a conference on the future of the Common Agriculture Policy (CAP).
a Describe in your own words one thing about which they both agree.
b Describe in your own words one thing that they might argue about.
c Which side of the argument would *you* be on? Why?

UNIT 2

▷ How does a farmer decide what to grow?

A farmer has to consider many things before deciding what crops to grow or what animals to keep on the farm. Not only must he or she consider the physical environment, the soils, climate and slopes (relief). There are also economic considerations, such as the CAP, the possibility of government subsidies, and whether or not there is a market for the product.

A farm can be thought of as a *system*. The physical and economic considerations are the *inputs*, and what the farm produces is the *output*. The farmer's success (or lack of it) will help to determine the next year's inputs.

In this section we will look at how the physical environment influences the decisions a farmer takes about what to grow. But remember all the time that physical influences are only one consideration. In deciding what to grow, a farmer will also think about the market for the farm's products. If the farm is close to a town, it might be worth producing eggs and cream, even if the farmer has to buy feed for the chickens and cows because the land is not suitable for growing sufficient animal feed.

2·12 *A farmer has many decisions to make.*

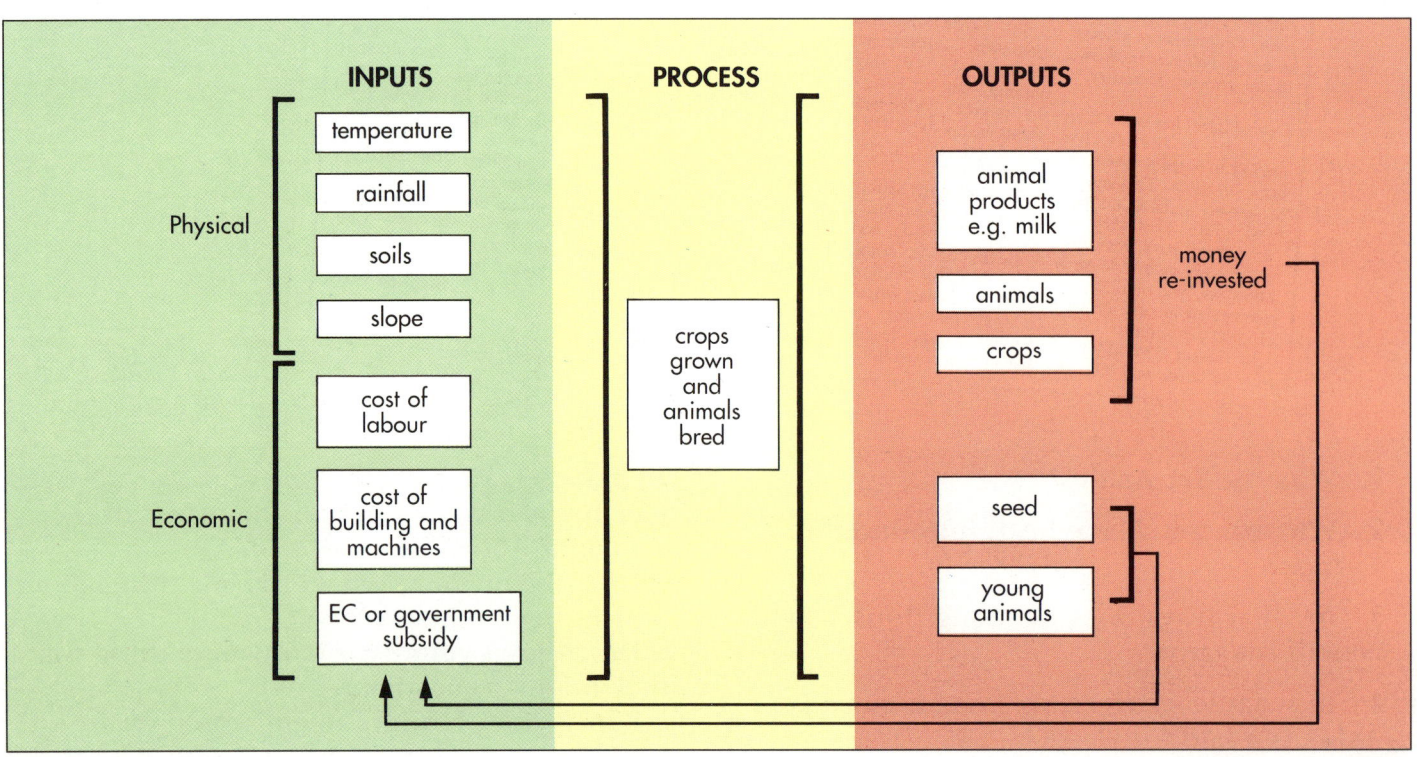

2·13 *A farm system.*

32

How do climate and physical features affect farming?

To consider the effects of climate and physical features on farming, look at the map below, and read on the next page what a weather expert, Sunni McCloud, has to say.

2·14 *The physical features of the British Isles.*

Along the western side of Britain there is considerably more rainfall for two reasons:

1 The wind blows mainly from the south-west (this is the *prevailing* wind). If you look at an atlas you will see that this means it is coming from across the Atlantic Ocean. So the winds pick up plenty of moisture.

2 On reaching Britain the winds are forced up over hills and mountains which are mainly on the western side of Britain (look at the map). As the air rises it cools and can hold less water, and it rains. By the time the air reaches eastern Britain it is drier and warmer, and here there is less rainfall.

The western side of Britain has milder winters. The prevailing wind blows off the Atlantic Ocean which stays quite warm even during the coldest winter months. However, in summer the west coast is windier because of the prevailing wind, and therefore cooler, whereas the eastern side is more sheltered, and warmer.

On hills and mountains, the land is higher and therefore cooler. Temperature falls roughly 1°C for every 200 metres in height above sea level.
Another influence on temperature is latitude. This means that *in summer* the north is cooler than the south. This is because the nearer a place is to the Equator, the stronger is the warming of the sun. Although Britain is a long way north of the Equator, it lies between latitudes 50° and 60° North, and this range in latitude means that there are differences in the summer temperatures between the north and south of the British Isles.

Physical features influence farming indirectly because of their effect on climate, but they also have a direct influence. Generally, the flatter the land, the easier it is to farm, in terms of both ploughing the land and harvesting the crop. It is difficult and sometimes dangerous to use machinery on steep slopes, so very few crops are grown in hilly areas.

The ideal physical conditions for different kinds of farming.

Crops/Animals		Climate	Physical features
Wheat		Rain less than 750mm, summer temperatures > 15°C.	Flat land for the efficient use of machinery.
Sugar beet		Rain less than 750mm, summer temperatures > 15°C.	
Barley		Rain less than 850mm, summer temperatures > 13°C.	Flat land for the efficient use of machinery.
Potatoes		Mild winters, rain less than 900mm.	
Cows		Mild winters, warm, moist summers for good grass growth.	Fairly flat land – steep slopes can be difficult for cattle.
Sheep		Can cope with all temperatures in Britain.	Hills are no problem.

As a very rough guide, Britain can be divided into four parts. Look at the map and information below, then work through the questions on page 36.

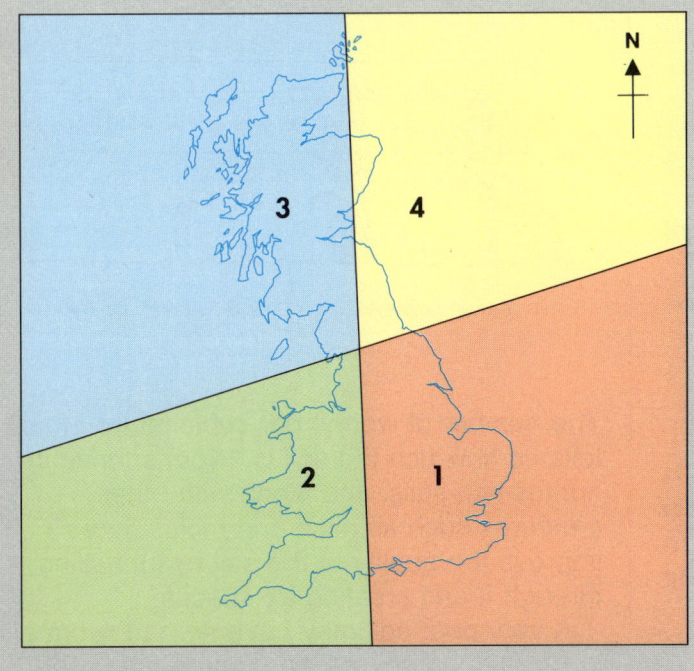

AREA 1 Cool winters, 4°C
Hot summers, 17°C
Low annual rainfall, 600 mm

AREA 2 Mild winters, 6°C
Warm summers, 16°C
High annual rainfall, 950 mm

AREA 3 Cool winters, 4°C
Warm summers, 13°C
High annual rainfall, 2,000 mm

AREA 4 Cold winters, 2°C
Warm summers, 14°C
Moderate annual rainfall, 850 mm

2·15 *The climatic regions of Great Britain.*

1 Draw up a list of the physical and climatic characteristics of each of the four areas.

2 Now look at the table on page 35 which shows the climate and physical features required for some crops and animals. Write a description of the type of farming you would expect to find in each of your four areas, and explain why.

3 This analysis gives you a general idea about the pattern of farming land use in Britain. But the general pattern is not followed by everyone.

Mr Helier has a farm in East Anglia. It is less than a mile from Cambridge. He has chosen to practise dairy farming, and has a herd of Jersey cows. Most other farms in the area are arable farms. Imagine that Mr Helier is explaining to you the reasons for his choice of farming. What do you think he would say?

Will the climate influence farming in the future?

Global warming could change Britain's climate. It could become warmer so that it is like the Mediterranean. Imagine Birmingham having a climate like Marseille! It has always been difficult to grow vines in Britain, and they are limited to a few areas, but *viticulture* (growing vines to make wine) could become widespread in southern Britain if temperatures rise by 2 or 3 degrees centigrade.

But there are problems too. East Anglia, one of the best areas for farming today, could suffer from increased flooding due to rising sea levels.

How important is soil?

A good soil is essential for good plant growth. It originates from weathered rock. Rain is the main cause of weathering. It seeps into small cracks in the rock, and when it freezes it expands, cracking the rock. There are also acids in the rain that dissolve rocks slowly. Over hundreds, thousands and even millions of years this combined attack results in rocks being broken down into tiny particles, forming the basis of soil.

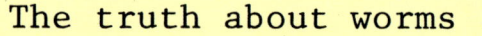

The number of worms per cubic metre of soil tells us how rich the soil is. Worms thrive in humus-rich soils, and along with other creatures such as mice and moles they improve the quality of the soil by tunnelling through it and creating air spaces.

A very poor soil may have no earthworms in it. But a good soil will have more than 400 worms in every cubic metre of soil!

Soils are basically of three main types:
1 *Clay soils*, which are made up of very small particles.
2 *Sandy soils*, which are made up of large particles.
3 *Loam soils*, which are a mixture of clay and sandy soils.

The size of soil particles is very important. This determines the speed at which rainwater passes through the soil. In sandy soils the water passes through very quickly, and the soil dries out quickly. In clay soils the water has difficulty in squeezing between the soil particles, so the soil can easily become waterlogged and muddy. In loam soils, however, the balance is just right.

Soil particle size is also important because it affects the amount of *nutrients* that are stored in the soil. Nutrients provide the nourishment for future plant growth. Many of these nutrients come from dead plants and animals which are rotted down by bacteria and creatures such as worms and millipedes into a thick sticky black stuff known as *humus*. The amount of humus in a soil shows how rich it is.

In a sandy soil the humus is washed out as the water passes quickly through the soil. In a clay soil the particles are so close together that there is little air and the dead plants and animals are not easily broken down into humus. Again, loam soils are just right, with enough space and air for the humus to enrich the soil.

Sandy soils are the easiest to plough, but they are not very fertile. Clay soils hold water, so are very heavy and difficult to plough. Yes – again, loam soils are just right.

Look at the two maps below. One shows the soil type, and the other the land use, for a small farm in Shropshire. The farmer says:

> The heavy clay soils, which would be hard to plough and are liable to flooding, have been left as permanent pasture. Although the best soil has been used for sugar beet, which needs a deep, well-drained soil, barley is grown on both the good and the poor soil. This is because I can use artificial fertilisers and even sewage sludge to increase the fertility of the sandy soil. I have built an intensive pig unit close to the main road. The type of soil here does not matter because these pigs are kept permanently indoors. More important is access to the road, to bring in the feed and to take the pigs to market.
>
> Every farmer has many things to consider before deciding what to grow and what animals to keep. And soil is only one factor to be considered.

▶ Is the land use determined by the soil type? If not, what else might have influenced the farmer's choice of land use?

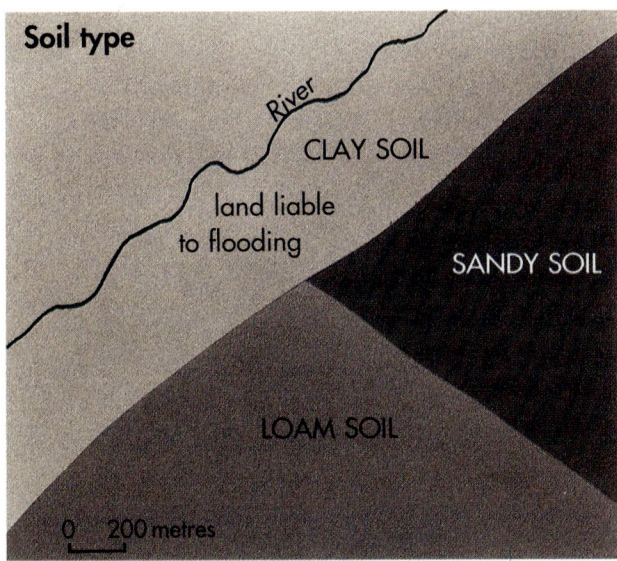
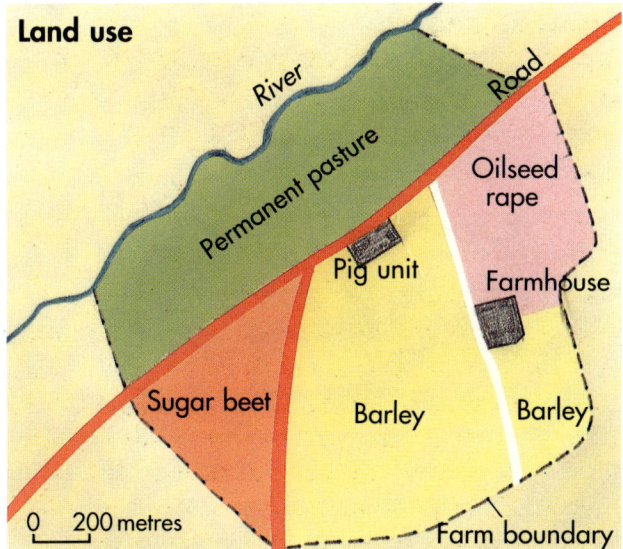

2·16 *Soil types and land use on a Shropshire farm.*

UNIT 2

▶ What kinds of farming might we see in the future?

In 'Setting the scene' on page 25 we found that consumers are often concerned about the *quality* of the food they eat. Modern 'high-tech' farming is successful at producing large quantities of food. Can it also produce good-quality food? Let us examine the arguments.

Anne Strad
HIGH-TECH FARMING

2·17 Ms Anne Strad's 'high-tech' farm.

To me, farming is a great challenge, and I look on it as a business. I get tremendous pleasure out of seeing the farm run ever more efficiently, and in continuing to improve productivity per hectare. By that I mean producing every year just a little more wheat or sugar beet on each field, or getting more milk from each cow.

In Britain we are now producing more of some foods than we need (as are other countries in the EC). I know there are butter mountains and a surplus of wheat. But that is not my problem – it is for the politicians to resolve. My job is to produce as much food as efficiently and cheaply as I can, ensuring also good quality.

I can produce 8 to 10 tonnes of corn per hectare, whereas my father, twenty years ago, only produced 5 tonnes. To do this I have to use plenty of fertiliser. I leave nothing to chance – everything is carefully calculated to ensure the perfect nutrients for each crop. Without this the high productivity for each field would be impossible. It also means that every piece of land is used to the full. None needs to be left fallow.

Some of my cows give 10 to 12 tonnes of milk per year compared with a national average of just over 5 tonnes. I'm careful to breed my 'super cows' with only the best sires to produce the next generation of dairy cows. It should soon be possible to use banks of frozen embryos instead to ensure a perfect herd. I'm investing in new technology to make sure the milking parlour operates efficiently – it looks more like a science laboratory than a farm.

I've got rid of most of my hedgerows. Hedge-trimming equipment is expensive, and it used to take one of my workers days to trim all the hedges. By getting rid of them there is no longer wasted land on either side of the hedge. If you have hedges you are supposed to leave a strip of land on either side of the hedge out of cultivation. By clearing the hedges and joining fields together they are now much larger, which makes it much easier to operate large machinery such as the combine harvester, and it's easier for aerial crop spraying against pests and diseases too. It is true that occasionally some of the topsoil can get blown away, but this is not often a problem.

If you want to run an efficient farm these days you need to use computers. The soil type does not matter as much as it used to – you can always add chemicals, lime, or whatever you need to improve it. But you do need to understand government and EC subsidies if you want to stay on top.

A lot of fuss is made about nitrates in the water system. They are essential for efficient agriculture. It is the responsibility of the water authorities to ensure that the water is safe to drink. I understand that it is not *really* a problem and that 96 per cent of the water supplied in Britain already complies with EC standards of water supply. If nitrates are banned it would reduce productivity and the price of food would go up.

Carrots	29p	Potatoes	17p
Onions	22p	Apples	35p
Cabbage	25p	Oranges	44p
Swedes	32p	Tomatoes	69p

PRICES DOWN?

All prices per ½ kilo weight.

2·18 'High-tech' food prices in January 1991.

UNIT 2

Al Green
ORGANIC FARMING

2·19 *Mr Al Green's organic farm.*

I used to farm using chemicals, but I've come to believe that they do far more harm than good. There may be short-term gains in terms of productivity, and I do not produce as much per hectare as I did. But it is vital for the future of our land and for our own health that we change to organic farming. Organic farming means that no artificial chemicals are applied to the land, to crops or to animals, and that only naturally occurring substances are used.

Good old-fashioned muck-spreading is more natural than all these chemicals, and does no harm to the environment. The land can take only so much nitrate. Many of the nitrates get washed through the soil and into the rivers, and eventually into our drinking water. It may not be a problem in most parts of the country, but here in East Anglia it is. In 1989 some 35 water sources were thought to exceed the EC's nitrate limit. Many people locally dare not drink the water. They have their own water filters or buy bottled water. It's ridiculous – Britain used to pride itself on having the cleanest water in Europe.

It takes years for chemicals to be completely washed out of the soil, and for the land to become truly organic again, but even within a few years there are plenty of worms back in the fields and more insects, including butterflies, in the air. This means there is an increase in the number of birds, and slowly the wildlife will increase.

People make jokes about organic food, for example that you can always tell organic produce because the cabbages have holes in them, and there are slugs in the lettuces. They may not always look as good, but they taste much better. And anyway, there are non-chemical ways of dealing with pests. For example, I use a soap solution and sprays made from nettles. The increased population of owls, spiders, frogs and ladybirds on my farm all help in natural control.

Britain produces too much food. To resolve this the government has introduced a 'set-aside' policy (see page 31). This is to encourage farmers to take some of their land out of production. It could just be allowed to remain out of use and go back to its natural state. But farmers are more likely to try to find other, more profitable uses for their land, for example by creating golf courses or shooting ranges. To me this presents the perfect opportunity for encouraging farmers to become organic. It is altogether a much better use of the land. Hedges can be planted to provide shelter for the fields, reducing soil erosion and providing a home for wildlife. Ponds and ditches provide natural drainage and another habitat for wildlife, including frogs and toads, which are especially useful for controlling insect pests.

Farming Questionnaire

1 Do you think farming in the future should be 'high-tech' or organic?

    High-tech ☐
    Organic ☐

2 Which do you think is better for you, food from a 'high-tech' or an organic farm?

    Food from a 'high-tech' farm ☐
    Food from an organic farm ☐

3 Would you be prepared to pay more for organic produce?

    Yes ☐
    No ☐

2·21 *Farming questionnaire.*

Data Collection Sheet

Question 1: Farms   Number of ticks
    High-tech ☐
    Organic ☐

Question 2: Food
    High-tech ☐
    Organic ☐

Question 3: Cost
    Yes ☐
    No ☐

2·22 *Data collection sheet.*

ORGANIC

Carrots	52p	Potatoes	25p
Onions	49p	Apples	74p
Cabbage	45p	Oranges	85p
Swedes	42p	Tomatoes	£1.49p

All prices per ½ kilo weight.

2·20 *Organic food prices in January 1991.*

Class activity

1 Look carefully at all the information on the farms belonging to Mr Al Green and Ms Anne Strad. Draw up a list of all the advantages and disadvantages of each farm. Compare your list with those of others in the class, and see if you can agree on a final list.

2 Use copies of the questionnaire on this page to conduct a survey of opinions on the two different types of farming. Each person in the class should interview one or two adults.

First, ask the person being interviewed to read through your list of advantages and disadvantages (see above). Then ask him or her to complete the questionnaire by ticking the appropriate answer box. (Instead of writing out the questionnaire twice, you can simply add more boxes if you interview more than one person.)

When you have collected enough answers, work in groups to put your results together. Use a copy of the data collection sheet (left) to list in the appropriate box the total number of answers to each question.

Discuss your results and compare them with other groups, perhaps finding a total figure for the whole class.
▸ Do people think organic farming is better?
▸ Are they prepared to pay more?

3 On your own, decide which you think is the better farming system for the future. Write a short piece with the title, 'Our Food in the Future'. Suggest which type of farming you think should be adopted, and give reasons to support your choice.

KEY POINTS KEY IDEAS

This unit is concerned with farming. But there is much more to supplying food to our tables than just farming. The large stores like Tesco and Asda are now so powerful that one farmer can easily sell all the farm's products to a single company. The 'market' is just one company. We could say that the big companies control the food business.

Food shortage

Planet Earth produces more than enough food for its people. But hundreds of millions of people – mostly in economically developing countries in Africa and Asia – still go hungry. Some starve, but most suffer a range of deficiency diseases. This situation is scandalous. The scandal will stop only when enough people – mostly in the economically developed countries of Europe and North America – decide that it cannot continue and ways to stop it must be found.

Shopping for food

In general we now have fewer, larger food stores, which are further apart than the small grocery shops of years gone by. These changes have advantages: there is a greater choice of food to buy from all over the world, all under one roof, and in a place where it is possible to park the car! There are disadvantages too. Is the food really any cheaper? What choice do we have if we have no car, or cannot drive for some reason?

Growing food

Both physical and human factors affect the type of farming practised by a farmer. In *Europe*, economic factors are the most important. Most of these are dictated by the *Common Agriculture Policy*, or CAP. This is the farming policy of the European Community (EC).

The CAP was created because the leaders of Europe decided they needed a system that would *guarantee* food production. Before the CAP, some people in Europe experienced hunger. The aim of the policy is to guarantee high prices to farmers. This acts as an *incentive* to grow as much as possible.

The CAP became a problem because farmers began to produce too much food. So the *Set-Aside* policy was introduced to encourage farmers not to use all of their land.

Quality of food

One reason for European farmers' success is the use of chemical fertilisers and pesticides. These chemicals help to produce large quantities of food (high yields). But has *quality* suffered?

Increasing numbers of people are willing to pay a higher price for food which has not been grown with the help of chemicals. This is *organic* food production. The big food companies are forcing more farmers to produce organic food.

42

What's the Weather Like Today?

UNIT 3

AN ELEPHANT ON THE ICE

Yesterday a fine elephant crossed the Thames a little below Blackfriars Bridge...
Morning Post, 3 February 1814

3·1 *In centuries past, winters were so cold that even the River Thames froze over, and fairs and other special events (see left) took place on the ice. This painting shows a Frost Fair on the River Thames in 1814. On this occasion the ice melted on 6 February. The Thames has not frozen over since.*

43

UNIT 3

What do you know about weather?

1 Imagine you went to the Frost Fair shown in the picture on page 43.
a Describe the things that were happening at the fair.
b Describe the clothes that the people were wearing. Why were they wearing these clothes?
c Explain why you think the River Thames has not frozen over since 1814.

2 Now think about other kinds of weather.
a Write a list of all the words you can think of that describe weather.
b Organise these words by putting them under the following headings:

Hot	Cold	Wet	Dry	Other

c Compare your list of words with those of the person sitting next to you. Explain to each other how you have organised your words. Together, can you think of a way of displaying these words in a diagram to show how some weather events overlap?

Setting the scene

Weather is an important part of our lives. We often talk about it. In this section let's see how different people react to different weather conditions.

Do you think it will snow at Christmas?

I hope it doesn't rain on holiday.

I'm scared of thunder and lightning.

A walk across a wilderness

It was a clear cold evening as I set out at 10 pm from Dundonnell in the Scottish Highlands. The tips of the mountains were lit by the last rays of the sun.

I spent a few minutes memorising the map. It became gloomier with the first star appearing at 11 pm. It would be dark until 3.30 am.

3·2 *Walking across a wilderness in the Highlands of Scotland. This walker is dressed well to deal with the wintry weather conditions.*

At first the track was easy to follow. After a while it became more difficult to see as cloud was blocking the moonlight. I reached a small loch and then began to clamber up some steeper slopes. It was now snowing and as I climbed above the 500-metre contour it was starting to settle. The rocks were horribly greasy and a slight slip could have left me with a broken leg. I had no gloves or ice-axe and my face and clothing were iced up and frozen.

I did not wait long at the top as strong winds were turning the snowfall into a blizzard. I began to descend the rocky slope very cautiously. As I got lower the wind dropped and the snow began to turn into rain.

It was a long and weary trudge back to the road and shelter. On my walk across the wilderness I had seen no one nor passed any farm or house . . .

I flopped into a chair and drank a mug of hot tea. I realised that even after many years of climbing Scottish mountains I had not been properly equipped for my walk. I should have known that it can still be winter on the last day of May.

The burst of the monsoon

With the passing of each week the tension grew. It was not only the awful heat that wore nerves finer and finer but terror as well, the terror of famine and disease. The terror of that burning sun which nerves could bear no longer. The storm, accompanied by a sudden fierce wind, came up quickly, covering all the stars which were like diamonds in the sky, as if a curtain had been drawn across them. The thunder and wild flashes of lightning drove the gigantic bats into wild flutterings above the pond.

At last, green drops began to splatter in the thick dust. The branches of the mango trees whipped black against the wild glare of lightning and the water fell in torrents on the parched thirsty earth. Tomorrow it would be green again, miraculously green with the miracle of the monsoon.

3·3 *The arrival of the monsoon. The monsoon is the name given to the seasonal tropical wind that brings much rain.*

UNIT 3

The Garden Year

January brings the snow,
Makes our feet and fingers slow.

February brings the rain,
Thaws the frozen lake again.

March brings breezes, loud and shrill,
To stir the dancing daffodils.

April brings the promise sweet,
Scatters daisies at our feet.

May brings flocks of pretty lambs,
Skipping by their fleecy dams.

June brings tulips like roses,
Fills the children's hands with posies.

Hot July brings cooling showers,
Apricots and gillyflowers.

August brings the sheaves of corn,
Then the harvest home is borne.

Warm September brings the fruit,
Sportsmen then begin their shoot.

Fresh October brings the pheasants,
Then to gather nuts is pleasant.

Dull November brings the blast,
Then the leaves are whirling fast.

Chill December brings the sleet,
Blazing fire and Christmas treat.

Sara Coleridge

This poem is not just about the weather. It tells us what conditions we can expect, usually, as the months and seasons go by. In other words, it also tells us about the climate. The *climate* is about *average conditions* from month to month over the year. The *weather* is about *day-to-day conditions*. The weather in Britain is very changeable, which is probably why we talk about it so often.

Weather affects us in all sorts of ways. To help us study this we ask three key questions in this unit:

▷ How does the British climate vary?

▷ Where does our weather come from?

▷ Have we affected the climate?

How does the British climate vary?

The weather forecast I hope for in the summer is '... and the outlook is for a sunny weekend.' I own a small hotel in Lulworth on the south coast. Britain's changeable weather is a nuisance for me as I cannot guarantee sunshine for the visitors.

The south coast is one of the warmest parts of Britain. Many visitors come here during the year, especially in the summer. At this time the best weather comes from the south-east, and it is warm and dry.

Lulworth is a pretty place. It began as a tiny fishing port, where boats could shelter from the weather's moods. In winter, the sea is sometimes whipped up into a furious rage by the gales blowing from the south-west.

Iain, a chairlift operator in the Scottish Cairngorms

In the Cairngorm Mountains we always hope that there will be a 'white Christmas'. Then the area will be busy with tourists. Most of them come to ski. This gives us jobs, which means we can earn a living. I run a chairlift, but friends of mine own hotels and restaurants.

In this area are the main ski resorts in Britain, and visitors come from far and wide.

The Cairngorms are very high. This means that there is snow on them even when it has melted down in the valleys. The ski season lasts until Easter.

We look forward to winds from the Arctic as they are bitterly cold and bring lots of snow.

Chris, a Dorset hotelier

Thomas, a farmer from Dyfed, south-west Wales

Most farmers around here keep cattle. Many are kept for the milk they produce. Others are reared for beef. The climate is very important to us.

We are grateful that the winter is rarely cold. If the temperature falls below 5°C the grass will not grow. Instead we must feed our animals on cattle feed, which is expensive. Fortunately this does not happen often.

There is plenty of rain which keeps the grass growing quickly. We know that when the weathercock on the barn roof turns to the south-west there is usually rain on the way.

Our summers rarely get very warm. We do not mind as it allows more water to sink into the soil before it evaporates.

Read what Chris, Thomas and Iain have to say about the places where they live.

1 Which place is the coldest in winter?

2 Which place is the warmest in summer?

3 Explain why very warm summer weather is not especially welcome in Dyfed.

4 Which area would you prefer to live in? Why?

5 For each of these three people, describe how the climate affects their lives.

6 For each of these three people, describe how some unexpected weather could be very upsetting to their lives. For example,
- a warm spell in winter in Scotland,
- a very dry and hot spell in Dyfed,
- a cool and wet August on the south coast of England.

UNIT 3

1a Make a list of the reasons why you think tourists visit Lulworth.
b Underline all those reasons that are to do with weather.
c Using your words from question (a), write a paragraph for a tourist guide to the Lulworth area.

2a Describe what is going on in the picture of a dairy farm.
b At what time of year do you think this photograph was taken? What evidence is there for your answer?

3a What is the weather like in the photograph of a skier in the Cairngorms?
b What must the weather have been like before the photograph was taken?
c How is the man dressed to suit the weather?

3·6 *Skiing in the Cairngorms.*

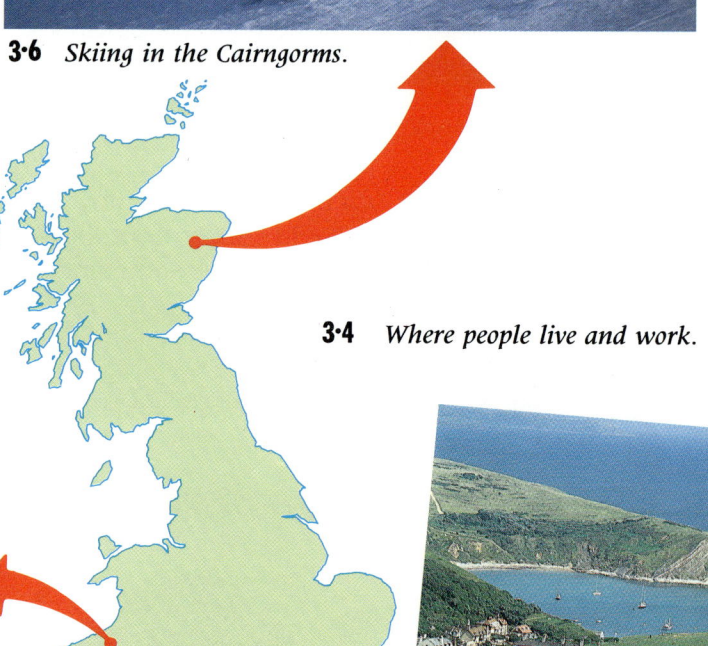

3·4 *Where people live and work.*

3·7 *A dairy farm in Dyfed.*

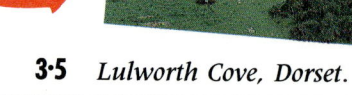

3·5 *Lulworth Cove, Dorset.*

Study the four maps opposite.
1 Copy out and complete the following table.

	Annual rainfall	Summer temperature	Winter temperature	Height of land
Lulworth				
Dyfed				
Cairngorms				

2 Which parts of Britain are the wettest?
3 Which parts of Britain are the driest?
4 Write a paragraph to explain how temperature varies in Britain, in summer and winter.

5 Describe the pattern of high and low land in Britain.

6 'Cool, wet areas can be found where the land is highest.' Investigate the truth of this statement. Write a report, giving evidence to say how true you think it is.

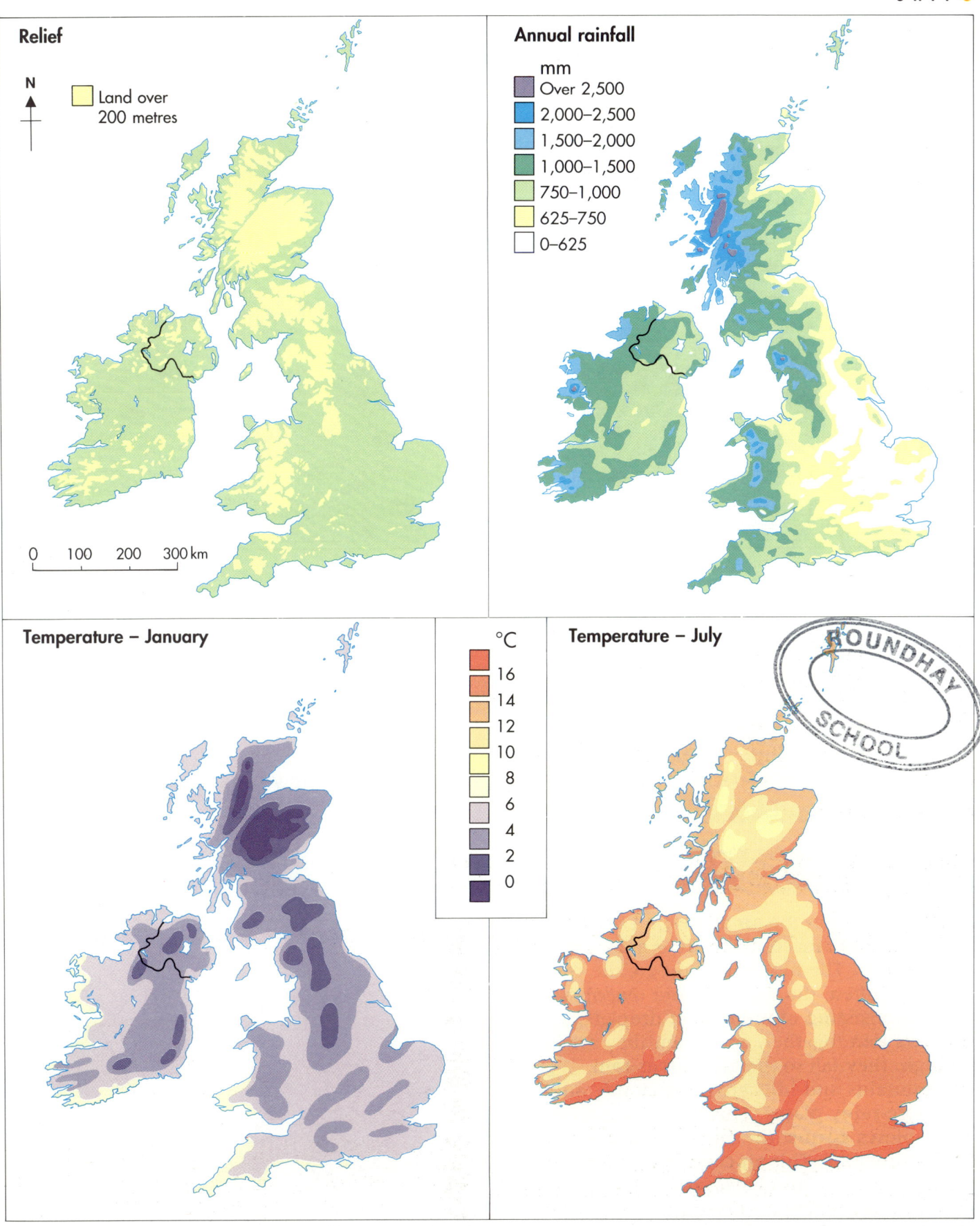

3.8 *The relief and climate of the British Isles.*

UNIT 3

▷ Where does our weather come from?

One way of finding out about what the weather is like is to look at a weather forecast. These can be found on the television and radio and in newspapers. Below is a weather forecast from a national daily newspaper for Wednesday 26 October 1988.

Today's weather forecast

General outlook
Much of central and southern England will be dry with bright spells. Most of Scotland will start cloudy with some rain, but many areas will benefit from the clearer weather spreading from Northern Ireland.
   Rain will be heaviest in northern England, Wales and south-west England. All areas will have temperatures near normal for late October. Winds will be mostly light to moderate from the south. Winds could be stronger in north-east Scotland at first.

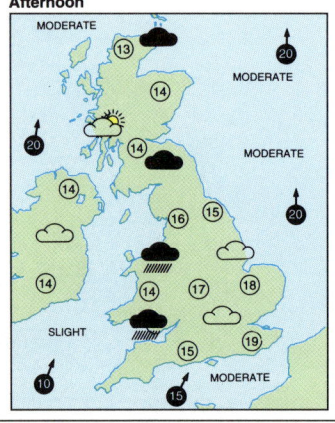
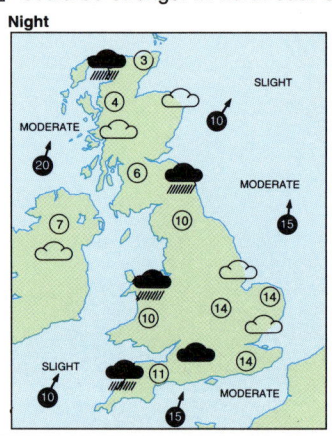
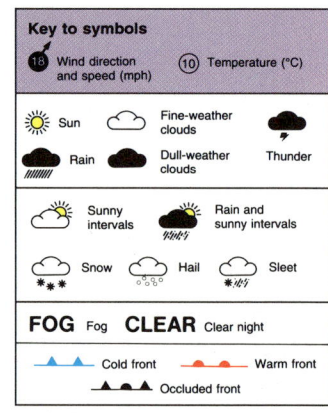

3·9 *The weather forecast for 26 October 1988.*

1 Using the maps and the key above, find the following temperatures:
a south-east England in the morning
b the highest afternoon temperature
c the lowest night temperature.

2 Describe the weather in Northern Ireland on the afternoon of 26 October.

3 Where in the British Isles will the strongest winds be expected?

4 Using an atlas, locate the cities of London and Liverpool. Write a paragraph giving a weather report for each city on 26 October 1988. Look at the paragraph on 'General outlook' to remind you about which features to include in your report.

Why are mountains rainy places?

There is water in the air all around us, but it is invisible. It is carried in the air as a dry gas called *water vapour*. The higher up you go, the colder it gets and, often, the water vapour *condenses* into clouds consisting of millions of droplets. The droplets join together, and when they are heavy enough, they fall to the ground, as rain.
   Mountains and hills are often cloudy and therefore rainy places. This is because air in the wind blows against the mountainside and is forced upwards. This air cools in the process, and the water vapour condenses into droplets to form clouds. Rain falling as a result of this process is described as *relief rainfall*.

3·10 *How clouds are created over mountains.*

How convection makes clouds

On sunny days the ground is heated up and the air above it also warms up. This warm air rises upwards. As it rises high up into the air it cools, and the water vapour it contains condenses to form water droplets and clouds.

This process, of hot air rising and making clouds, is called *convection*. These clouds can produce rain and even thunderstorms, especially in the summer. Rain falling as a result of this process is described as *convectional rainfall*. Convection is the main source of rain in tropical regions.

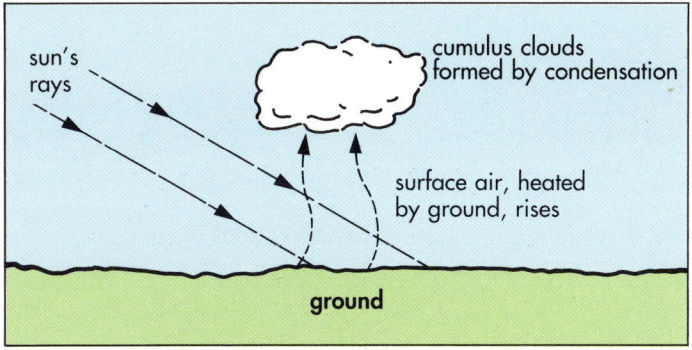

3·11 *How clouds are created by convection.*

Look at the two diagrams showing how clouds are created.
1 How are clouds over mountains formed?
2 Using only a labelled diagram, explain why mountains and hills are often cloudy and have a high annual rainfall.
3 What does *convection* mean, and how does it create clouds?
4 Look back at the map on page 49 showing the relief of the British Isles. Compare that map with the weather map on page 50 for the afternoon of 26 October 1988. Can you see any connection between high land and rainfall? Explain your answer.

Rainfall records

The wettest place on Earth is Cherrapunji in Meghalaya, in north-east India. The wettest year recorded there was 1861, when it received a total rainfall of 26,461 millimetres.

Cherrapunji has a *monsoon climate*. Water vapour is carried by warm air blowing from the Bay of Bengal onto the landmass of Asia. Rain falls because
- the air is forced to rise over the hills, and
- convection rain is created by the heat of the landmass.

The wettest place in Britain is Sprinkling Tarn in Cumbria. During 1954, a total rainfall of 6,527 millimetres was recorded at this point, which is high in the hills of the Lake District.

Where do our winds come from?

Some of our weather can be predicted by finding out where the air comes from. The diagram on the next page shows four air masses, each one having its own conditions. Air masses can move and invade other areas. As they do so they cause the weather to change.

Study the map and information on the next page.
1 Describe the weather you might expect in summer if the wind was from the south-east.
2 Which two air masses might give snow in winter?
3 You are going on holiday for the New Year. The forecast is for a north-east wind. Describe what clothes you might take away with you, and explain why.
4 It is summer. What air mass would you hope Britain to be affected by if you were
a a gardener,
b a holidaymaker?
Explain your answers.

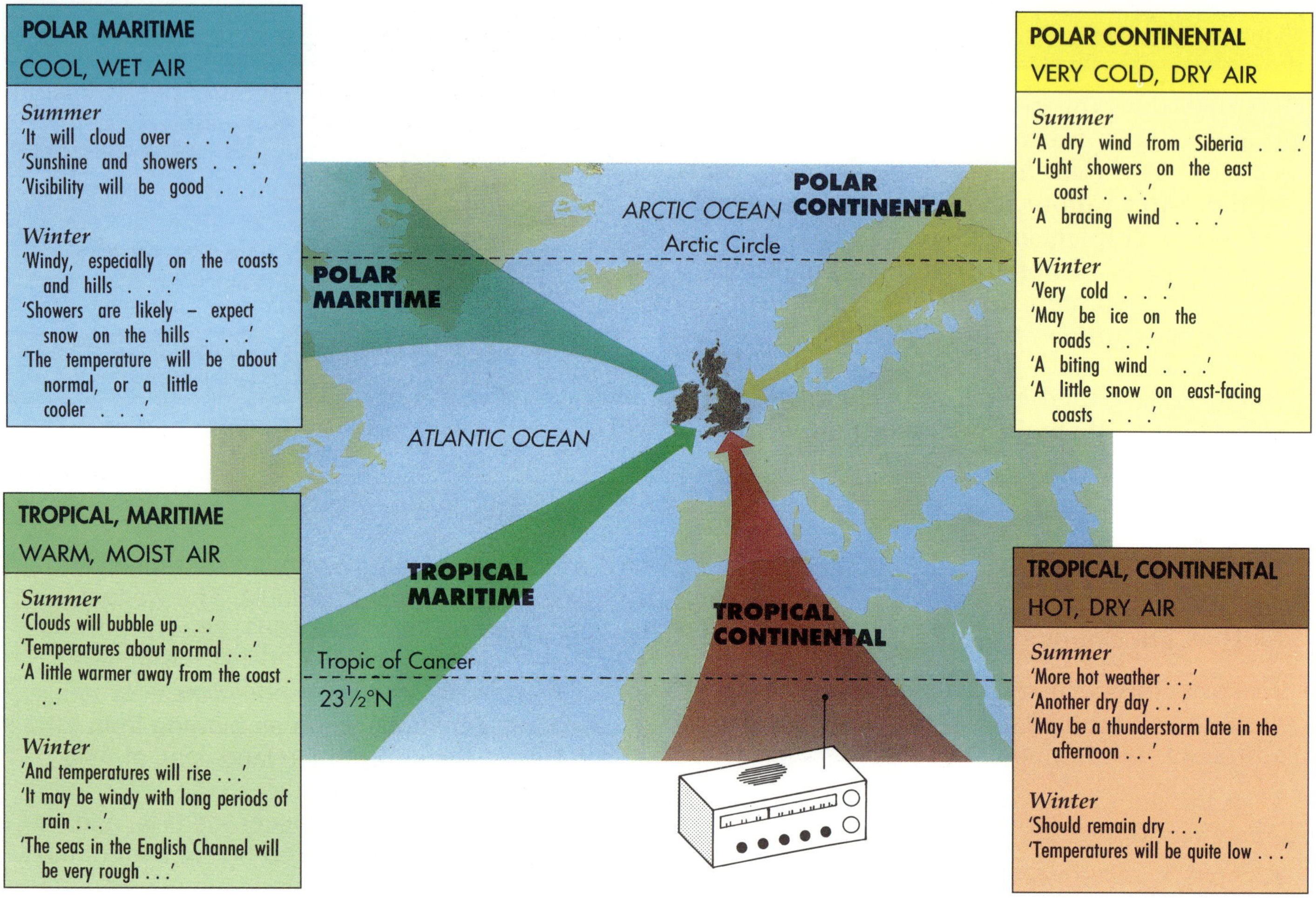
POLAR MARITIME
COOL, WET AIR
Summer
'It will cloud over . . .'
'Sunshine and showers . . .'
'Visibility will be good . . .'
Winter
'Windy, especially on the coasts and hills . . .'
'Showers are likely – expect snow on the hills . . .'
'The temperature will be about normal, or a little cooler . . .'
POLAR CONTINENTAL
VERY COLD, DRY AIR
Summer
'A dry wind from Siberia . . .'
'Light showers on the east coast . . .'
'A bracing wind . . .'
Winter
'Very cold . . .'
'May be ice on the roads . . .'
'A biting wind . . .'
'A little snow on east-facing coasts . . .'
ARCTIC OCEAN
Arctic Circle
POLAR CONTINENTAL
POLAR MARITIME
ATLANTIC OCEAN
TROPICAL MARITIME
TROPICAL CONTINENTAL
Tropic of Cancer
23½°N
TROPICAL, MARITIME
WARM, MOIST AIR
Summer
'Clouds will bubble up . . .'
'Temperatures about normal . . .'
'A little warmer away from the coast . . .'
Winter
'And temperatures will rise . . .'
'It may be windy with long periods of rain . . .'
'The seas in the English Channel will be very rough . . .'
TROPICAL, CONTINENTAL
HOT, DRY AIR
Summer
'More hot weather . . .'
'Another dry day . . .'
'May be a thunderstorm late in the afternoon . . .'
Winter
'Should remain dry . . .'
'Temperatures will be quite low . . .'

3·12 *Air masses and how they affect the British Isles.*

Fronts

A front is where different types of air, warmer and cooler, meet each other. Where they meet a lot of clouds form, sometimes giving rain. Rainfall as a result of this process is described as *frontal rain.*

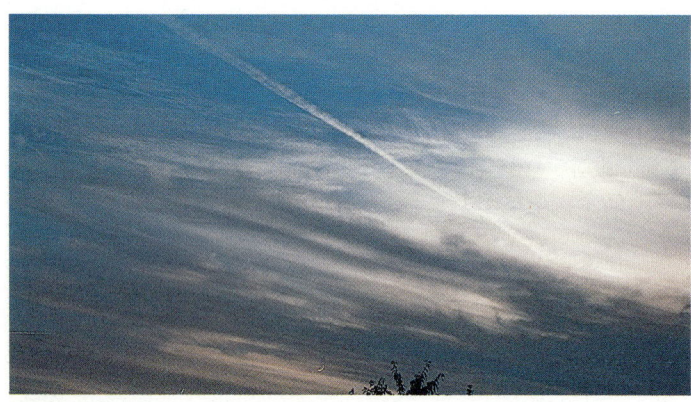

3·13 *An approaching front, as seen from the ground.*

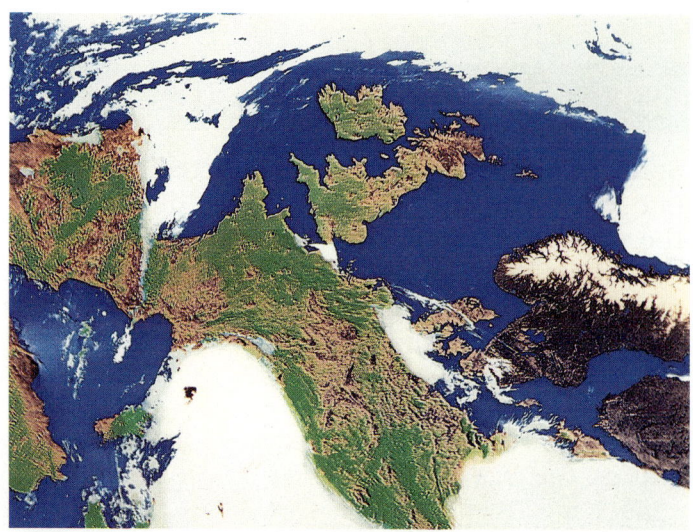

3·14 *A front moving over the Atlantic Ocean, approaching Britain, as seen from a weather satellite in space. When the photograph was taken, Britain was under high pressure.*

Air pressure

The force of the air pressing down on the Earth.

Low pressure

The air is quite 'light', and it tends to rise. It moves around freely, scattering dust and smoke in the air, far and wide. The air feels clean and fresh. Low pressure usually brings clouds and rain because the air is rising.

High pressure

The air is quite 'heavy', and it tends to sink. It moves slowly, so any pollution in it takes a long time to scatter. This means that the quality of the air may be poor, with lots of dust and smoke in it. High pressure usually brings clear skies, with no clouds. In winter, this means bright, cold and frosty days. In summer it means bright, hot and dry days.

1 What is a weather front?

2 Describe what a weather front looks like from a satellite in space.

3 Describe what a weather front looks like to us on the ground.

4 Look back to the weather map for the *afternoon* of 26 October 1988 on page 50. Copy the outline of the British Isles, and on your map draw in a line where you think the front is. Give reasons for your answer.

'And the outlook for today...'

'... and now for the forecast for midday, 12th November...', ... see page 54.

Ian McCaskill, 'the weather man'.

3·15 *Weather map of the British Isles.*

The *south-east corner of England* will have thick cloud, although it should soon stop raining. The temperature will remain quite high for the time of year, so expect 12°C in London and 13°C in Southampton. With a wind speed of only five miles per hour it will take all afternoon for the last of this gloomy but mild air to cross over to mainland Europe.

Now to the forecast for *south-west England, Wales, the Midlands and East Anglia*. A gentle wind is pushing some fresh and clean air in from the south-west. It should be mostly dry, with sunny spells. Cloud will bubble up, perhaps thick enough to give a few short showers over the hills in Wales and Devon. It will be a pleasant day with good visibility. Expect temperatures of 9°C or 10°C over Cardiff, Birmingham and Norwich. Winds will be light and not more than 10 miles per hour.

Moving on to *northern England and Scotland as far north as a line between Glasgow and Aberdeen*. The winds will strengthen to 15 miles per hour as they blow from the south-west. There will be a sheet of cloud, with a few sunny spells. This will keep the temperature down to 8°C over Newcastle, cooling to 6°C over Glasgow and Aberdeen. It should keep dry, but expect the wind to strengthen by the evening.

Lastly I will look at *north-west Scotland and Northern Ireland*. It will be a blustery day with winds from the west of about 25 miles per hour. On west coasts and in other exposed places it may be much windier than this. It will be a day of short sunny patches separated by heavy showers, especially over the hills. With temperatures down to 5°C at sea level at Inverness and Belfast, it will be cold enough for snow on high ground. Between showers the visibility will be very good.

Class activity

Work in pairs or in groups of three. You will need to *discuss* the information above and decide on how best to use it.
Begin by answering these questions 1–4.
1 Where is the mildest weather expected?
2 Where is the windiest weather expected?
3 In which parts of Britain do you think it might rain today?
4 Where is most sunshine expected?

Now you will each need a blank copy of the weather map of the British Isles and its key. You are going to produce your own weather report for the 12th of November.
5 Using the description above, draw symbols on your map to show what the weather will be like in the various parts of the country. Make sure that
- you place the symbols in the right places (an atlas will be useful)
- you match the right symbols with the right weather conditions.

6 Write a paragraph to describe the weather for that day in Dover, Liverpool and Fort William.

7 Two fronts are passing over the British Isles today, the 12th of November.
a Mark on your map where you think these two fronts are.
b Explain how they are affecting the weather.

8a Which areas will have sleet and snow?
b Explain why this is to be expected.

Follow-up activity

Weather forecasts are not always accurate. Collect your own weather information. Your teacher will help you with this. You should collect information over at least a week. For the same week, collect weather reports from local and national newspapers. Compare your own weather information with the forecasts from local and national newspapers.
▸ How are they similar?
▸ How are they different?
▸ Why do you think there are these differences between your own information about local conditions, local newspaper forecasts and the national forecasts?

▶ Have we affected the climate?

We have already seen that people's lives are influenced by climate. Can people also influence the climate? There is now evidence that people have begun to change the world's climate.

This section looks at some of this evidence. Is the climate really changing? If so, by how much? Whom will it affect? And what should we do about it?

Surprises of the 1980s!

- Hurricane Joan (1988) was the strongest ever to hit Nicaragua, with winds of up to 170 miles per hour.
- The 1980s was the warmest decade on record.
- A summer heat wave in China killed hundreds of people. Local hospitals could hardly cope with the number of sunstroke victims.
- Drought in North America meant that in 1988, for the first time, more grain was consumed than was produced.
- The winter of 1988–89 was the mildest in Britain since records first began in 1659. Temperatures were found to be 2.5°C above average. (Scientists warned that this could just be a freak mild winter. They said that this winter weather alone did not prove that the climate is changing.)

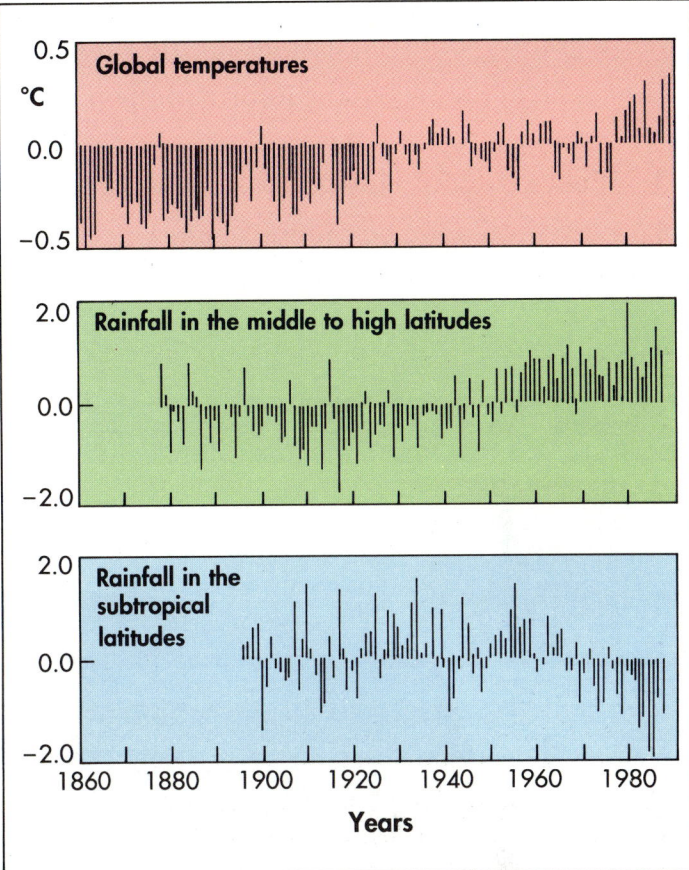

3·16 *Has our climate changed? These three graphs show how temperatures and rainfall have changed during the years between 1860 and 1990. The 'normal' line on which each graph is based was calculated as an **average** of weather records between 1951 and 1979. Rainfall is based on a simple index to show relative amounts, not actual units.*

Now read what Professor V. R. Whett has to say.

The climate is always changing. Parts of Britain have been covered with ice several times. Between the ice ages, there are warmer spells. We are in one now. It is no surprise that the seas should rise slightly as a little ice melts.

Only 200 years ago we had much colder winters than we do now. It got so cold that the River Thames froze over several times.

We should be careful about jumping to conclusions. For example, many of the rising temperature figures were taken in big cities. It is quite likely that they are higher in cities because of all the fuel that people use. This may not mean that temperatures are rising everywhere else.

UNIT 3

Study the three graphs on page 55.

1 Describe what has happened to global temperatures since 1860.

2 Write a short paragraph to describe what these graphs could suggest about the future.

Now look at the rest of the information on page 55.

3 What evidence is there for climate change?

4 Why should we be cautious before deciding that the climate has changed?

Carbon dioxide (CO_2)

- It is a natural part of the atmosphere.
- In 1850 the amount of CO_2 in the atmosphere was 280 ppm (parts per million). Now it is 350 ppm.
- Plants take in carbon dioxide. With water and sunlight they use carbon to build up plant tissue. This process is called *photosynthesis*. In exchange, plants release oxygen back into the air. Plants are the 'lungs' of our planet Earth.
- Experts are worried that by chopping down the forests of the world, there will be fewer plants to carry out this process.

Carbon dioxide and the greenhouse effect

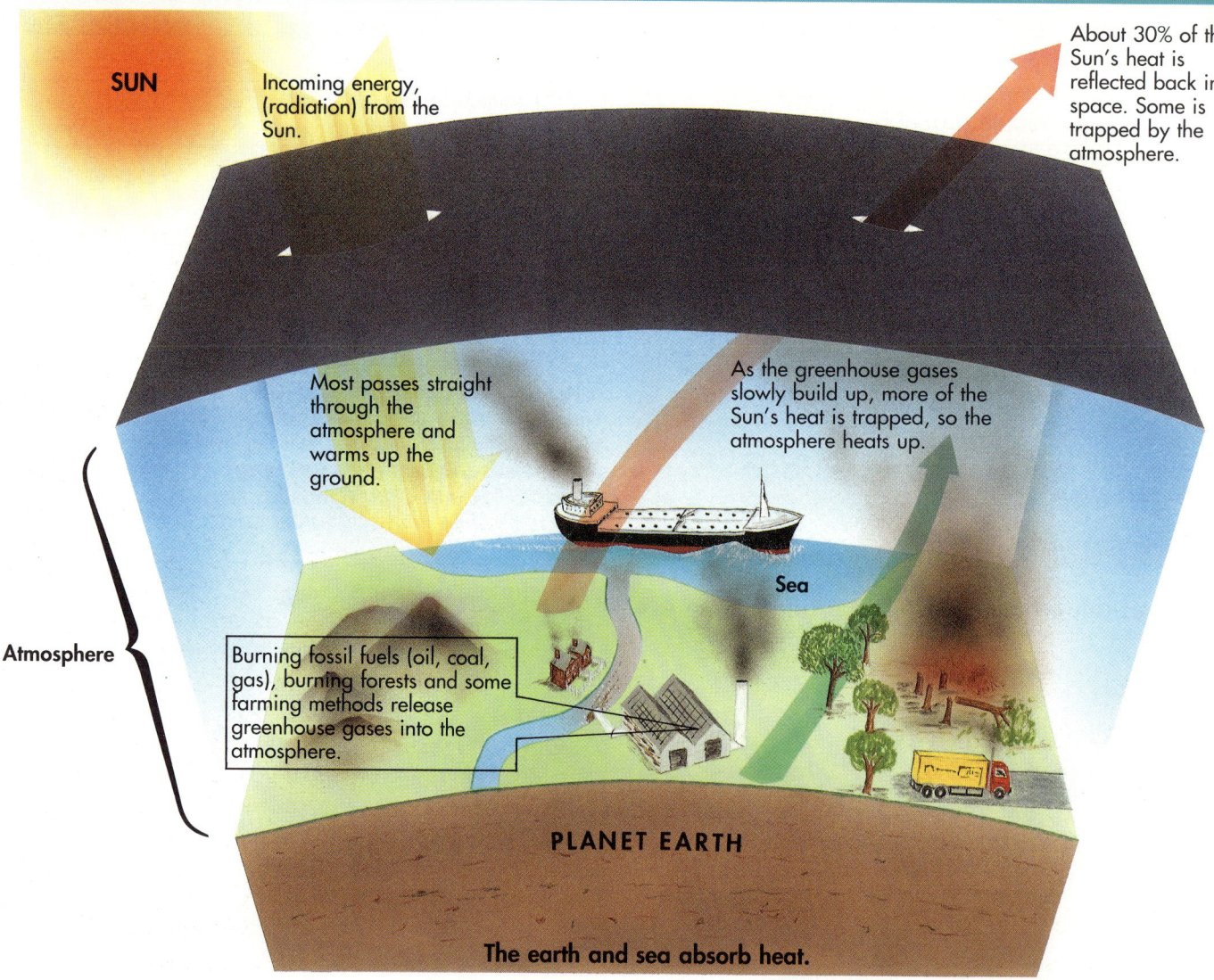

3·17 The 'greenhouse effect'.

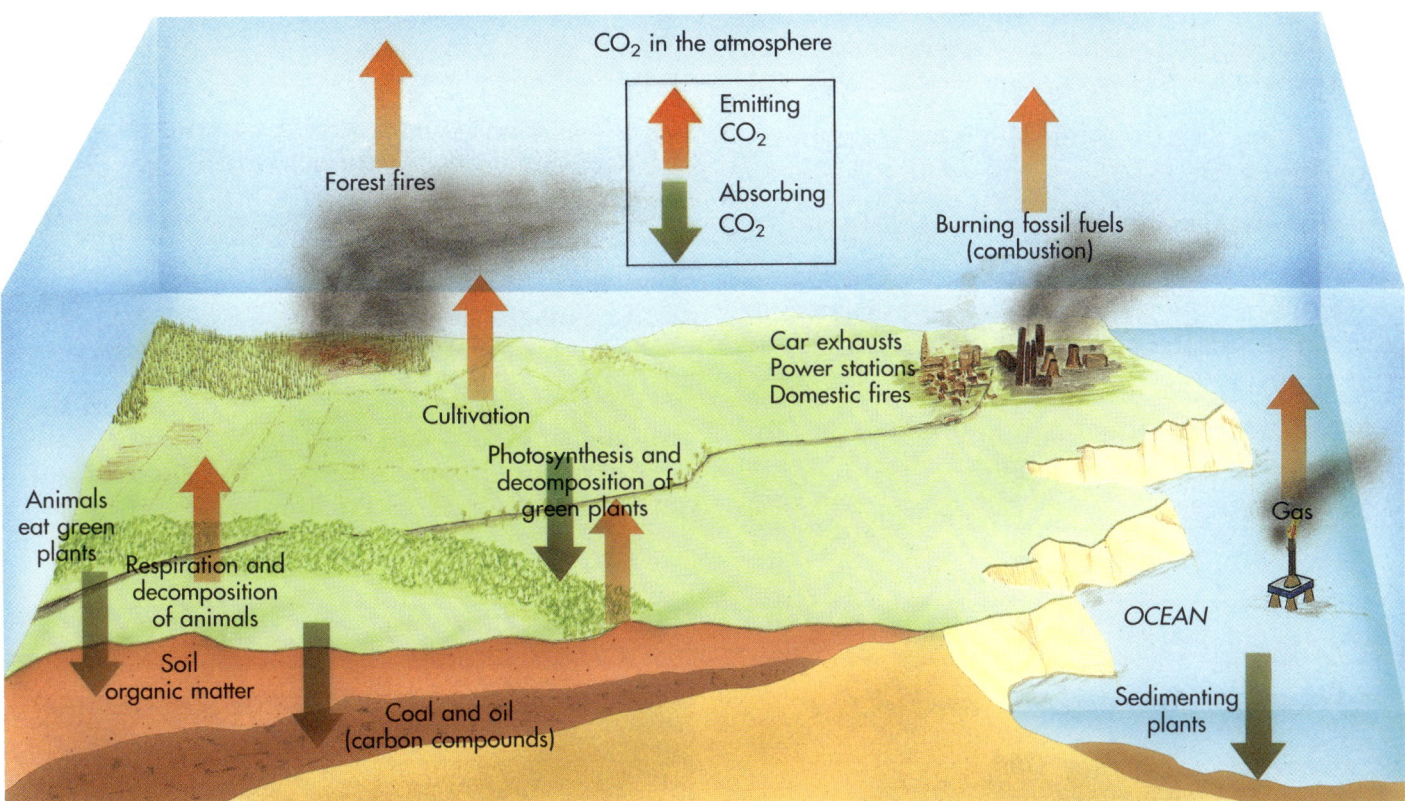

3·18 *The carbon exchange.*

3·19 *A power station emitting polluting smoke, steam and gases.*

3·20 *Burning the rainforest of Trinidad. Every year, worldwide, an area of rainforest larger than the size of Scotland is destroyed.*

Study all of the facts about carbon dioxide on pages 56–57.

1 How much carbon dioxide was there in the atmosphere in 1850?

2 What has been the increase in carbon dioxide since then?

3 Explain how plants play an important part in controlling the amount of carbon dioxide in the atmosphere.

Look carefully at the diagram on page 56 which explains the 'greenhouse effect'.

4 Describe what happens to the sun's energy after it hits the Earth.

5 What effect does an increase in carbon dioxide have on the atmosphere?

6 From the diagram on page 57 showing the carbon exchange, make a list of the processes which
a are caused by people,
b happen naturally.

7 Describe what is happening in each of the photographs on page 57. For each photograph explain how people are changing the amount of carbon dioxide in the atmosphere.

A tropical paradise ... but for how long?

'When will they stop talking and do something?'

Maumoon Abdul Gayoom, the President of the Maldives

About 1,500 islands make up the Maldives, although this number changes as new islands form, whilst others are washed away. The people of the Maldives live on the larger islands. Wherever you are in the Maldives the sea is never far away.

The highest point of the Maldives is about the same as the height of two adults standing one on top of the other. Although these islands are beautiful, they may eventually all lie beneath the sea.

Global warming is a big issue here. Scientists expect the sea level to rise between 15 and 30 centimetres by the year 2030. It may not sound much, but it is worrying when there is no high ground to escape to.

The flooding will not happen overnight. First, the high tides will push waves further up the beach, and some will break over sea defences during storms. The sea may wash away some beaches, reducing the vital buffer between the

3·21 A beach on the Maldive Islands. Find out from an atlas where these islands are.

sea and the people. Gradually more salt water will seep under the islands. Salt water is undrinkable without expensive treatment, and it will ruin crops in the soil.

The people of the Maldives are anxious and a little angry: anxious because even though leaders of the world's powerful countries have done lots of talking, there has not been enough action; and angry because they feel they are paying the price for damage to their environment that has been caused by other people.

1 Imagine you are on holiday in the Maldives. Write a postcard home describing the islands' problems.

2 By how much do scientists expect the sea level to rise in the next 40 years?

3 How will global warming affect the people?

4 Explain whether you think the people are right to be angry about the rise in sea level.

▲ 3·23 *Damage caused by flooding in Bangladesh in 1991. Just a one-metre rise in sea level could mean that 50 million people across the world are made homeless. That is three times the number of homeless in the world today.*

3·22 *Bangladesh today – and tomorrow?* ▼

Today

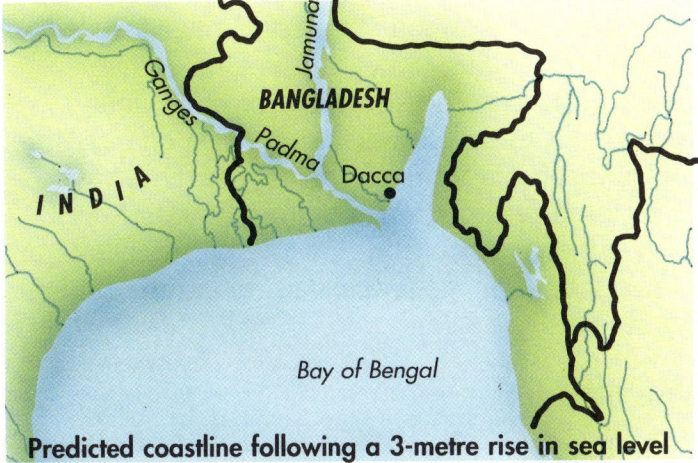

Predicted coastline following a 3-metre rise in sea level

1 Use an atlas to explain why Bangladesh would be seriously affected by even a small rise in sea level.

2 Write a paragraph describing your feelings about the photograph above showing recent floods in Bangladesh.

Investigation

In groups, read the following item.

At the mercy of a natural killer

Bangladesh suffered serious floods from the sea in 1985, 1986, 1989 and 1991. Perhaps as many as *two million people* died as a result.

Bangladesh today resembles Holland in the 15th and 16th centuries. Then, the fast-growing population of 'the low countries' colonised new farmland on the Zuider Zee, which was protected by fragile dykes. But North Sea storms washed the dykes away and killed tens of thousands of people in the St Elizabeth's Day floods of 1421, and again in 1570.

Faced with untameable natural forces, the Dutch abandoned the Zuider Zee to the sea for almost 400 years. Today in Bangladesh — as the sea level rises and cyclones rage — that country may have to do the same thing. For the flood peril is going to remain for a long time to come. But where will the people of Bangladesh go to?

From a newspaper article, 29 May 1991

1 Find out the answers to the following questions.
▸ Where is the Zuider Zee? Draw a map of the area.
▸ What can you learn about the St Elizabeth's Day floods of 1421?
▸ How have recent floods affected Holland?
▸ How do the Dutch people now use the Zuider Zee?
▸ How have the Dutch people reclaimed the land in Holland?

Present your answers to these questions as a poster.

2 Do you think the comparison between Bangladesh and Holland is a fair one?

KEY POINTS KEY IDEAS

In this unit we concentrated on some of the processes at work in one part of the physical environment, the atmosphere. We came across several important key points.

The weather

The British are famous the world over for their willingness to talk about the weather. This characteristic comes from the most obvious feature of the British weather: it is so changeable and unpredictable that there is nearly always something new to talk about or comment on.

Weather is about the day-to-day conditions of atmosphere that we feel: the temperature, rainfall, wind, sunshine, cloud, etc.

The climate

Even the British do not talk much about the climate. This is because it is not so noticeable. It is predictable and does not change much. There is the annual passage of seasons, but *on average* – climate is always about averages, over at least 35 years – temperatures and rainfall are fairly constant.

Occasionally, in Britain, a very hot summer is experienced, or an extremely cold winter. But it is the exception that proves the rule!

Climatic change in the past

Scientists who examine the growth rings in trees, the pollen found in peat bogs and the sediments at the bottom of lakes all agree that the climate of any place does slowly change. And we know by examining landforms and landscapes that only 10,000 years ago, during the last Ice Age, much of the British Isles was covered in ice. No one is sure exactly why climates have changed in the past.

Climatic change in the future

During the last 200 years, but especially during the last 50 years, people around the world have themselves started to change local and global climates. This is mainly a result of burning oil and coal and destroying large forests. No one is sure exactly what the effects of future climatic changes will be.

Global warming

Many scientists and politicians agree that the global climate is warming up. This does not mean that the whole Earth warms up evenly. Nor does it mean that all people will suffer (or benefit) in the same way. For example, the poor of the world will be the first to suffer from the effects of a rise in sea level caused by global warming. This is because many such people are forced to live on *marginal* land. This means dangerous, low-lying land, unprotected from floods.

Forecasts

It is difficult to forecast the effects of climatic change. It is easier to forecast changes in the weather. It is also extremely useful to do this: farmers, ferry operators, builders and people who live in marginal areas all find forecasts useful.

Weather experts are becoming more accurate with their forecasts, because they have a better understanding of *processes* in the atmosphere (that is, what *causes* the weather). The processes we came across in this unit include those that cause rainfall: frontal rainfall, relief rainfall, convectional rainfall.

Water Shapes the Land

UNIT 4

4·1 This photograph was taken from an aeroplane about 500 metres above the ground. It shows the River Thames in flood in February 1990. On this occasion houses were flooded and people had to be evacuated. It was the worst flood for many years.

UNIT 4

Water, rivers, land and people

The Earth is the home of people. Sometimes we study the Earth ('physical geography') and sometimes we study people ('human geography'). As this Venn diagram shows, it is often difficult to draw the line between the two. Studying rivers is a bit like this: the physical and the human aspects are mixed up together.

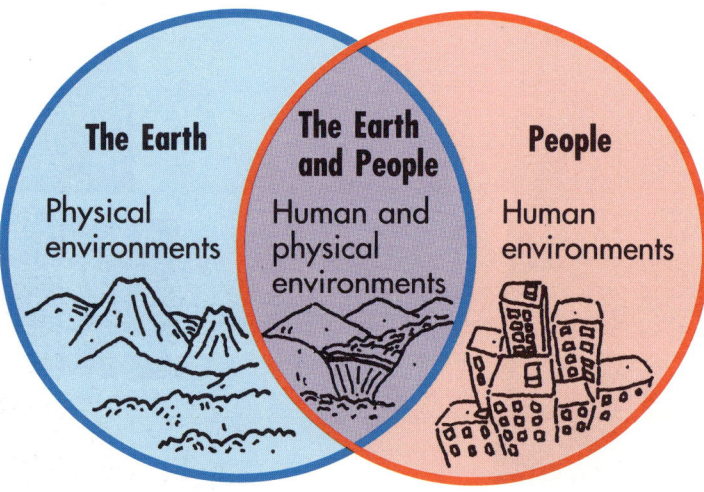

4.2 *A Venn diagram to show the relationships between physical and human environments.*

Class activity

The aim of this activity is to give you a chance to think about water, and especially rivers, using the Venn diagram as an *organiser*.

Your first job is to discuss among yourselves what the differences are between 'physical' and 'human' aspects of water and rivers. Some pupils were given this question to answer:
▸ What is a river?
Some of their answers are written down above.

1 Decide what you think is the main point that the student is making in each case. This is like trying to make up a heading for each piece of writing. Write down your headings as a table like this:

No.	Heading	Question
1	Rivers transport water	

Some 12-year-olds were asked, 'What is a river?' This is what they wrote.

1 I think a river is a means of transportation of water to get into the sea from the ground, when it has landed. You see, when it has been raining the rain lands on the ground. From there it could flow straight into a river, or it could soak into the ground and eventually get into the river. From there it will go along lots of streams and rivers, and at the end that river will flow into the sea.

2 They have different personalities some are calm and some are very wild rivers.

3 The main job of a river is carrying water to the sea.

2 Now try to make each heading into a question. For example, if you thought that extract 4 was mainly about *how rivers are all different*, the question could be: 'How are rivers different?' or 'How do rivers vary?'

3 On another piece of paper, draw three columns. These columns represent the three parts of the Venn diagram, and they should be headed 'Physical', 'Human' and 'Physical/Human'.

4 Now take your questions one by one and write them down in what you think is the correct column.

5 Then look carefully at the photographs on page 75 (Exmoor). In your pairs, note down for each photograph any questions that come into your mind about the river itself or its surroundings.

6 Copy out these new questions in the correct column.

By now you will have quite long lists of questions. This unit should help you to answer some of them – possibly all of them.

UNIT 4

4 All rivers vary. Mountain rivers are different to rivers by the sea as they flow faster and are much cleaner. Rivers can be beautiful or dull and dirty. When the rivers flow fast rocks debris crash against the sides of the river bank this is called erosion. I like rivers and when there are thoughts in my head about them, I think of the rippling current and the fresh, cool clear water.

5 I think the most important thing about rivers is pollution in the river and how we could stop it.

6 Rivers run through towns, cities and villages. The big rivers are normally in cities but small ones are in towns and villages. Streams run into rivers.

7 A river carries water down it and it takes it into the sea. It is made up by little streams which join together to make a bigger stream, then the bigger stream joins another big stream and so on. Then it joins to the river. If there weren't any rivers then when it rains there would be a lot of surface water.

8 Rivers can be dangerous to people and to other things. A river can destroy things, overflow its banks and destroy animals and homes.

9 The river I can remember was in Cornwall. I was about 9 at the time. This river was about 2 feet deep with big rocks poking through all along that stretch of river. I can remember it well because I was always falling in.

Setting the scene

What is a river?

To some people, a river is a friend: it provides clean water and a source of food. A river can also be a foe, for when it floods it can kill and destroy. A river which floods can be both a foe *and* a friend because after a flood the stinking black mud that is left on the floodplain around its banks is fertile; the grass grows greener and the crops grow stronger as a result.

Mark Twain, the American author who wrote the stories *Tom Sawyer* and *Huckleberry Finn*, lived near the Mississippi River in the USA. He was always amazed at its size (it is the third largest river in the world), and he wrote about its huge floods in his book *Life on the Mississippi*, in 1883. He noticed that rivers, even enormous ones like the Mississippi, do not always stay in the same place. They sometimes change their course. They usually do this when they flood. On the next page is Mark Twain's description of such a change in the river's course.

4·3 *The Mississippi River and the Mississippi Delta.*

The town of Delta used to be three miles below Vicksburg. A recent cut-off has radically changed the position, and Delta is now *two miles above* Vicksburg. Sudden cut-offs could also mean someone in the State of Louisiana could find themselves transferred with their land to the State of Mississippi.

The diagram below helps to explain how the two towns 'changed positions'.

4·4   *Meanders on the great Mississippi River.*

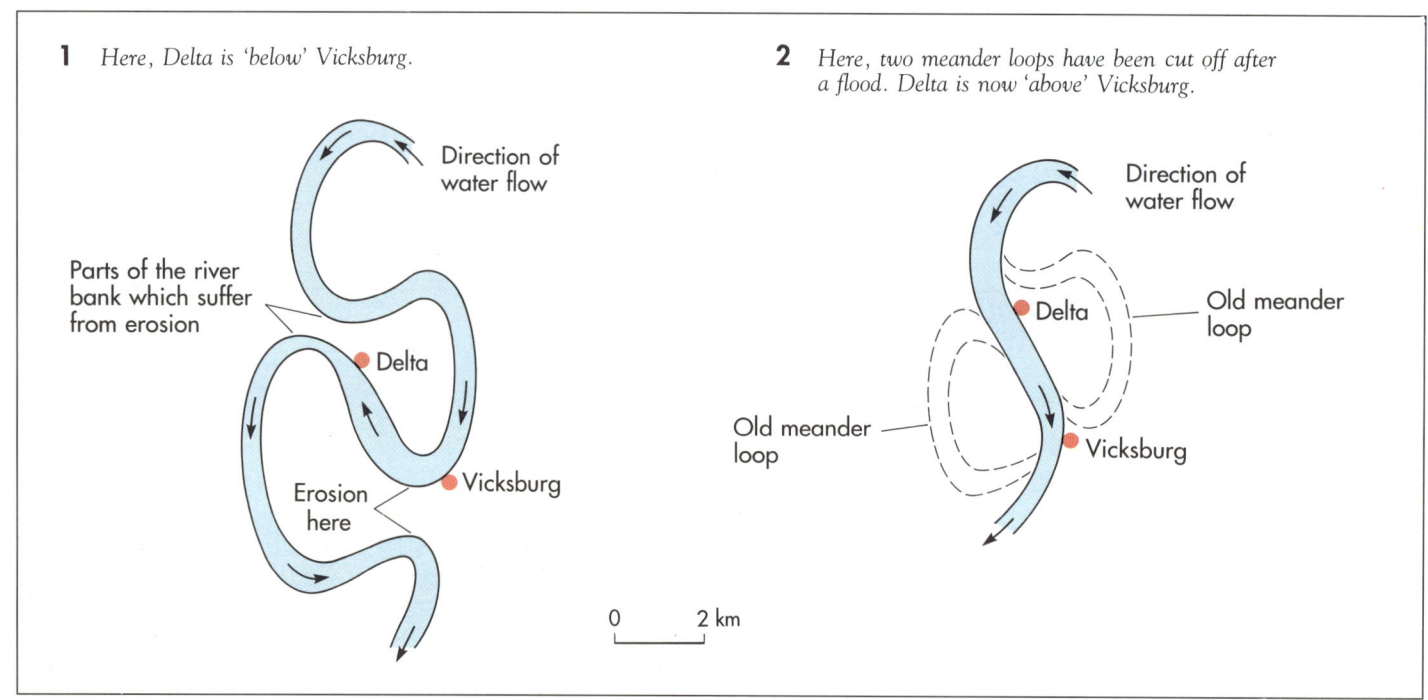

4·5   How Vicksburg 'moved' to a new position below Delta on the Mississippi River.

1 What did Mark Twain mean when he wrote that the towns of Delta and Vicksburg 'changed positions'?
Clue: Which way does water always flow?

2 Why could a change in the position of the river channel mean that people suddenly find themselves in a different state?

3 *Either* find some local examples of rivers which have changed courses, *or* find an example on an OS map of a river in Britain which has changed course.

At Vicksburg, on average the amount of water which flows by is 14,000 cubic metres per second (m^3/sec). This can easily double in times of flood and it is then that the channel bursts and a new one is sometimes cut. After the flood, the old channel is left high and dry.

In addition to all this water, the Mississippi River *transports* large amounts of sand and mud (*sediment*), most of which is *deposited* in the sea. Here the river finally stops flowing and the sand and mud simply falls to the bottom. Gradually, a *delta* has grown, made out of all this deposited sediment.

But these days, less sediment reaches the sea. Many experts have noticed that now the delta is being attacked by the sea and is becoming smaller as a result! This is probably happening as a result of the building of dams. Several large dams were built on rivers flowing into the Mississippi during the 1950s. This was done to control the flow of water. But dams also trap the sediment. One day they will fill up with sand and mud.

Over the years the average flow of water in the Mississippi has not changed much. But the flow of sediment has fallen. The great Mississippi Delta itself may now slowly disappear.

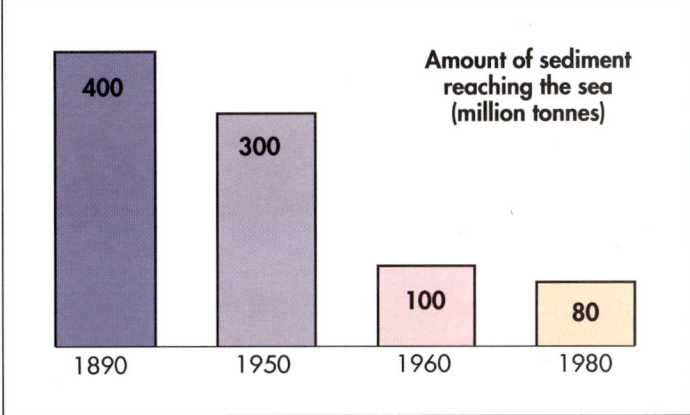

4.6 *A century ago, much more sediment was carried to the sea by the Mississippi River.*

Rivers in our lives

Another writer, named Graham Swift, lived near a much smaller river, in Britain. This is how he describes it in his book *Waterland*. Use an atlas map to try to identify the river from this description.

> It flows out of the heart of England to the Wash and the North Sea. It passes the sturdy English towns of Bedford, Huntingdon, St Ives, Ely, Gildsey and King's Lynn, whose inhabitants see the river which flows only one way – downstream. Its name derives from Sanskrit for 'water'. It is a hundred and fifty-six miles long. Its catchment is 2,067 square miles.

It is a tiny river compared with the Mississippi, but there are similarities:

> It is a feature of this footloose and obstinate river that it has several times during its brush with human history changed direction, taken short-cuts, long loops, been coaxed into new channels and rearranged its meeting-place with the sea.

And people have also tried to control this river, especially a famous Dutch water engineer named Vermuyden in the eighteenth century.

> Then Vermuyden came to put matters right, and dug the Bedford and New Bedford Rivers – straight strings to the bow of the rebellious river – to the glee of the people of Huntingdon who now had better access than ever to the coast.

This work stopped the river from flooding so often. But perhaps people can never totally change the character which a river can give to a place or a region. Will the Fens, a part of East Anglia, ever change its image of being flat, low-lying and damp?

The New Bedford River, or 'Hundred Foot Drain'.

UNIT 4

Graham Swift has a *feeling* for the river he describes:

> The Great Ouse. Ouse. Say it. Ouse. Slowly. How else can you say it? A sound which exudes slowness. A sound which suggests the slow, sluggish, forever oozing thing it is. A sound which invokes quiet flux, minimum tempo; cool, impassive, unmoved motion. A sound which will calm even the hot blood racing in your veins. Ouse, Ouse, Ooooooouse . . .

The River Ouse near Huntingdon.

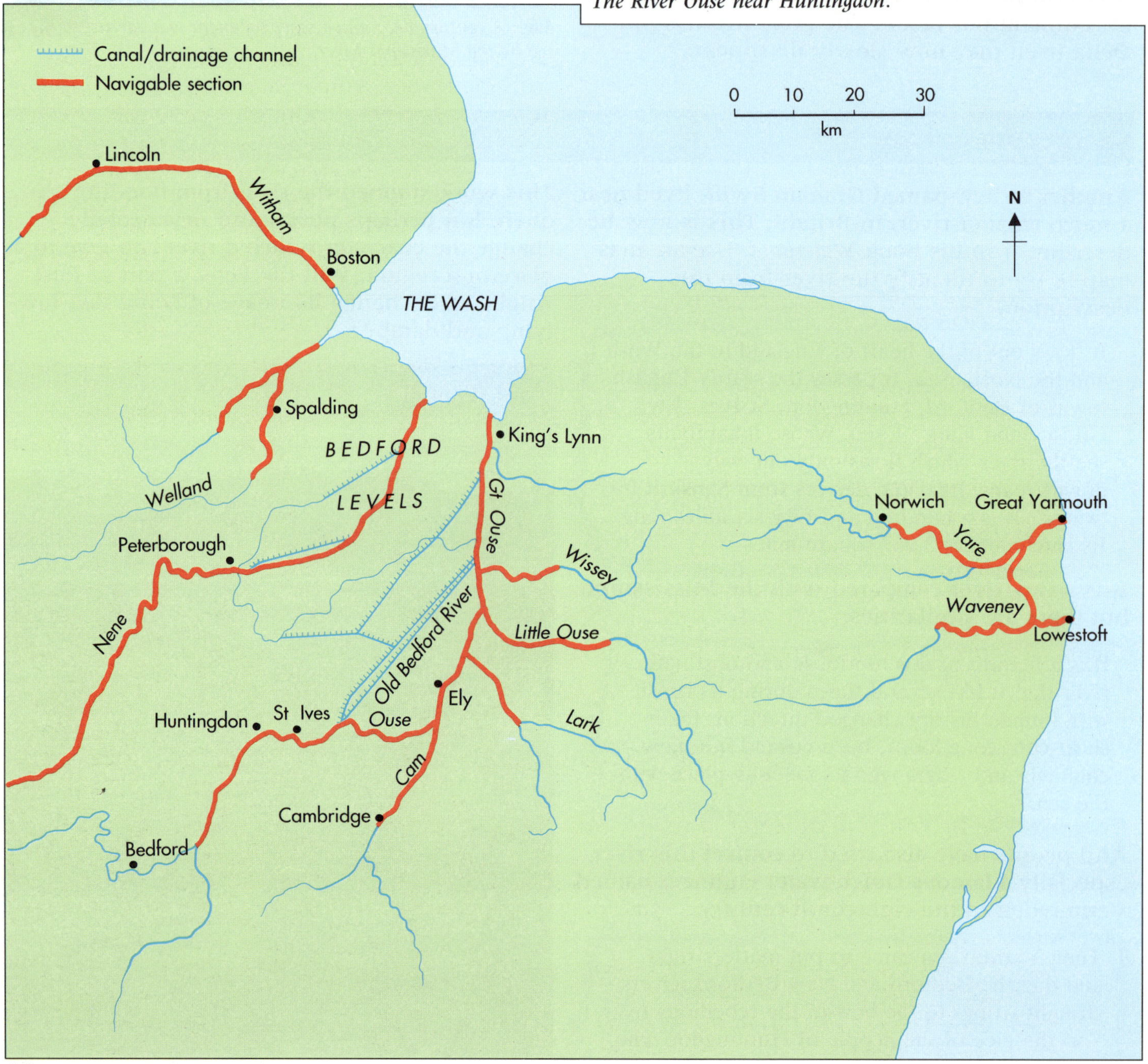

4.8 *The Rivers of East Anglia.*

Rivers: part of the water cycle

Students were asked to write an answer to the question: What is a river? One student wrote this poem.

*A river H_2O flowing deep over a landscape
Filling gaps and draining the land for, well
nearly ever.
You see,
a river can stop.
When it is warm it drys up,
and stops.
But when it rains again,
It starts to flow again
Regaining its territorial path.
A river helps to provide
water to live
'A river of Life' is what comes from the sky
that comes from the sea
To which we all
swim.*

Graham Swift, in his description of the River Ouse, wrote this:

> It flows – oozes – on, as every river must, to the sea. And as we all know, the sun and the wind suck up the water from the sea and disperse it on the land, perpetually refeeding the rivers. So that while the Ouse flows to the sea, it flows, in reality, like all rivers, only back to itself, to its own source; and that impression that a river moves only one way is an illusion.

These two writers have the same idea: that rivers are a part of a large water system. This is an important idea which we can see when later in this unit we investigate the water cycle.

But we already know that rivers are not *just* conveyor belts for water. In this unit we will investigate water, rivers and their effects on the landscape – both the 'human' and the 'physical' landscape. To help us do this we have three key questions:

▷ Where does our water come from?

▷ How do we investigate the work of a river?

▷ In what ways do river landscapes vary?

▷ Where does our water come from?

Many people would answer this question by saying, 'From the sky!' But how does water come to be in the sky? And what happens to it when it falls to the ground? To help us with these questions we can refer to a very useful idea: the water cycle.

The water cycle

There is a limited amount of water in the world. We cannot really *make* any more than there is already. But there is a lot of it, though most of it is not easy to use, either because it is too salty, or because it is frozen.

This means that the same water is used over and over again. There is a never-ending *water cycle*. When you study the diagram on the next page, look first at the surface of the sea where warmth, wind and sun *evaporate* the water.

4·9 *A mountain stream, part of the water cycle.*

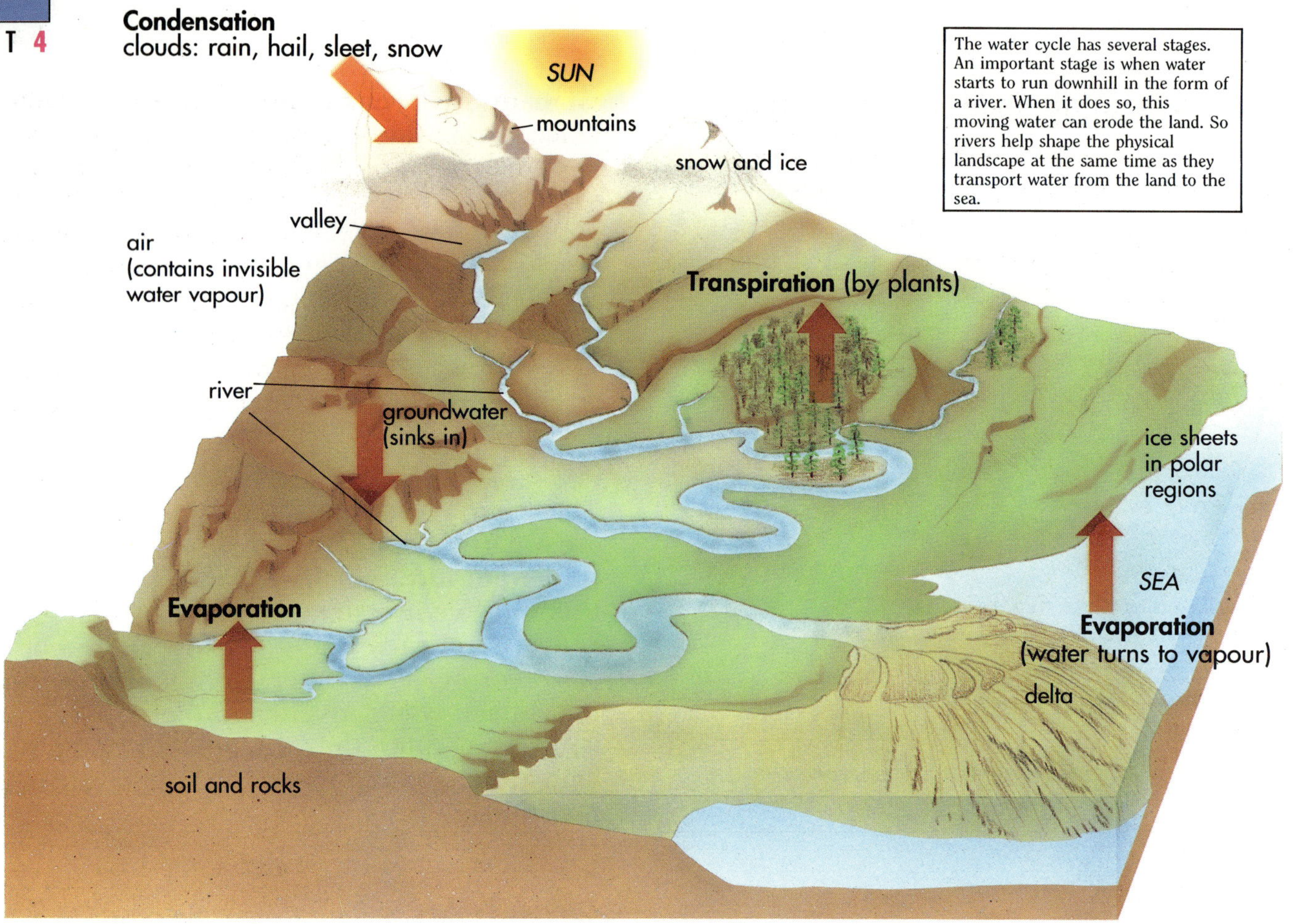

UNIT 4

Condensation clouds: rain, hail, sleet, snow

SUN

mountains

snow and ice

valley

air (contains invisible water vapour)

Transpiration (by plants)

river

groundwater (sinks in)

ice sheets in polar regions

Evaporation

SEA

Evaporation (water turns to vapour)

delta

soil and rocks

> The water cycle has several stages. An important stage is when water starts to run downhill in the form of a river. When it does so, this moving water can erode the land. So rivers help shape the physical landscape at the same time as they transport water from the land to the sea.

4·10 *The natural water cycle.*

People in the water cycle

The water cycle goes on for ever. People are also part of this cycle because they use water. The flow diagram below shows this. You can find out *how much* water people use by reading 'Setting the scene' in Unit 5 (pages 82–85). Unit 5 also helps us investigate how people have tried to change the water cycle in a big way – with disastrous results.

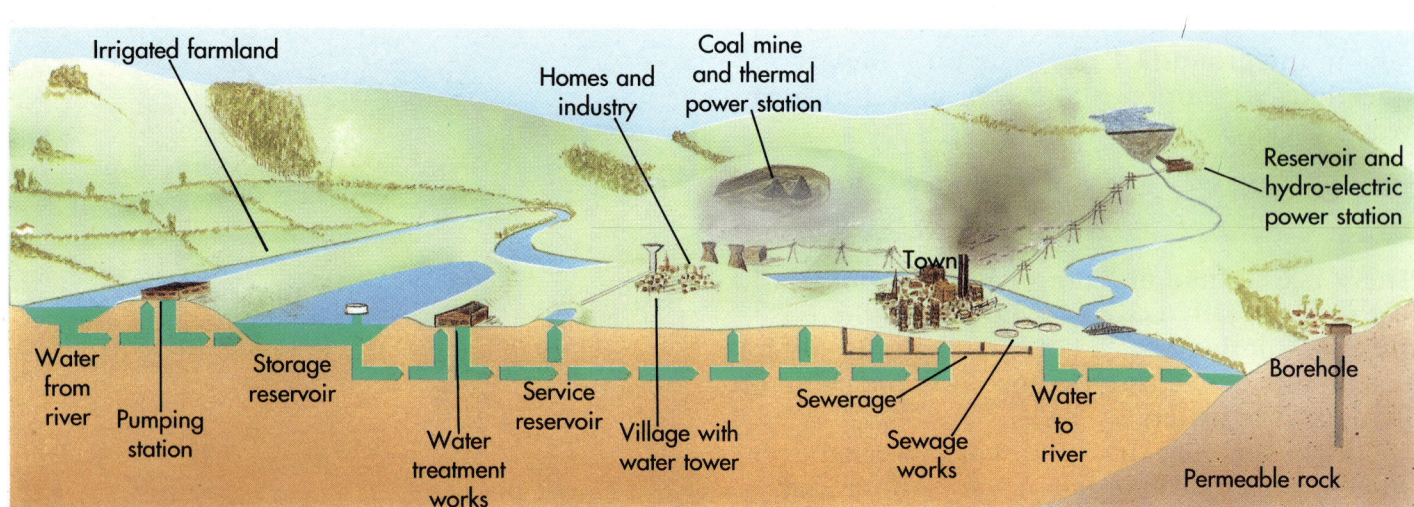

4·11 *The human water cycle. By building reservoirs, pumping stations and pipelines, people can change the natural movement of water.*

68

An enquiry to the local water company

Two pupils were beginning a project to answer the question, 'Where does our water come from?' They decided to telephone the local water company to help them find out.

A man answered and they asked him what it was like having to supply more and more people with more and more water. This was his reply:

> It gets more and more difficult! People have to learn that water costs money – money to build reservoirs, pipes, and sewage works. You can see from a map that one of the problems is that water users do not always live in the best place! I think users should pay more. This way we would make more profit and users might try to use less water.

Mr Bourne.

Mr Bourne sent the pupils some extra material to look at. Place a piece of tracing paper over the map on this page (bottom left) and trace it, then mark two points: one where the River Tees meets the sea, and the other where the River Exe meets the sea. If you join these points with a straight line you now have the Tees–Exe line. This divides Britain into two parts: Upland Britain and Lowland Britain. It may be a useful line in other ways too. (See questions 4 and 5 on page 70.)

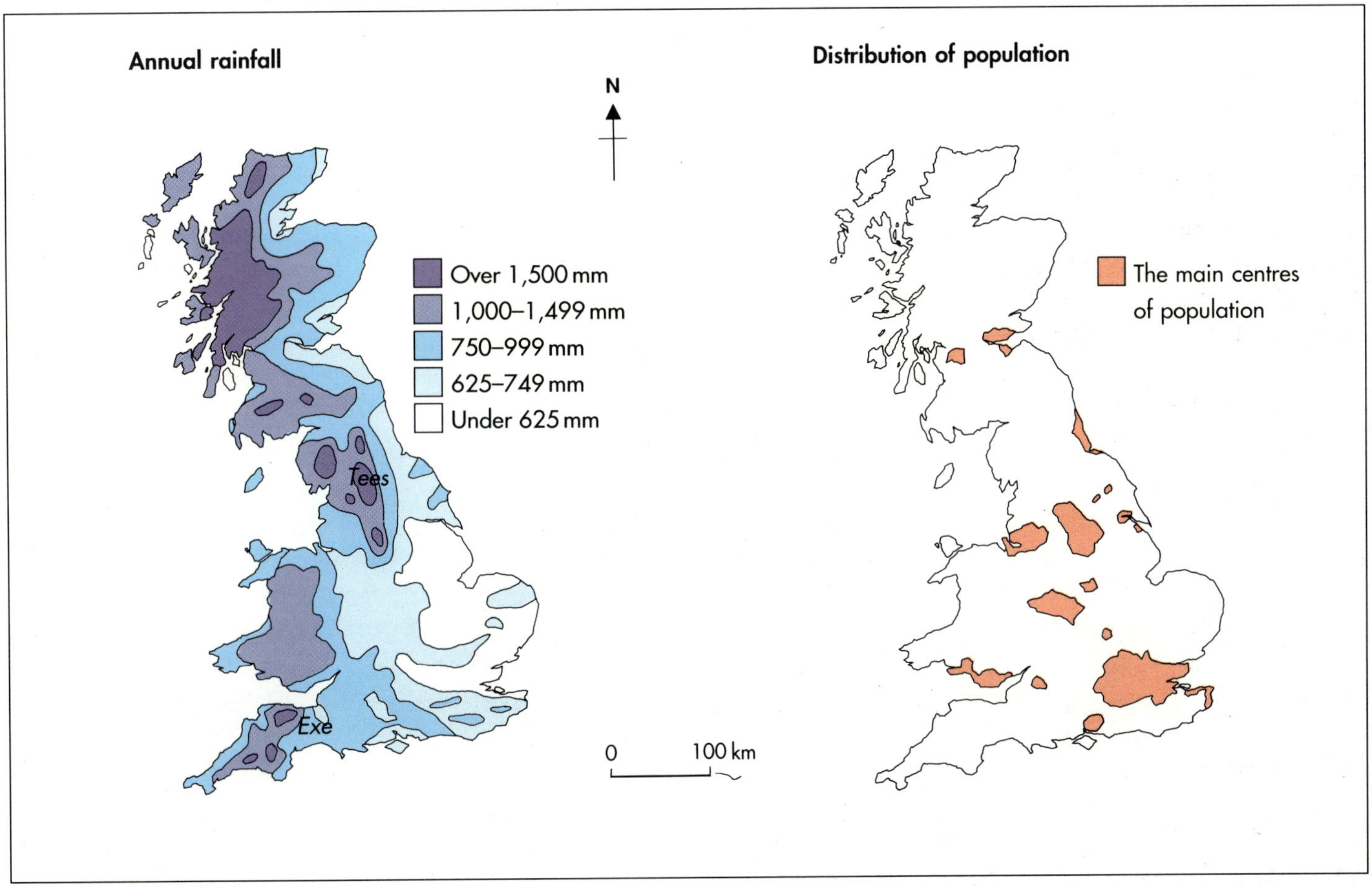

4·12 *A comparison of the annual rainfall and distribution of population in Great Britain.*

UNIT 4

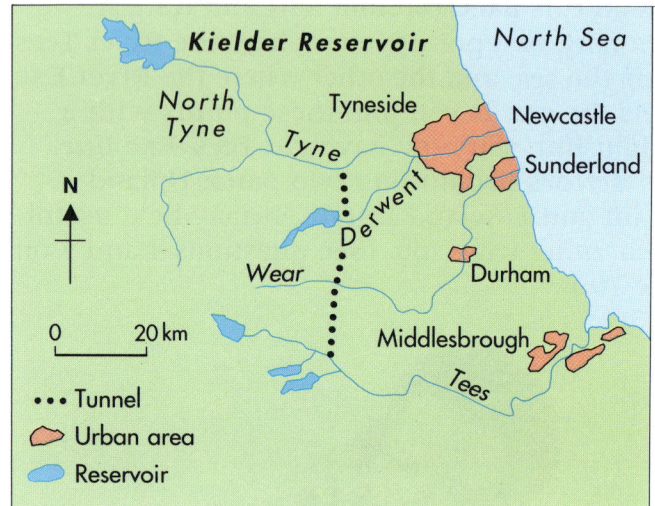

The Kielder Reservoir is the largest artificial lake in Europe. It was built in the 1970s. People and industry in the north-east of England should have plenty of water for many years to come.

Other parts of England are still short of water. In the dry, sunny summers of 1989 and 1990, parts of south-east England, including London, had strict water controls. The drought continued into 1992 and became the most severe for 200 years.

The Kielder scheme consists of two parts. The reservoir at Kielder is a regulating reservoir which releases water into the North Tyne river and increases its flow. In this way the Water Company can take more water from the river. The second part of the scheme is a tunnel which links the rivers Tyne, Wear and Tees. By means of this tunnel, the industrial areas of the North East can all use water from the Kielder Reservoir.

4·13   *The Kielder scheme.*

Classroom activity

Work in pairs.

1 Look at the diagram of the water cycle on page 68. Imagine one drop of water swirling around on the surface of the sea. Follow the *cycle of events* from the moment it is evaporated until the moment it is returned to the sea. Write down the events as a story under the heading, 'The Journey of a Water Droplet'.

2 Join up with another pair. Have they written the same journey as you? Under a new heading write a list of the different things that could happen to the water droplet during its journey. Your heading could be, 'There is more than one way to go through the water cycle'.

3 You can draw a picture of the water cycle in the form of a flow diagram. Your teacher may be able to help you with this, but if you wish to devise your own, start by listing all the *changes* that happen to the water. Then arrange the changes on a piece of blank paper in boxes. Connect up the boxes with arrows.

4 Look carefully at the map on page 69. The Tees–Exe Line divides Britain into two parts:
a the North and West (or Upland Britain)
b the South and East (or Lowland Britain).
What *three* differences can you find in the geography on either side of the line? A *relief map* of Britain, showing the *shape* of the land, will be very useful (see page 33).

5 Study your answer to question 4, because it will help you with this one. Look back at the phone call the two pupils made to Mr Bourne. One of you take the part of the students, and one of you be Mr Bourne. Try to continue with the conversation. The students go on to say, 'What do you mean, Mr Bourne, when you say *water users do not always live in the best place*?'

Mr Bourne:

Students:

What happens to water after it has reached the ground?

The diagram on this page shows all the things that can happen to rain after it has fallen on the ground.

Look at the diagram on this page.

1 Find the symbol on the diagram for each of the following:
- rain falling on the ground
- evaporation
- water sinking into the ground
- water accumulating on the ground.

2 On a copy of the diagram, label arrows to show each of the processes identified in (1).

3 Now label your diagram with these additional items:
- water table
- groundwater
- soil water.

4 When a lot of rain falls, the soil cannot hold any more water and the ground becomes *saturated*. What do you think happens to any further rain reaching the ground?

5a In Britain, during which season of the year do we find most puddles? When does the soil stay wet for the longest time?
b Using the figures supplied below, draw a graph. Your graph should have two lines, one to show the amount of water that falls as rain each month, and the other to show the amount of water that is evaporated each month.

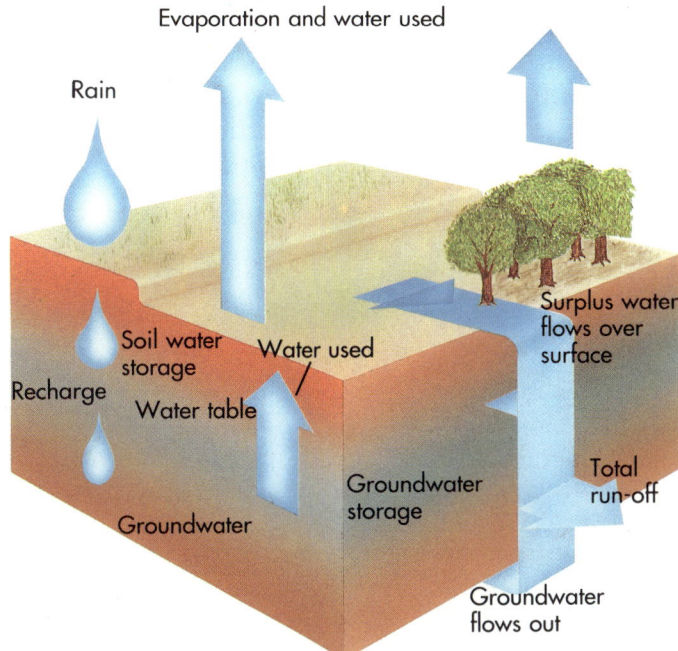

4·14 *What happens to rainwater after it has fallen to the ground.*

c Choose two colours and shade in the spaces between the two lines on your graph. Which *two* spaces should have the *same colour*?
d Now label these spaces. Choose from 'water shortage' and 'water surplus'.
e Imagine asking someone:
'Why do you think puddles last much longer in winter?' He or she answers, 'Because it rains more in winter!' What would you say in reply? Use your graph to help you.

	J	F	M	A	M	J	J	A	S	O	N	D
Rainfall (mm)	74	75	76	78	82	86	85	84	81	80	80	81
Evaporation (mm)	16	24	39	68	106	127	129	118	93	56	30	17

UNIT 4

▷ How do we investigate the work of a river?

Rivers on the land

Much of the rain that falls on the land soaks through the soil. In a country like Britain, where it rains quite a lot, there is often a water surplus. Even in the summer months, when evaporation rates are high, there is still usually plenty of water stored underground. This groundwater is vital for keeping rivers flowing even through periods when there is little or no rain.
Study the diagram below, which shows how a river gets its water.

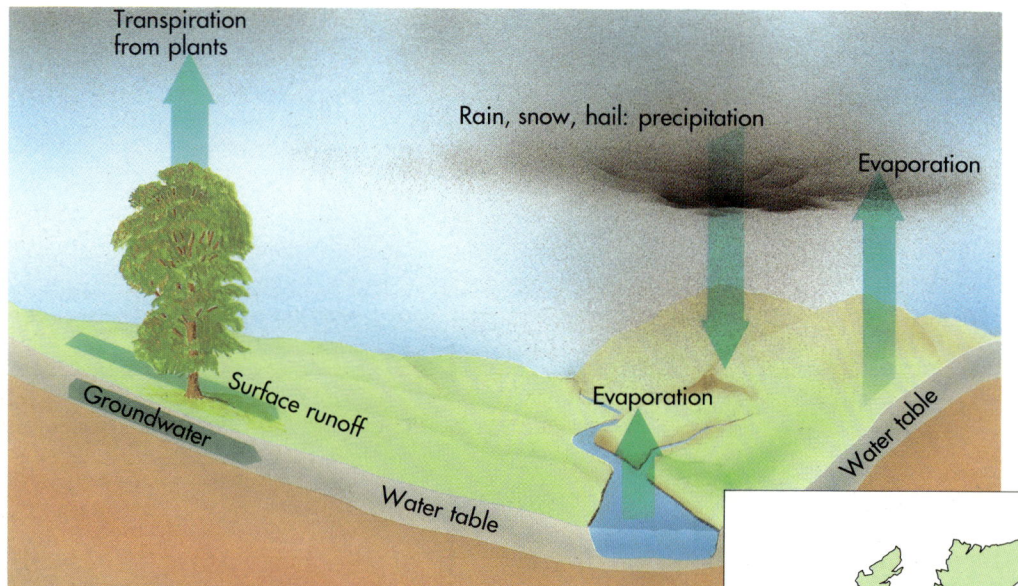

4·15   *How a river gets its water.*

1   How does a river manage to continue flowing through periods of no rain?
   In some parts of Britain the rock beneath the ground is *permeable*. This means that it allows water to pass through it. Examples of such rock are *chalk* and *limestone*. These parts of Britain (see the map, right) do not have many rivers. The rivers that do exist dry up during long dry periods.

2   Draw two diagrams to show why a river in chalk country dries up after a period of no rain (a drought). Your diagrams should show the area
   a before the drought, and
   b after the drought.
Diagram (a) could be similar to the one above.

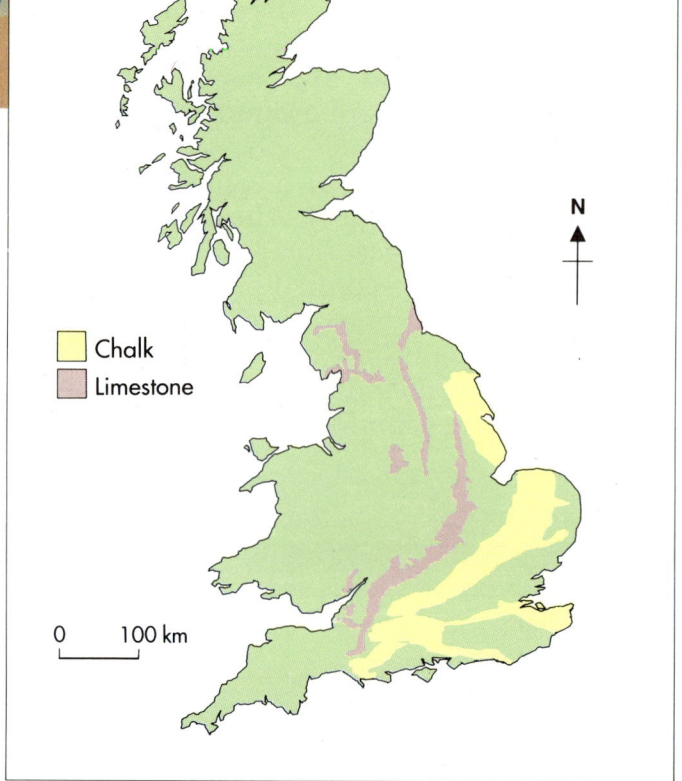

4·16   *Chalk and limestone areas in Britain.*

A field trip to Exmoor

You need to look at the map on page 74 as you read this.

Describing how a river channel changes downstream

A class is going on a school trip. The evening before, Ms Avon, the geography teacher, explains that as soon as they have finished breakfast, the minibus is going to drop off one group of four – Sharon, Desmond, Tracy and Tom – at the telephone box on the B3226 near Mockham Down (grid reference 665364). The day's work is to investigate a river. The aim is to find the *source* of a particular river. The group then have to follow it downstream, and study how the river changes on its journey downstream.

Well, here they are. Other groups have been dropped at other places near Barnstaple (which is where everyone is staying). They have other rivers to study.

The group's first job is to find *their* river. Ms Avon has told them the grid reference for the source of their river: 657373.

'I saw a river on the right-hand side when we were coming up the hill from Brayford,' announces Tracy. 'That must be it.'

'That was miles away,' says Sharon, who is always a bit short with her friend at moments like this. Tracy is always jumping to conclusions!

'No it wasn't,' answers Tracy. 'Look, you can almost *see* it from here. Come on, let's get going. It sounds as if we've got a lot to do.'

'Hang on a moment!' shouts Desmond. 'Ms Avon told us that this road, going north, almost follows the *watershed*. So we can't just take any old river. We have to make sure that it's flowing in the right direction.'

'And what *is* the right direction?' asks Tom.

'Well, we have to meet the others at the bridge near Riversmead, on the River Yeo, according to these instructions,' answers Tracy. 'You've got the map, so you work it out!'

4·17 *At Mockham Down Gate, Sharon examines the map. It's a gloomy day, and could soon turn to rain.*

Tom chose the correct river. The group quickly found the *source* of the river. Their instructions were to follow the river and make observations about how the valley and the channel *changed* downstream. They did this using their sketchpads and cameras. They also had a stopwatch and a metre ruler – using these they could measure the speed of the water and the depth of the water. Some of their results are shown on page 75.

UNIT 4

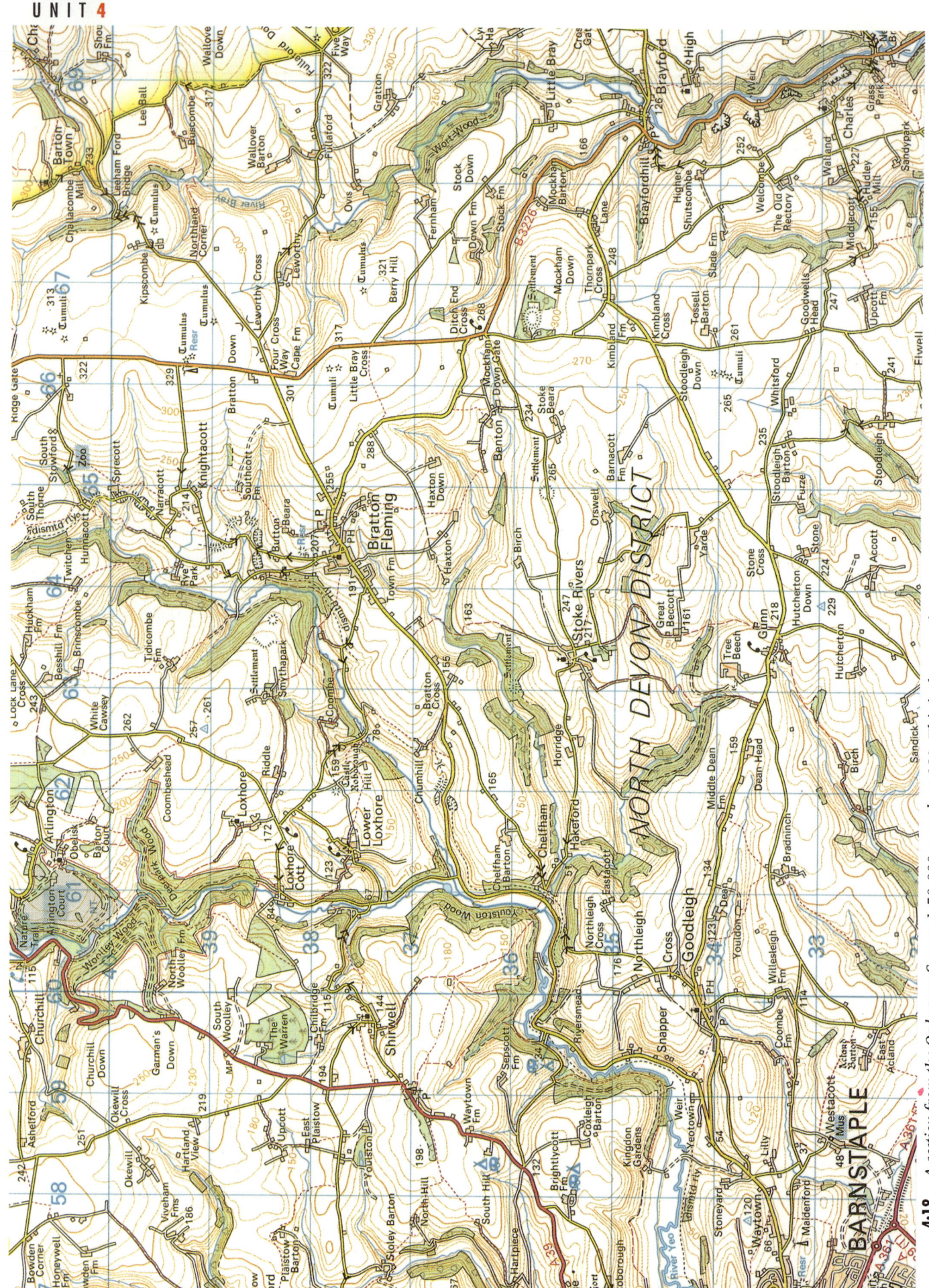

4·18 *A section from the Ordnance Survey 1:50,000 map sheet 180. This is the map that was given to the group. Can you find which is 'their' river? The pupils have a long walk ahead of them. Luckily it is all downhill and they do the whole day in which to do it! After looking carefully at the map, can you suggest a suitable place for them to have lunch?*

RIVER STUDY: RECORDING SHEET

	Grid ref.	Channel width	Channel depth	Bed load	Flow	Comments
Site 1	650 365	1m 31cm	62mm	12cm	swirling rapid shallow	At the bottom of a very steep valley. Loads of trees and bushes.
Site 2	645 363	2m 78cm	336mm	10cm	turbulent swirling	The valley is still quite deep, but the sides are not so steep. Trampling cows seem to help the river erode its banks.
Site 3	614 356	3m 82cm	631mm	5cm	deep calm	The river is so large now it is difficult to measure. Although the valley is still deep the bottom of the valley is quite flat. Desmond says it probably gets flooded from time to time because it is quite boggy.

INSTRUCTIONS

Channel width: Use your tape measure to measure the full width. For example, here the channel is wider than the part with water in it. This could be after a dry spell.

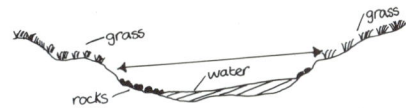

Channel depth: Always take three measurements with your ruler – or long pole – at intervals across the river. Then calculate the average: add them up and divide by three.

Bed load: From the points where you measured the depth, choose the largest piece of bed load (pebble or boulder). Measure it along its longest axis. Then calculate the average size: add them up and divide by three.

Flow: Use one or two of these words to describe the flow of water: rapid, slow, calm, turbulent, still, swirling, cloudy, clear, deep, shallow.

A pebble's longest axis

Comments: In this column write down any extra information. Any special observations about the valley? Any signs of the channel being eroded by the river?

4·19 *River Study: Recording Sheet.*

4·20 *A photographic record of the life of a river:*
a The source: from 657373 looking southwards.
b The valley: from 652364 looking westwards.
c The channel: from 650365.
d The first confluence: from 646364 looking eastwards.
e A wider view of the channel and the valley bottom: 613355.

UNIT 4

Classroom activity

For this activity it is best to work in pairs. Try to put yourselves in the shoes of the group who did the fieldwork. You will each need a piece of tracing paper.

1 The first job is to make sure that you know the proper words for describing a river.
▶ What is a *river channel*?
▶ What is a *river valley*?
▶ What is the *source* of a river?
▶ What is a *confluence*?

Think of some more questions of your own. Help each other to understand the answers to these questions.

2 Take your piece of tracing paper and place it over the Ordnance Survey map on page 74. Your task is to draw a simple sketch. This will help you understand the OS map, which has lots of lines on it and looks quite complicated. Do it like this:

a Mark a little + over the *fort* on Mockham Down. This is the very top of the hill.
b Mark an × for each of the following: Brayford (687348), Stoke Rivers (634354), Bratton Fleming (645378), Shirwell (598374), Goodleigh (599342).
c Shade in the built-up area of Barnstaple.
d Carefully draw the main course of the River Yeo.
e Carefully trace the course of 'your' river (the river followed by the school party), and *all* of its tributaries.
f Trace the course of the river which Tracy wanted to follow at first.
g With a red pen, try to mark the line of the watershed which the teacher mentioned in her instructions.
h On each of the rivers that you have marked on your tracing paper, draw a small arrow to show which way the water is flowing.
i Finally shade all the land that is higher than 250 metres above sea level.

3 You can now carefully stick your tracing paper onto a large piece of plain white paper. Stick it in the middle of the paper because you need to leave space above and below it for some writing.

On the tracing paper, mark with a small black dot the exact position of each of the photographs shown on page 75.

4 For this next part you should practise first, before writing your final version. Imagine that you are Tracy, Sharon, Tom or Desmond. For each of the photographed positions, describe exactly what you see and write down what you find out. Use the photographs and the Recording Sheet on page 75 to help you do this. You should use sketches or drawings and write some detailed notes.

Then, when you think you have got it right, copy your writing and drawings onto your plain paper. Put each description in a box. Draw an arrow between each box and the correct position on the river (on the tracing paper).

5 Imagine being back in the field study centre at the end of the river study day. Write a postcard home, or to a friend, describing the day.

Describing a meander

Another group of pupils on the Exmoor field trip followed a different investigation. This group had to investigate in detail just one point along the river. The point chosen was where the river flowed around a bend. Ms Avon called the bend a *meander*, and explained that meanders are important because they are the part of a river where the river does most of its work of *erosion* and *transportation* of sediment (pebbles, sand and mud).

The bottom diagram opposite shows the measurements collected by the fieldwork team investigating a meander.

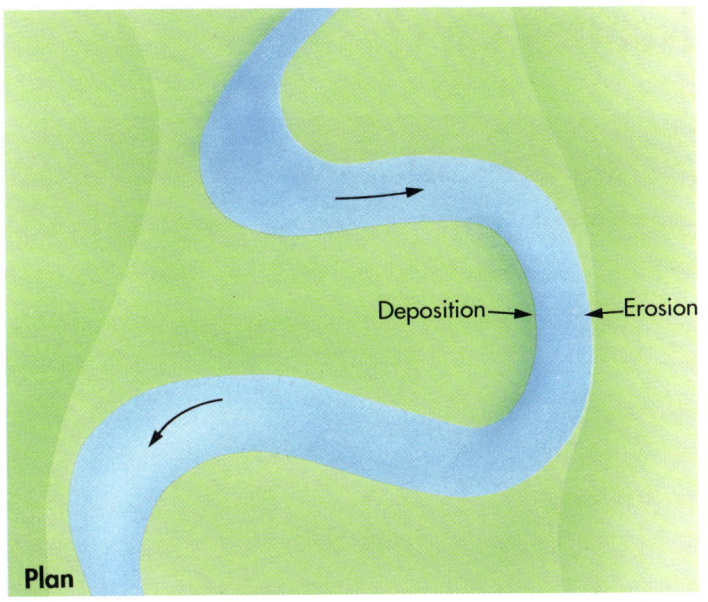
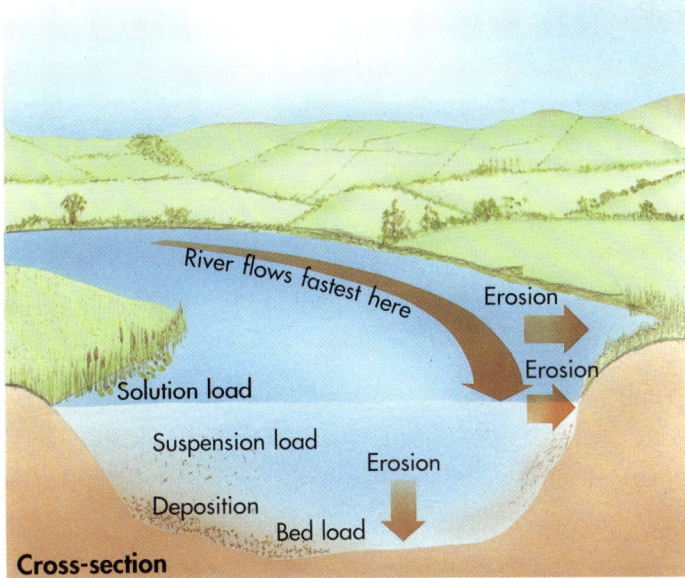

4·21 *Plan and cross-section of a meander.*

1 Make a copy of the *cross-section* above.

2 Label on your diagram *where* you expect to find:
a most pebbles, sand and mud
b evidence of erosion of the bank
c the fastest flow of water.

3 Now draw a *plan* view of the meander (like the one above). Write on this diagram *where* you would expect to find (a), (b) and (c).

4 Finally, look back at page 64 on which we learnt about how the Mississippi river has changed course. Mark Twain described what happened in his book. Imagine writing to Mark Twain to *explain* to him how the river changed course. You will need to remember what you have learnt about meanders.

A meander.

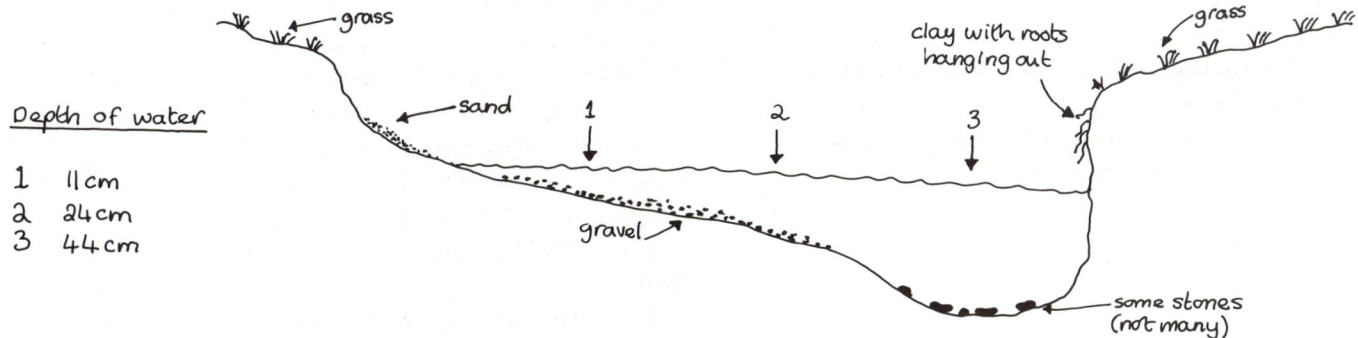

Depth of water
1 11 cm
2 24 cm
3 44 cm

4·22 *The pupils' cross-section of a meander.*

UNIT 4

▷ In what ways do river landscapes vary?

Channels and valleys

a *River racing through a narrow V-shaped valley.*

b *River flowing across a broad, flat floodplain.*

4·23 Two different river landscapes

During their field trip to Exmoor, pupils investigated river *channels*. Channels vary a lot depending on how much water the river has and how much mud, sand or pebbles it has to carry.

River *valleys* also vary a lot. Over thousands of years, rivers can shape whole valleys. Over millions of years rivers can shape whole landscapes.

The two photographs above show different river valleys and landscapes. The river in (a) flows along the bottom of a narrow, steep-sided valley, while the other river flows over a wide valley. On the river (a) you will find waterfalls and rapids, but on the river in (b), many meanders twist and turn across a moist floodplain.

4·24 A waterfall.

Trying to control rivers

River landscapes are rarely totally 'natural'. People who live near to floodplains or use floodplains for farming have often tried to prevent the river from flooding. Here are two photographs of river landscapes which have been shaped by people as well as by the river itself.

4·25 *River landscapes shaped by people.*
Left: *River X, in the Lake District of England. After a long drought the water table has fallen and the river has dried up. You can see the large boulders that have been carried by the river when it was full of water.*
Right: *River Y, in Cambridgeshire. After heavy rain the river is full.*

Mr Bourne, the water company engineer whom we met on page 69, is an expert on flooding. Read what he has to say, and look back at the picture of the Thames at the beginning of this unit.

> Flooding happens when it has rained so much that the river channel can no longer hold all the water. Water spills over its floodplain. But we can prevent floods. If we change the channel so that water flows away more quickly, or build up the banks to a safer level, we can help a river get rid of the water more efficiently.

1   Examine the two rivers carefully. Choose one:
▸ Find evidence that the channel has been changed in order to stop flooding.
▸ Draw a sketch or a cross-section of the channel to illustrate your answer. (You will have to guess the shape of the channel of the river with water in it.)

2   'One of the best ways to improve a river channel so that it does not flood, is to straighten it,' said Mr Bourne, the river expert.
a Why do you think this is so?
b Can you see evidence in *either* river which shows that the river has been straightened?

KEY POINTS KEY IDEAS

At about the same time as people began to accept the theory of evolution in science, geographers began to develop theories about how the landscape had changed through time. It was difficult at first for some people to accept that the landscape has not always been the same as it is today.

The most important factor in shaping landscapes all over the world is water. In this unit we studied the action of water in rivers. These are some of the key points.

Hydrological cycle

A 17th-century geologist called James Hutton was the first scientist to describe the water cycle. He likened it to the circulation of the blood in our bodies. It is not quite the same, of course: water takes on different states – solid, liquid or gas – at different stages of the cycle.

But the idea of a cycle or circulation – sometimes called a system – is very important in helping us understand how the world works.

Erosion

Erosion of the land means *wearing it away*. Running water wears away the land – by the action of the water itself (*hydraulic action*) and by the water 'armed' with fragments of rock (*corrasion*).

Through erosion, a river shapes many distinctive features and, over a long period of time, carves out a valley.

On steep gradients (slopes) a river cuts downwards, carving a deep V-shaped valley. On gentler gradients, a river erodes sideways, widening the bottom of the valley.

Deposition

Eventually rivers run into lakes or the sea. Eroded material is carried by the river's turbulent flow. When the river enters the lake or sea the current slows and the material is dropped. (It is now called *sediment*.) Much material is also deposited on the bed of the river and, during times of flood, all over the valley floor (which is known as the *floodplain*). Floods happen because the channel can no longer hold all the water pouring into it after a period of heavy rain. The banks 'burst'.

Meanders

Most rivers meander. That is, their channels twist and turn through the landscape. Meanders happen on steep gradients and on gentle gradients. No one is quite sure why this is. Water seems to *want* to flow in this way.

Meanders can be a problem because they slow down the flow of water. This can make rivers flood more easily.

Controlling rivers

To people in many parts of the world, river floods are seen as good. The sediment fertilises the land, and the water can be channelled onto crops. A flood can be a source of easy-to-catch fish and an excuse for a huge celebration of water sports and feasting.

In Europe, floods are often seen as bad. Houses are damaged, transport is cut and wet, soggy soil is not good for growing crops. Europeans have, therefore, become clever flood controllers. Perhaps the most common way to stop a river flooding is to straighten its channel and to raise its banks. Raised banks are known as *levées*.

Water: a Scarce Resource?

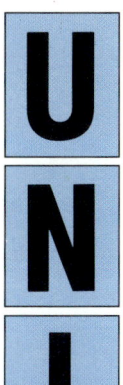

UNIT 5

5·1 *The south-western states of the USA are sometimes known as the Sun Belt. Dramatic scenery and wildlife, such as seen here in Arizona (above), make this an attractive part of the USA to live and work in.*

An atlas map will show you that this is an area of hot desert. But the lower photograph shows the desert blooming. How is this done?

UNIT 5

Brainstorm: How do we use water?

Water is one of the world's most precious resources, although it is often taken for granted. The lower photograph on page 81 shows one result of using water in the Arizona Desert in the USA.

1 Working with a partner, list all the different ways in which a household in Britain uses water.

2 Now add to your list any other uses that you can think of outside of the home.

3 Join up with another pair and compare your ideas. Make further additions to each other's lists.

4 In your group of four, attempt to categorise the uses of water under three or four headings. Each heading should show a type of water use. A couple of examples are given below.

Still in your groups, try to find the answers to these questions. You may need to ask your teacher for some help.

5 How much does water cost
▸ at home
▸ at school?

6 On average, how much water do people in Britain use in a day?

7 What is water most used for in Britain today?

8 What happens to water after it has been used?

Water in the home	Water for producing food		

Setting the scene

Where does water come from?

Nearly three-quarters of planet Earth is covered with water. But was it always there?

One theory is that water originally came from within the Earth. When the Earth was not very old, lava spilled onto the surface releasing water vapour into the atmosphere, where it formed clouds. As the Earth cooled, rain fell regularly from the clouds, and over a long period of time the oceans were created.

The amount of water that exists today is the same as it has been for many millions of years. As you learnt in Unit 4, water is constantly moved around in a process that is known as the *water cycle* or *hydrological cycle* (see page 68). In this cycle 97 per cent of all the Earth's water is stored in the oceans. Because of the minerals it contains, especially salt, sea water is difficult for people to use. However, the oceans are a very important source of food.

The other 3 per cent of the water in the hydrological cycle is fresh water. Most of this is held in the world's ice sheets and glaciers, especially in the polar regions. In fact, although water is constantly being recycled, less than 1 per cent – in lakes, rivers, the soil and rocks – can be used easily by people.

Although the amount of water on our planet is fixed, its *distribution* is uneven. This is because the *climate* varies from place to place. For example, tropical rainforest regions can have more than 2,000 millimetres of rainfall, while desert regions receive less than 200 millimetres in a year.

UNIT 5

TOTAL ANNUAL PRECIPITATION

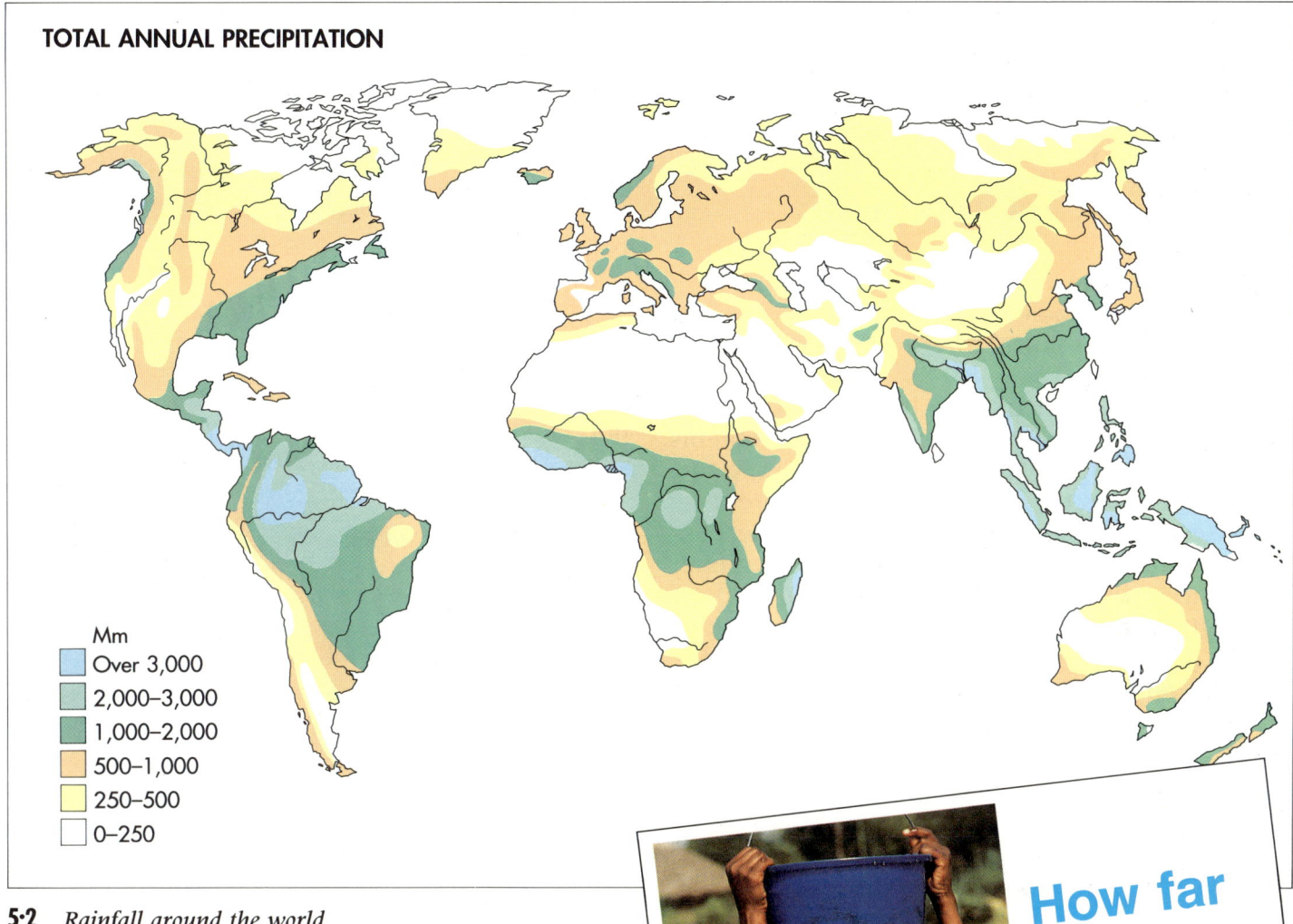

Mm
- Over 3,000
- 2,000–3,000
- 1,000–2,000
- 500–1,000
- 250–500
- 0–250

5·2 *Rainfall around the world.*

Is quality more important than quantity?

If people do not have enough water, they die of thirst. But all around the world, and especially in the continents of Africa, Asia and South America, many more people die from the effects of drinking dirty water. It is estimated that 25,000 people die each day as a result of water-borne diseases. The United Nations (UN) declared the 1980s the International Water Supply and Sanitation Decade. The aim was to ensure that by 1990 all people would have clean water and sanitation.

Sanitation

Good sanitation means that homes are clean, germ free, healthy and unpolluted. This is difficult to achieve in a country unless the government makes sure that water supplies are kept clean, and sewage is treated.

The most frightening water-borne disease is *cholera*. In 1991, more than 25,000 people died of this disease, in Peru, Bolivia and Brazil.

How far are *you* prepared to go to turn on a tap?

5·3 *We need to improve the quality of water world wide.*

Throughout the 1980s the UN helped countries devise National Action Plans to improve their water and sanitation services. In countries such as our own, many charity appeals were made to raise funds to improve water supplies in other less fortunate countries.

By 1990 the ambitious target set by the UN had not been reached and 300 million *more* people lacked sanitation than in 1980. However, by 1990, over the whole world, 75 per cent of urban and 50 per cent of rural dwellers had an adequate water supply.

In terms of water quality, both the rich and poor countries of the world face major problems. In the economically developing countries, poor water quality is the source of many different diseases. There are two main causes of these: water-borne parasites, and inadequate hygiene.

Malaria probably affects more people throughout the world than any other water-borne disease. It is caused by a parasite which is transferred from one person to another through the bite of the mosquito, an insect which breeds in stagnant water. People with malaria find it difficult to work, and are less able to fight off other diseases.

There are two main ways of dealing with these diseases: they can be treated with drugs – but a better way is to remove the cause and provide a clean water supply.

Water pollution

In the economically developed countries, most people enjoy clean water supplies and do not suffer from these diseases. However, there is growing concern in these countries about water pollution.

Often the waste water containing pollutants from homes and industries re-enters rivers. A variety of chemicals produced by different industries may find their way into water courses. The effects of these chemicals are disputed, but it is thought that a number of them damage organs such as the liver and may, in large doses, cause cancer.

One example of this kind of pollution is in the River Rhine, which flows from Switzerland to the North Sea. Over 40 million people live in the area that is drained by this river, with 20 million relying on it for drinking water. However, one-fifth of the world's chemical production takes place along its banks and to date over 50 different chemicals (not all from the industries) have been found in the river water. To make the Rhine fit for drinking it has to be treated with even more chemicals!

Who uses water?

On average, each person in the world uses about 750 cubic metres of water a year, but even though the population is increasing there is still more than enough water for people to use. People do not use this water directly – the pie graph below shows how the water is used by people.

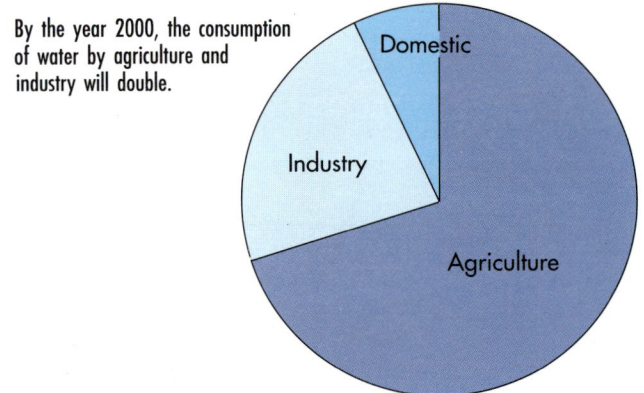

5·4 *How water is used by people.*

5·5 *Water being used to irrigate crops.*

The main use of water in agriculture is for irrigation. Farmers in the economically developed world can afford the technology to transfer water from one place to another and irrigate even the most unproductive land. However, in economically developing countries, although there are a number of large water control projects, such as those along the Rivers Nile and Ganges, many farmers are dependent on an unreliable water supply.

Industry also uses large amounts of water, especially in manufacturing processes. For example, it takes 30,000 litres to make one family car. Most manufacturing industries are found in the richer countries, and they use large quantities of water for this purpose.

5.6 *Water is essential to many industrial processes – pulp and paper making, for example.*

The consumption of water by individuals also varies considerably between richer and poorer countries. People in North America, for example, consume on average 20 times more water than their neighbours in South America. The graph below shows how much water is used in different ways in the United Kingdom.

For two-thirds of the world's households the water source is outside the home, and the people who have to fetch the water are almost always women or children. The water may be carried in pots or cans which can hold up to 18 litres. Many women have to make up to ten journeys a day to fetch water, and this may take as long as five hours. This reduces the opportunities women have for education, other work, or leisure.

▸ **Work out a method of weighing 18 litres of water. How far do you think *you* could carry this weight comfortably?**

5.8 *A woman in Sudan carrying water home to her family.*

Clearly, there are many issues involved in the storage, transport and use of water. This unit helps us to examine some of these issues, and is organised into three key questions:

▷ Why is California so thirsty?

▷ Whose water? Whose waste?

▷ How has the chase for water caused an environmental catastrophe?

Each person uses 160 litres of water a day:

Drinking/cooking	9 L
Garden/washing car	13 L
Washing dishes	15 L
Washing clothes	18 L
Personal washing	50 L
Flushing toilets	55 L

5.7 *The consumption of water in the United Kingdom.*

UNIT 5

▶ Why is California so thirsty?

'California, here we come!'

Since 1848 many people have been attracted to California, a state in the south-west corner of the USA. Just before California became part of the United States, only a few thousand people lived in the area. These people were soon to be overwhelmed by 'invaders'.

In 1848 gold was discovered in the north of the state and within a year thousands of prospectors were moving into the area. This 'gold rush' led to the rapid development of the region and in 1850 California became the 31st state of the USA. Over the years it has earned the nickname 'The Golden State'.

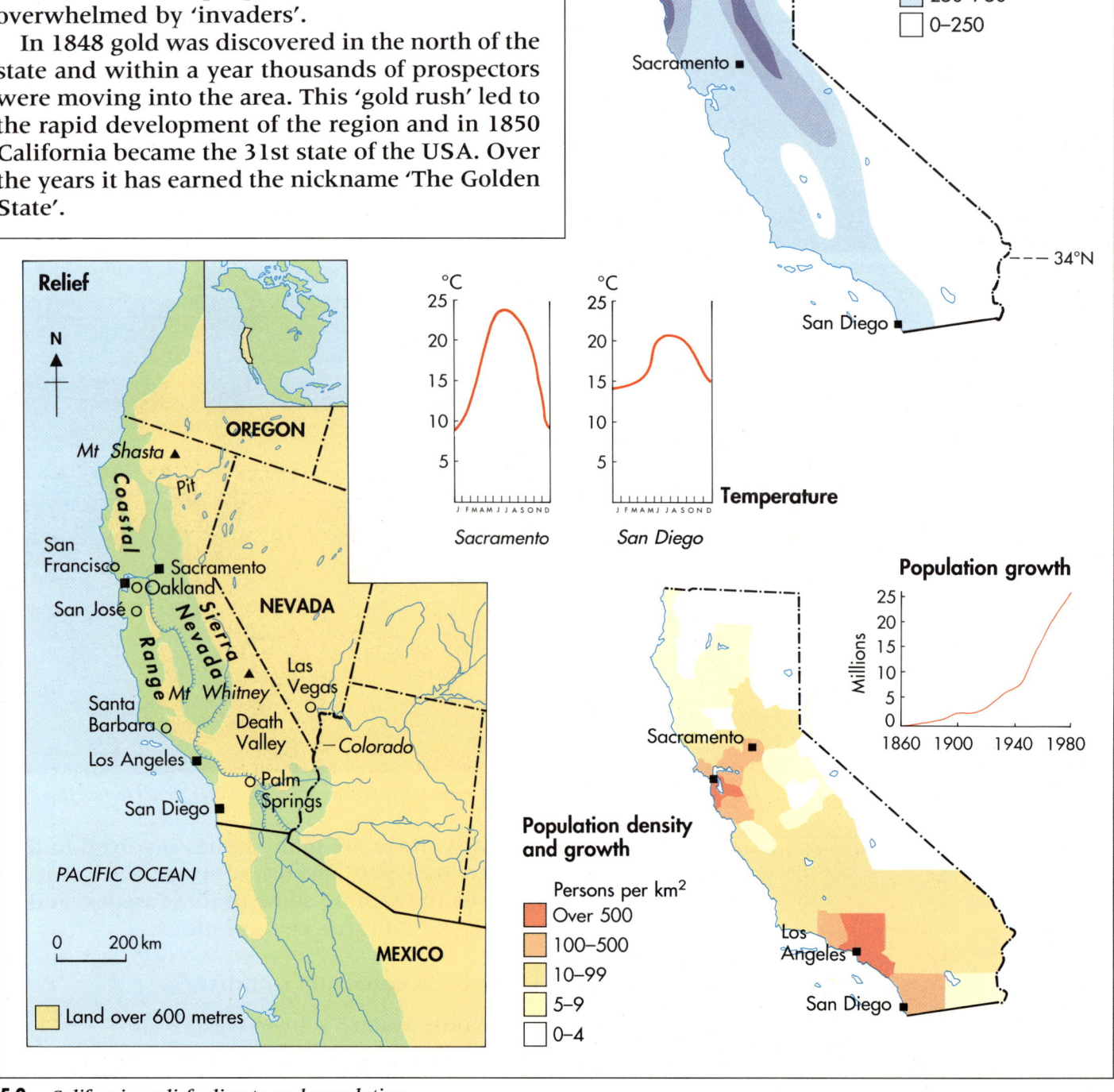

5·9 *California: relief, climate and population.*

Look at all the information about California on the opposite page, and then answer these questions.

1 Describe the locations of Sacramento and San Diego.

2 Describe the annual temperatures of these two cities. Use such words as *hot, cold, warm* or *cool*, and use actual figures. Start your answer: 'Winters in San Diego are warm at 15°C . . .'

3 Write a paragraph describing the rainfall pattern in California. Key phrases you should use are: *north-west, 250–750mm, over 750mm, central band, below 250mm, rest of California*. Start your answer: 'In the south-east of the state the rainfall is . . .'

4 The population map opposite also shows a clear pattern. Is there any link between the climate of California and the pattern of population distribution? Describe the climate of the places which have the highest and lowest population densities.

5 California's climate poses a water problem for its inhabitants. What do you think the main problem is, and which areas are likely to suffer most?

What is California like today?

Have you an image of California in your mind? California is famous for a number of reasons. For example, there are occasionally news reports of earthquakes that affect the area. Or we hear about or see films that are made there, and see the way of life of some of the people. All these things help shape our image of California.

The 'Golden State' is attractive to migrants from all over the world. By the year 2000 California's population is expected to reach 35 million. People of European origin will then make up less than 50 per cent of the population. In some parts of California, Spanish, not English, is the most commonly spoken language. This is the main language spoken by migrants from Central American countries like Mexico, who are known as 'Hispanics'. Links with Asia are also strong. For example, 40,000 Kampucheans live in Long Beach, and Fresno is home to 30,000 Laotians.

If California were a nation, and not a state of the USA, it would be the eighth richest country in the world. Only Japan, Germany, the former USSR, France, Italy, Britain and the rest of the USA produce more than California.

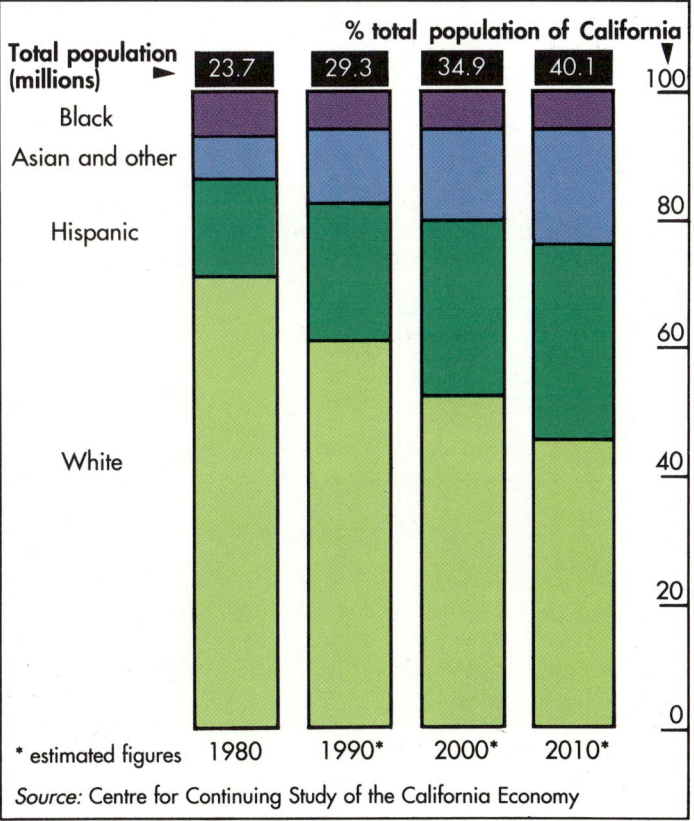

5·10 *California's population by ethnic group.*

The price of a medium-sized home in California is US$200,000 and only 19 per cent of Californians can afford this, but the growth of cities is a major problem to be faced. Some people fear that in time a continuous 'supercity' will stretch from San Francisco in the north to San Diego in the south. Its name? San-San!

Big Green

California suffers from several pollution problems, for example the *smog* that often lies over Los Angeles. 'Big Green' is a collection of ideas that are meant to improve the environment. It includes the creation of an oilspill fund, the phasing out of cancer-causing agricultural chemicals, ways of cutting carbon dioxide emissions by 40 per cent, and tree planting. Other environmental suggestions include the banning of the use of petrol in cars by the year 2007.

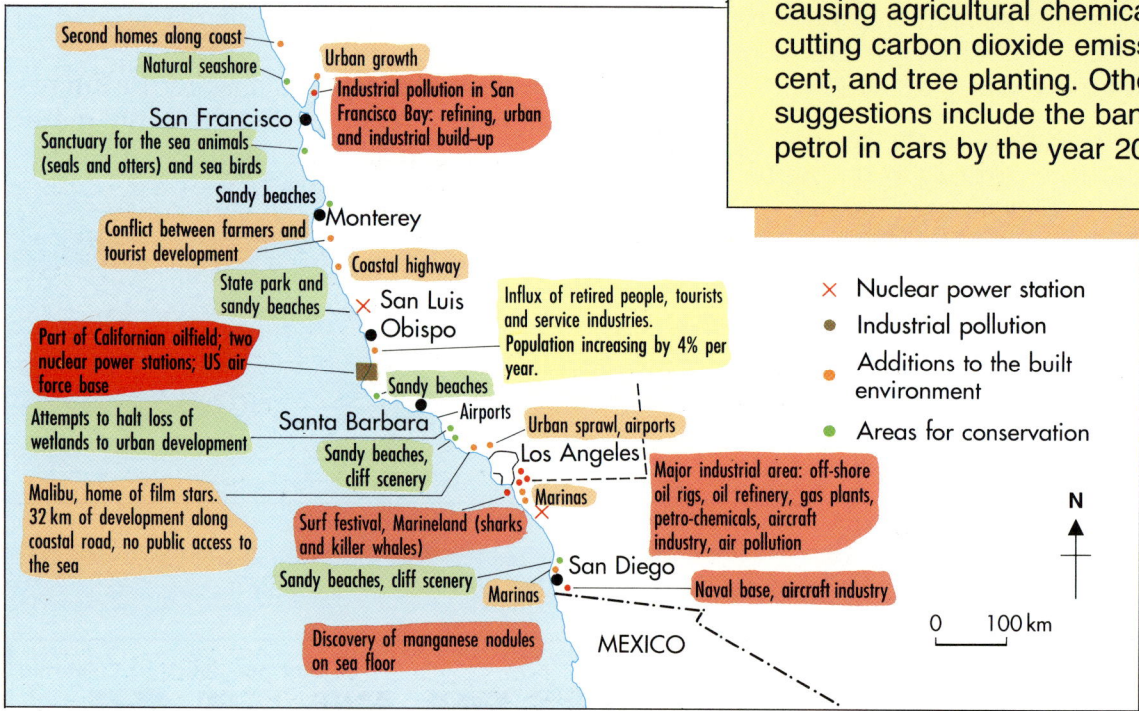

5·11 *Competition for land in California.*

5·12 *Busy roads in Los Angeles. Voters have recently agreed to add an extra tax to petrol to raise money for road and rail improvements.*

5·13 *Agriculture is big business in California. The 80,000 farmers here consume 85 per cent of the available water. Irrigating the alfalfa crop alone uses as much water as a city of 41 million people!*

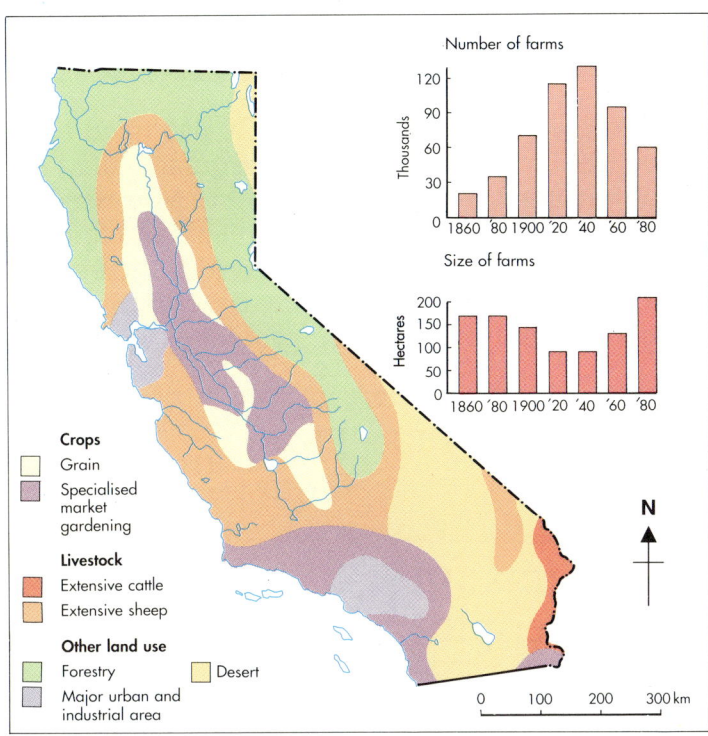

5·14 Land use in California. The state grows much of the USA's fruit and vegetables, including more than half of its tomatoes, grapes, lettuces, olives and cauliflowers.

5·15 A pumping station on the California Aqueduct.

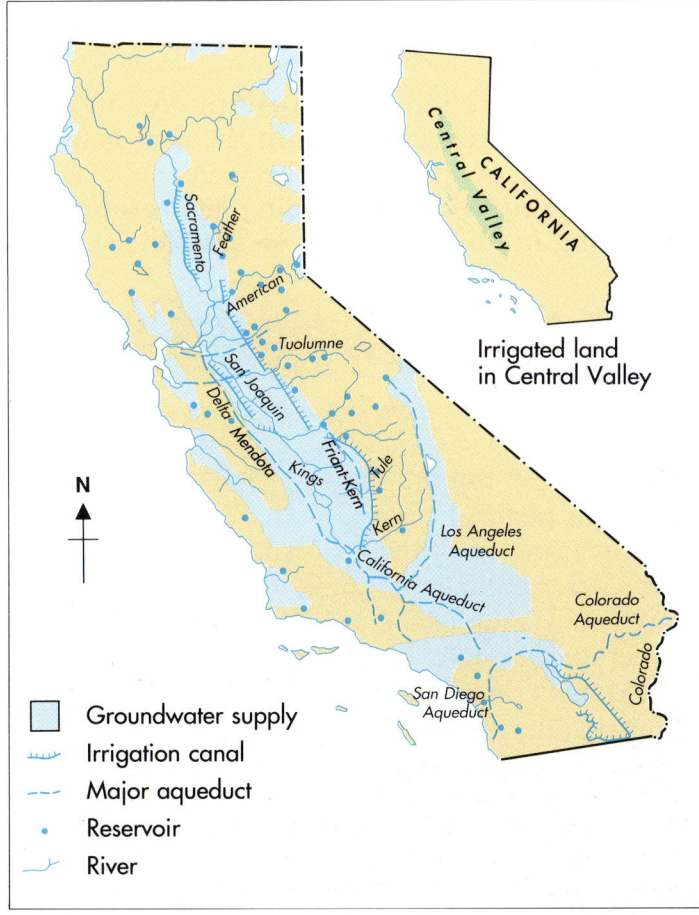

	Total consumption of all water per day (million litres)	Total consumption of fresh water per day (million litres)	Consumption of water per capita per day (litres)
1970	217,920	99,880	10,896
1975	231,540	104,420	10,850
1980	245,160	113,500	10,314
1985	225,638	95,794	6,446

5·16 California's water supply. More than 50 years ago, Californians knew that the **demand** for water in the Central Valley would soon outstrip the **supply** from rivers and from underground (groundwater). So the Central Valley Project was set up, and work began in 1937. Twenty dams were built, and canals to carry water from the wetter north to the drier south.

UNIT 5

California Today!

Working in groups of three or four, use the text and information on pages 86–89, and an atlas, to produce articles for a new magazine entitled *California Today!*

1 The first issue aims to provide 'A Portrait of the Golden State'. Use these headings for your articles:

- What the People Do
- California: A Changing World
- Where the People Work
- California: The Land
- Problems for the People
- The Future

2 The second issue, which you also need to prepare, is to have a two-page spread called 'California's Unquenchable Thirst'. You need to show in your pages the problems of supply and demand for water in California. Include also a glimpse into the future, describing possible solutions to these problems.

▶ Whose water? Whose waste?

California has a huge demand for water, and much of this is now supplied from *outside* the state. This has posed some tricky questions. For example, who owns the water in a river? This is not an easy question to answer, especially when a river flows through a variety of places, all of which make a demand on it. In the past it was often the first people to use the water who claimed the rights to it, stopping later groups from using it. Today it is not so simple.

The Colorado – whose water?

The Colorado River is probably the most controlled river in the world. At present seven US states and Mexico lay claim to a share of its water.

1 Study the map opposite of the south-west USA and describe the course of the Colorado River. In your description refer to at least some of these points:
- the general direction of river flow
- the approximate length of the river
- the source and mouth of the river
- the places it flows through.

2 Study the rainfall map of the Colorado Basin on page 91.
▶ Which section of the Colorado Basin receives the most rainfall, and how much each year?
▶ Which section of the Colorado Basin receives the least rainfall, and how much each year?
▶ A considerable amount of Nevada, Arizona and California is desert. Using the map to help you, write a definition of a desert.
▶ Summarise in a few lines the reasons why the Colorado River is such an important source of water for the south-west USA.

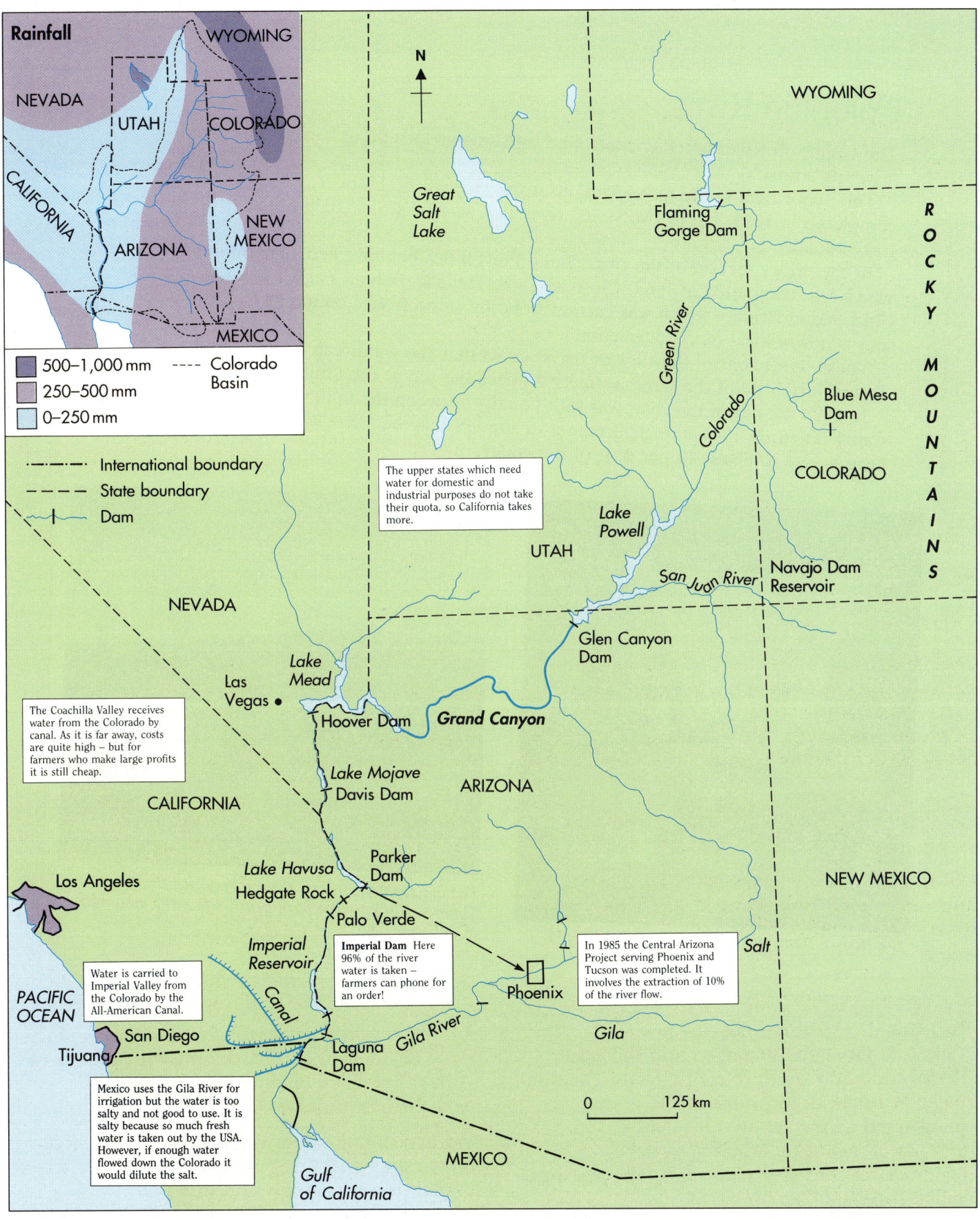

5.17 *The Colorado Basin.*

Colorado River

The Colorado River is today controlled by 19 dams located at various intervals along its course.

The major dam in the lower section of the river is the Hoover, which was completed in 1935. Up to two years' river flow can be stored behind the dam, in Lake Mead.

In the upper section of the river, Lake Powell lies behind Glen Canyon dam, which was completed in 1963. Close by Lake Havusa, behind Parker Dam, is the old London Bridge, which was carried stone by stone from London to California, and is now a local tourist attraction.

These dams control the flow of the river so that the water can be extracted. Today very little of the water actually reaches the sea at the Gulf of California.

In 1922 the use of the river was split equally between the upper and lower river states. Then, in 1944, the government of the USA agreed that Mexico should have access to about 10 per cent of the water.

The Hoover Dam, at the west end of Lake Mead.

The old London Bridge. Once it spanned the River Thames, but now the park benches face the mountains of Colorado.

3a Read the account above of how the Colorado has been managed and the water distributed and used, referring to the map on page 91 to check locations of the places mentioned in the report.
b What is meant by *extracting* water?
c Which are *the upper states*, and why are they called this?

4 The report goes on to say: 'The upper states have decided to extract double the amount of water they have been using, for new agricultural purposes.'

Write a dialogue between the governor of a lower state and the governor of an upper state, explaining their views on this plan.

UNIT 5

Whose waste?

When water is used it usually becomes dirty. Millions of gallons of dirty water are produced each day. This water needs to be disposed of or cleaned.

But who is responsible for doing this? This question is just as difficult as the previous one, on who owns the water in a river. Mexico and the USA have had a heated argument over this question for many years, particularly where it affects southern California.

A sea of waste: but whose waste?

California's southern boundary forms part of La Linea, the name given by the people of Mexico to its 3,000-kilometre border with the USA. On the American side of this border is the city of San Diego, whilst across the frontier is Tijuana. Both of these cities are growing fast, with populations now over the 1 million mark. Many experts think that in time these two cities will merge to form a huge border supercity with a blend of cultures.

Already the two cities are linked. Over 7,000 Tijuanans cross the border each day to work in San Diego, whilst an average of 1,200 people officially migrate each month, leaving Tijuana for ever.

In Tijuana itself 45,000 Mexicans work for as little as a dollar a day in the 450 assembly plants. These are owned by American companies which choose to locate here because it is so cheap. There is also another feature that these two cities share: pollution.

Class activity

Working in groups of four, study the information below on the pollution problem that faces this area.

1 When a problem becomes a crisis!

Read this magazine article:

> Since the 1930s sewage has been flowing intermittently into the Pacific Ocean from Tijuana. However, in 1980 a major failure of the city's sewage works led to the spilling of 15 million gallons of untreated effluent into the sea south of Imperial Beach, forcing the closure of four miles of popular beaches. Most of the sewage enters the sea via the Tijuana River which picks up the waste from the 60 per cent of Tijuana's houses that are not connected to the city's sewage system.

Prepare a 20-second newsflash on the 1980 leak, and the local response to it.

5·18 *Warning notices of pollution on a Californian beach.*

5·19 *The San Diego/Tijuana area.*

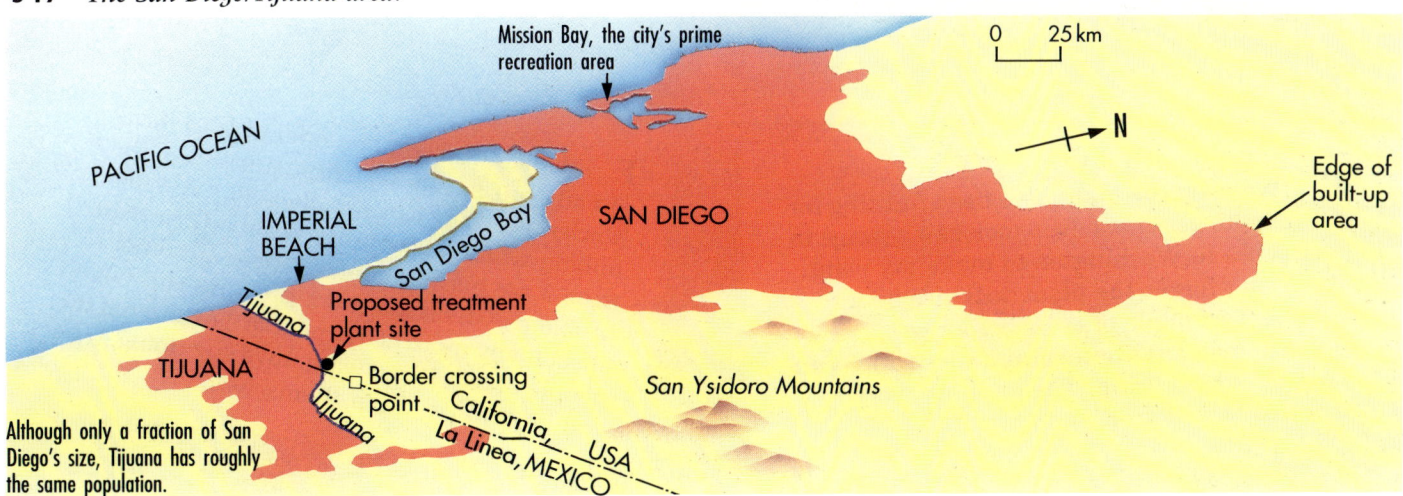

2 Tackling the problem

After the 1980 incident, officials in San Diego decided that it was time for a permanent solution to the problem. A spokesperson outlines the proposal.

> An international treatment plant is proposed. The idea is to build a plant which can deal with 25 million gallons of sewage a day, and provide a 3½-mile pipeline which would stretch out into the ocean. The cost of the works would be in the region of $200 million and the site would be just outside Tijuana.

A large number of people have commented on the proposal, and six points of view are outlined below. The people who made these comments are as follows:

- a Mexican factory worker
- a working-class San Diego resident
- a biologist
- an American government official
- the Mayor of San Diego
- a Mexican government official.

In your group:

a Match each person with a statement.
b Note the position that each person takes regarding the proposal to build a treatment plant. (Who is in favour, neutral, or against?)
c Take each person in turn and explain why he or she holds this point of view about the treatment plant.

A 'If we start paying to clean up our neighbours' waste using taxpayers' money, it could be the start of us having to subsidise many things they do, each one probably costing more than the last. I'm sure the ordinary American citizen wouldn't want us to do that.'

B 'I came to work in one of the American factories in Tijuana. The Yankees want us to work for them for low wages, yet they complain when we pollute the coast – how do they expect us to pay for it when they pay us so little in the first place?'

C 'We need the plant. I've been fighting for 10 years to get one. I even took raw sewage in test tubes to Washington to make my point. And don't forget the plant will also be an excellent example of cross-border co-operation on environmental issues which can only be a good thing. The more we work together, the better.'

D 'When I go down to the local Burger King I can't see the river as it is half a mile away but I can sure as hell smell it! The rich people don't have to live near it, we do, and it's about time something was done and I don't care who has to pay for it.'

E 'An international sewage plant is a stupid idea. Both Mexico and California face water shortages, and dumping treated effluent in the bay is simply a waste of water. Anyway, Tijuana will continue growing and the plant won't be able to cope by the next century. What is needed is a low-cost treatment which allows Mexico to recycle waste water for irrigation.'

F 'We would like to co-operate and have already put in one system just south of the border, but how can we afford to pay $100 million when our country is already in debt? Even if we had the money, there are other problems which are more pressing and which affect many more of our people. I'm afraid if the people of San Diego want anything doing, they will have to pay for it themselves.'

3 The art of persuasion: carrying people with you
a As a group, decide what *you* think. Do you wish to support the international sewage treatment plant? Have you a better idea?
b Design a large poster which aims to persuade people in San Diego *and* Tijuana to agree with your group's point of view.

How has the chase for water caused an environmental catastrophe?

The control of rivers and water supply is now common in many countries. As people demand more water, the control schemes become bigger. This means larger dams and larger and longer pipelines to get the water to where people need it – in their homes, on farms and in factories. There is now a proposal to control the water supply throughout the whole of North America. Huge schemes like this are planned in every continent.

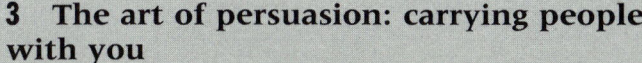

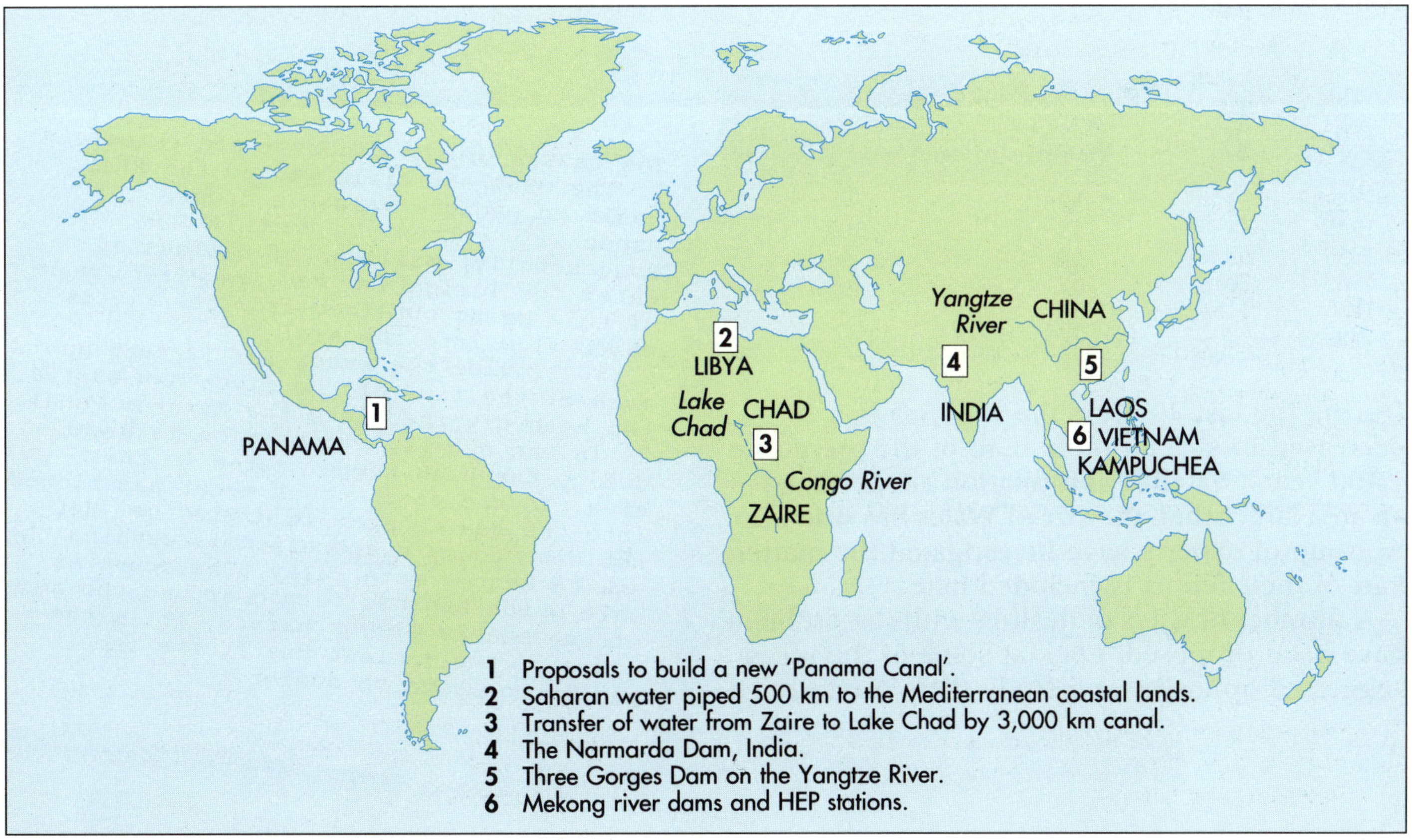

PANAMA
1
2
LIBYA
Lake Chad
CHAD
3
Congo River
ZAIRE
Yangtze River
CHINA
4
INDIA
5
LAOS
6
VIETNAM
KAMPUCHEA
1 Proposals to build a new 'Panama Canal'.
2 Saharan water piped 500 km to the Mediterranean coastal lands.
3 Transfer of water from Zaire to Lake Chad by 3,000 km canal.
4 The Narmarda Dam, India.
5 Three Gorges Dam on the Yangtze River.
6 Mekong river dams and HEP stations.

5·20 *Water 'mega-' projects worldwide.*

UNIT 5

Water control

Aral Sea disaster

The control of water supplies, whether on a small scale or large scale, has an effect on the environment. The impact of large-scale water control is being experienced in the area surrounding the Aral Sea, in Kazakhstan and Uzbekistan. The map on this page shows the Aral Sea area as it was in 1989. The blue dotted line shows the shores of the Sea in 1960. The Aral Sea has shrunk.

Aral Sea : The facts

- In 1961, the fourth largest lake in the world.
- Up to 53 metres deep in 1961.
  By 1981 had dropped by 13 metres to a maximum depth of 40 metres.
  Average depth in the 1980s 24.5 metres.
- Salt content 10 – 11% in 1961.
- Area in 1961 68,000 km².
- Area in 1987 41,000 km².

5·21 *The Aral Sea area.*

Year	Water inflow (km³)	Height of Aral Sea above sea level (metres)	Area irrigated by rivers feeding the Aral Sea (million ha)
1935	54	53	—
1945	64	53	4.3
1955	53	53	—
1965	30	52	5.0
1975	11	48	—
1985	2	42	6.0

During the last 30 years the Aral Sea has decreased in size far more than in the preceding 1,300 years. Satellite information suggests that an area larger than the size of Wales has dried up. A group of experts have investigated the matter. Part of their report is included here.

A number of ways of dealing with the problem have been proposed. Look at some of the ideas suggested opposite, and study them carefully.

The causes of the disaster are threefold:
1. The USSR officials wanted the Aral basin to produce valuable crops, especially cotton. To do this successfully, millions of gallons of water for irrigation were required, most of this being obtained from the rivers which flow into the Aral Sea.
2. To provide the water for irrigation much of the flow of the river Amu Dar'ya has been diverted into the Karakum Canal.
3. In the summer, evaporation is great due to the high temperatures in this area. In the past enough water has flowed into the sea to stop it drying up. But not now; today evaporation is causing the sea to become more salty. The crust of salt which has now formed around the edge of the sea is also a hazard. It is the cause of the violent duststorms the people now have to suffer.

UNIT 5

★ Ration water for irrigation.

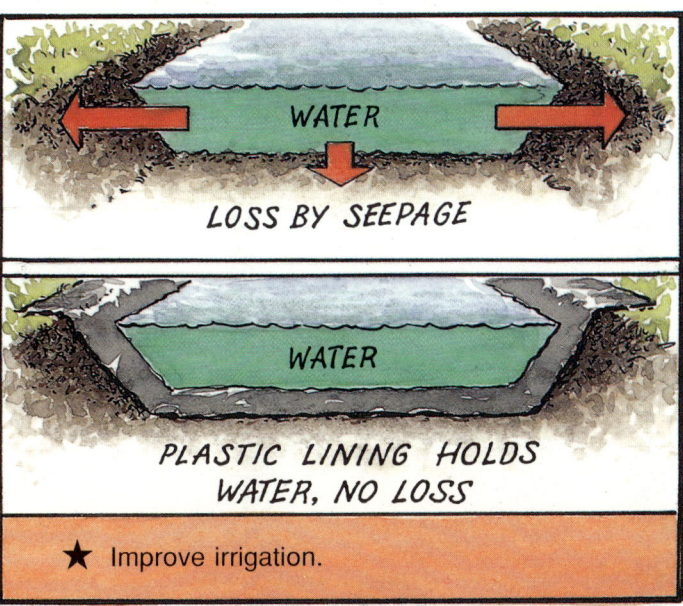

★ Improve irrigation.

★ Change land use.

5·22 *Aral Sea solutions.*

★ In the past, farmers have not had to pay for the water they have used. If they were charged they might use water more carefully.

★ Introduce new crop strains.

★ Find new sources of water.
★ Use alternative forms of energy – wind power, for example – to pump water into the area.

▸ What do you think are the advantages and disadvantages of these solutions?

UNIT 5

Investigation and presentation

Working in small groups you are to investigate the issue that has become known as the 'Aral Sea Disaster'. You are members of ASDAC, the Aral Sea Disaster Action Committee, and have relatives living in the area.

To persuade the government never to allow this kind of disaster to happen again, you have arranged a meeting in Moscow to which politicians, experts and specialists have been invited.

Your aim is to produce a presentation for this meeting. You need to prepare a short speech. You also need to design a *leaflet* (on one piece of folded A4 paper) to get your message across to a wider audience. Use the information in this unit to help you. Some points to consider:

▶ What is the disaster?
▶ What are the causes of the disaster?
▶ What are the views of the people involved?
▶ What are the effects of the changes and the solutions suggested?

5·23 *Boats stranded on the dried-up bed of the Aral Sea.*

UNIT 5

5·24 From the 'Soviet Weekly', 18 November 1989.

If you visited the Aral Sea in the early 1960s you would remember the vast blue expanse and fishermen bringing large fat bream and barbel ashore.

Uzbekistan journalist

The two rivers which fed the Aral only do so on maps today. The area which was once the sea bed is now desert, with up to 70 million tonnes of salt dust rising into the atmosphere from it – these dust clouds are sometimes so large they can be seen from space.

The USSR gets 90 per cent of its 'white gold' (cotton) and 40 per cent of its rice from this region. With its hot summers, this area is ideal for agriculture but it is very dry, so the land needs to be irrigated – the cotton fields are watered 10 times a year. Imagine a column of water 5½ metres high over each square metre of soil – that is how much water is used.

Russian geographer

WATER SHORTAGE MADE WORSE BY POLLUTION

Vast amounts of fertilisers and pesticides have been used and these have washed through the soil into the Aral Sea, causing severe pollution which has killed much of the plant and fish life. The soil has also been poisoned in many areas, making it impossible to continue growing crops. However, the saddest aspect of this story is the effect this is having on the people. Pesticides have made their way into the food chain as cattle are fed on waste matter. To make harvesting easier crops are sprayed while people are working in the fields – this has led to the highest infant mortality in the USSR and children being born with deformities.

From a magazine article

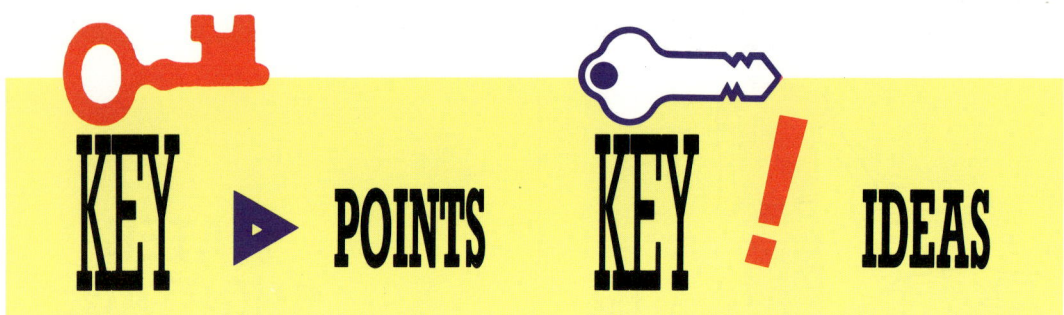

KEY POINTS KEY IDEAS

Water is a valuable resource which is consumed in huge quantities by people, especially people in affluent nations. We can discuss water in the same way as we discussed food: it is not simply a matter of the *quantity* of water, for there is a colossal amount of water on planet Earth. There are an estimated 35 million cubic kilometres of *fresh* water. The discussion here is about water *quality* and the *distribution* of water, and this unit helped us think about the following key points.

Water quality

'Fresh' water means water which is *not saline* (like sea water). It is water which can be consumed by people and used to irrigate crops.

Fresh water can be dangerous. It can contain human sewage and can, therefore, spread disease. Water can also become polluted with industrial or agricultural chemicals.

It is important and expensive to ensure good water quality.

Water consumption

It usually surprises people when they learn for the first time how much water is consumed per person. We use water *directly* to drink and to keep clean. We use far more *indirectly*, through the farmers who grow our food, and the factories which make our cars, for example.

Generally, the more economically developed a country is, the more water is consumed.

Water supply

Some parts of the world have a water shortage. Such areas in economically developed regions, like California, overcome this problem by building pipelines and canals from places which have a water surplus.

An interesting problem arises when a river flows from a region of surplus to a region of shortage. Whose water is it? This problem can be serious if an international boundary is crossed.

Water control

People have tried to control water for *thousands of years*, often by building small dams and irrigation channels to catch and distribute flood water.

Now, technology is so powerful that people are able to divert whole rivers and create enormous artificial lakes.

However, although people have the technology to do these things, we need a greater understanding of the *effects* on the environment of doing these things.

Industry and the Environment

UNIT 6

6·1 *A factory in Russia. For many years the smoke belching from factory chimneys was seen as a sign of progress. Now it is seen as a symbol of environmental disaster, which may put people's lives at risk. What should be done about it?*

What do you know?

1 Look at the photograph above.

2 Working with a partner, give yourselves one minute to write down as many words as possible to describe the photograph.

3 Ring all those words which you think are 'good'. Underline those you think are 'bad'. What do you notice about your numbers of good and bad words?

4 If you were a person working in this factory and living nearby, how do you think this factory would affect your everyday life?

5 For the next week, look through daily newspapers and cut out any articles on industry and how it affects the environment. Your class should make a display of these, perhaps arranging them around a suitable map.

101

Setting the scene

Many of us at one time or another have found ourselves in a different country. For a number of people it is for a holiday lasting just a week or two. For others it is a more permanent move.

As we travel to other countries there will be much that we recognise but there will also be many things that are unfamiliar to us.

Here, six people write about their experiences of living in a different country, and how it compares with the United Kingdom.

Steve Allen, a teacher from London, describes his first visit to what was then the Soviet Union.

Steve Allen.

6·2 *St Basil's Cathedral in Red Square, Moscow.*

I first visited the Soviet Union in September 1985. Most of my stay was spent in Moscow, easily the largest city, with a population of over eight million people.

At this time nobody had heard of the words 'glasnost' and 'perestroika'. Mikhail Gorbachov had only just come to power as General Secretary of the Soviet Union. He had started to make changes in the way the country was run. One of these was with a poster campaign against alcoholism. Apart from this there were few advertisements to be seen in Moscow, except for the odd hoarding publicising 'Pepsi' which was then the only Western-style product available.

Before visiting the city I had imagined Moscow to be a drab, grey place. Nothing could have been further from the truth. There were sophisticated boulevards lined with grand eighteenth- and nineteenth-century buildings as well as more modern constructions. Red Square is one of Moscow's most famous tourist attractions. It contains the Kremlin and Saint Basil's Cathedral.

I was impressed with Moscow's underground train system. The fare was a flat rate of five kopeks (five pence) and the trains and stations were spotlessly clean. Many stations, with their splendid murals and chandeliers, looked more like art galleries!

I learnt that most Muscovites live in state-owned flats which are basic and far from luxurious. In the shops there appeared to be a shortage of many foods, and there were often long queues in the shops.

Yuko, Tomoko and Ryo, who have recently moved to the United Kingdom from Japan, describe the area where they used to live.

Yuko, Tomoko and Ryo.

6.3 *Street scene, Tokyo, Japan.*

We all lived in apartments in Tokyo, just as many other Japanese do. This is because land is scarce and expensive. In some parts of Tokyo, land is so expensive that a patch about the size of a telephone box can cost as much as £70,000.

Yuko's apartment block was in the fast-growing Chiba district of Tokyo. At first it was a quiet neighbourhood, but now it has been surrounded by a shopping centre, swimming pool, department store and other big buildings. We found that owning a car in the Chiba area could be a problem, especially when trying to find a space to park! Luckily a new station has meant that the journey into the centre of Tokyo takes only twenty minutes.

Chiba is just part of the massive growth taking place in Tokyo. Experts think that Tokyo will continue to spread and will soon join up with other cities nearby.

Molly and Bonnie have just moved to London from Washington DC in the United States of America. Here they describe what Washington was like.

Our house in Washington was very big. We had a bedroom each and a spare room. From our sitting-room you could look out to the garden. The house was in a quiet tree-lined street, and nearby there were parks to play in. It was only a short walk to the grocery and video stores.

The city centre was twelve minutes' drive away. It was much busier there, with tourists coming to see famous landmarks such as the White House and Capitol Hill. Occasionally some roads were closed while the President and his guards travelled in convoy through the streets from the airport.

Washington is a city of contrasts. In Britain we often see the city on news-reports as a rich and successful place, but this image hides many problems. One-fifth of Washington's population have so little money that they find it hard to lead comfortable lives. There were some parts of Washington that we were scared to visit at night because there was so much crime.

Molly and Bonnie.

6.4 *Capitol Hill, Washington DC, USA.*

These six people have written about the environments they lived in. In this unit we will look at how industry affects the environment, and we will try to answer three questions:

▷ What are the former USSR, the USA and Japan like?

▷ What is it like living in an industrial environment?

▷ What can be done about pollution?

UNIT 6

What are the former USSR, the USA and Japan like?

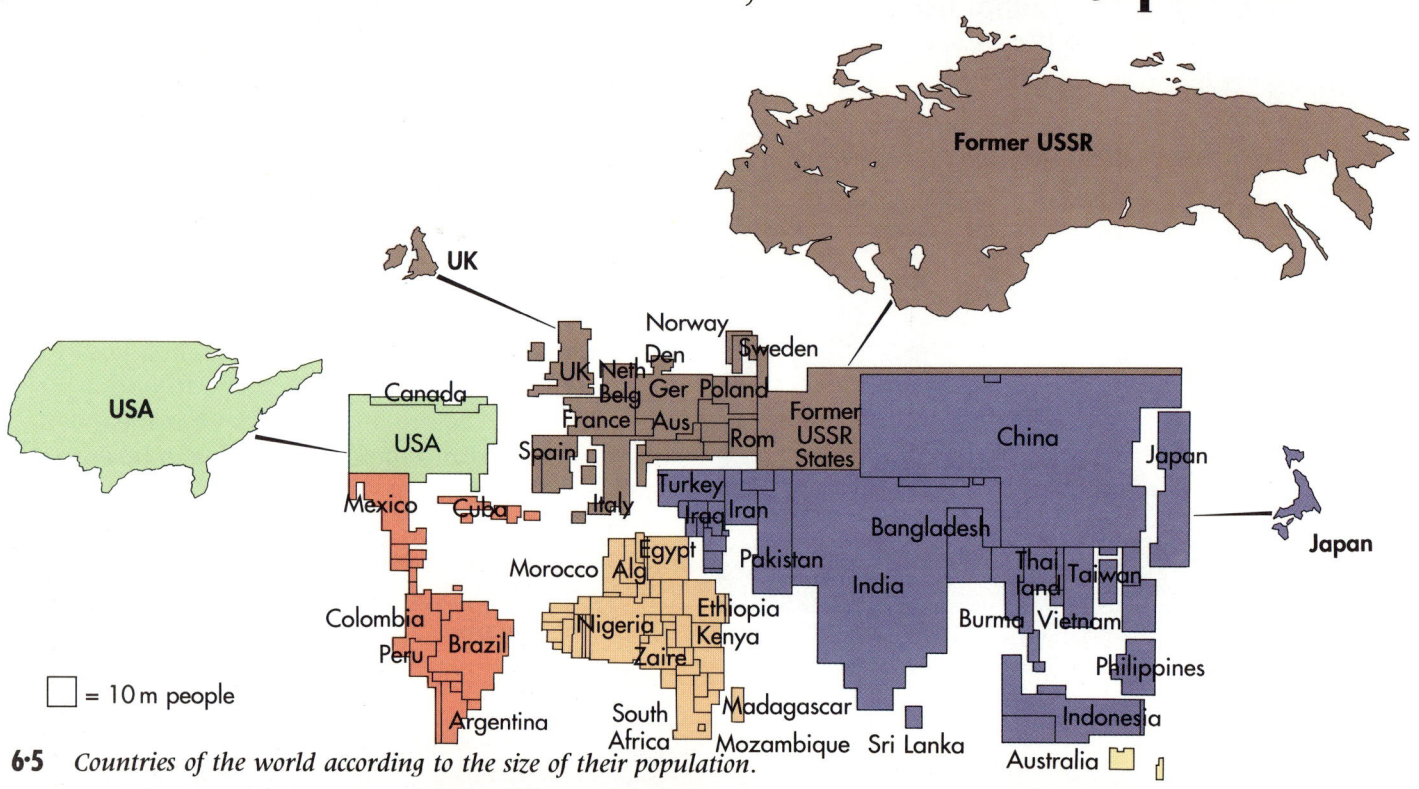

6·5 *Countries of the world according to the size of their population.*

The population

Look at the population map above.

1a Which continent has most people living in it?

b Which continent has least people living in it?

Now look at the table below.

2a Rank these four countries in order of area (size), from largest to smallest.

b Now rank them in order of population size, from largest to smallest.

3 Explain why the map is a good way of showing population sizes.

4 Population density measures how many people live in an area of land. It can be worked out by dividing a country's population by its area. In the United Kingdom, for example, there are 56 million people living in an area of 245,000 square kilometres, so:

$$\frac{56,000,000}{245,000} = 229 \text{ people per km}^2.$$

Now work out the population density for the other three countries in the table.

5 Look at Japan's population growth rate and population density. Why might experts be worried by these figures?

	Population (millions)	Area (km²)	Population growth rate per year (%)*
Japan	122.6 (1988)	372,000	1.2
UK	57.1 (1988)	245,000	0.1
USA	245.8 (1988)	9,363,000	0.8
Former USSR	286.7 (1989)	22,402,000	0.9

* The rate of increase changes from year to year. The mean annual rate of increase in population is the average indicated by the national censuses, which are held every ten years. Between census years, figures are estimates.

UNIT 6

USSR?

The world is constantly changing. This means that the 'facts' of geography also change. It is important to try to keep up with the changes, but it is almost impossible to predict exactly where the next changes will happen.

The Union of Soviet Socialist Republics (USSR) came into being after the 1917 revolution, and was one nation until 1991. But several of the individual states that were part of the USSR now want to be independent.

The USSR is history. In 1991, 11 of the original 15 states signed a new agreement. They called themselves the *Commonwealth of Independent States* (CIS). But no one knows how long this will last, or what the future holds for the people of what was once the USSR. So when you read 'USSR', remember to check the current situation in this fast-changing part of the world.

What the people do

Look at the photographs A, B and C.

1 Describe what is happening in each photograph.

2 These photographs show examples of *primary*, *secondary* and *tertiary industries*. What is meant by these terms?

3 'Together the USSR, USA and Japan make half the world's wealth.' If this is the case, why is it important to study the USSR, USA and Japan?

Look at the table below.

4a Which country has the lowest unemployment?

b Which country has the highest percentage of people of working age?

5 You are to investigate the figures for the three different types of industry. To do this you must choose a way of displaying these figures (bar graphs or pie charts, for example) and describe what your graphs or charts show.

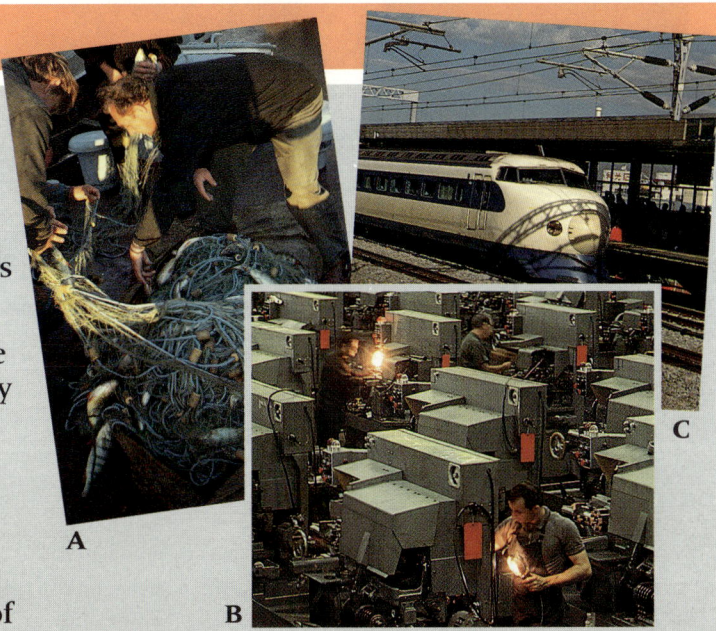

6·6 **A** *Primary industry: fishing in the USSR.*
6·7 **B** *Secondary industry: manufacturing in the USA.*
6·8 **C** *Tertiary industry: the 'bullet train', Japan.*

	Percentage of unemployed		Percentage of population of working age	Percentage of people working in		
	Male	Female		primary industry	secondary industry	tertiary industry
Japan	3	3	68	12	39	49
UK	16	10	64	2	42	56
USA	7	8	66	2	32	66
Former USSR	5	3	66	14	45	41

UNIT 6

Quality of life

The photographs on this page give you an idea of the quality of life in the former USSR, USA and Japan. They should give you some clues about how well people live in these countries.

6·11 *A street scene in Kiev, Ukraine.*

6·9 *A busy station in Tokyo, Japan.*

6·10 *An industrial complex in Denver, Colorado, USA.*

1 Look at each of the photographs. For each one, imagine that you live here. Describe the things that you like and dislike about it. Study the table below.

	Life expectancy	Quality of life figures		
		Murders per 100,000 people	Number of birds and animals facing extinction	Money spent on defence compared with money spent on health
Japan	77	Below 2	20	Less
UK	74	Below 2	4	About the same
USA	75	6 – 10	51	Twice as much
Former USSR	72	2 – 5	31	Three times as much

2 Explain which two 'quality of life' measures you think give the best idea of how well people live.

3 If you were comparing the quality of life in these countries, describe *five* other measurements you might use. Look back at all the information on pages 104–106.

4 You have won a holiday to *either* the USA, Japan, *or* a country in the former USSR.
a Write down the name of the country you would most like to visit.
b Give your reasons.

What is it like living in an industrial environment?

In 1985 Mikhail Gorbachov took charge of the Union of Soviet Socialist Republics (USSR), or Soviet Union. Through a process called 'perestroika' he tried to transform the way in which the Soviet Union was run. Perestroika has also led to 'glasnost', a new openness in society. This openness has allowed people to find out more about environmental problems in the Soviet Union.

One such problem happened in 1986, when a nuclear power plant at Chernobyl exploded. In this accident, 31 people died, and the 116,000 others who lived in the area will have to undergo regular medical check-ups for the next ten years. Many of these people face an increased risk of cancer.

Food supplies all over Europe were contaminated as the cloud of radiation from the accident spread as far afield as the United Kingdom.

The Chernobyl accident shocked the world, and yet 'glasnost' helped to reveal the sorry state of industrial standards in the USSR.

This article from a national newspaper describes a more recent case of environmental pollution, in the town of Sillamaa in Estonia, which was also in the Soviet Union.

THE POISONED CHILDREN

The children of Sillamaa have left their homes, but their faces stare up from the page of a local newspaper. They are hairless.

Nearly 300 children are bald, suffering from a condition called alopecia. The nursery schools they went to were built on top of a uranium waste dump, which was covered only with a thin layer of sand.

Uranium is a dangerous radioactive material. Although not all of the information is available, it is thought that the uranium found under the schools had been used in military weapons. A special committee was set up by the Soviet Health Ministry. It found that radiation levels around the nursery schools were higher than those found at the Chernobyl site today.

The children of Sillamaa have been sent to hospitals in Moscow. The Government promised to turn the factory which made the uranium in the first place, into a plant manufacturing magnets. The local people are demanding more: they want the radioactive topsoil to be dug up and taken away. For people living in what was the Soviet Union the case of Sillamaa is just one more example of how the Government allowed industry to damage the environment. The people of the former USSR want stricter controls on industry so that their environments are not poisoned.

6·12 *A car close to Chernobyl being checked for radiation.*

The location of Sillamaa in Estonia.

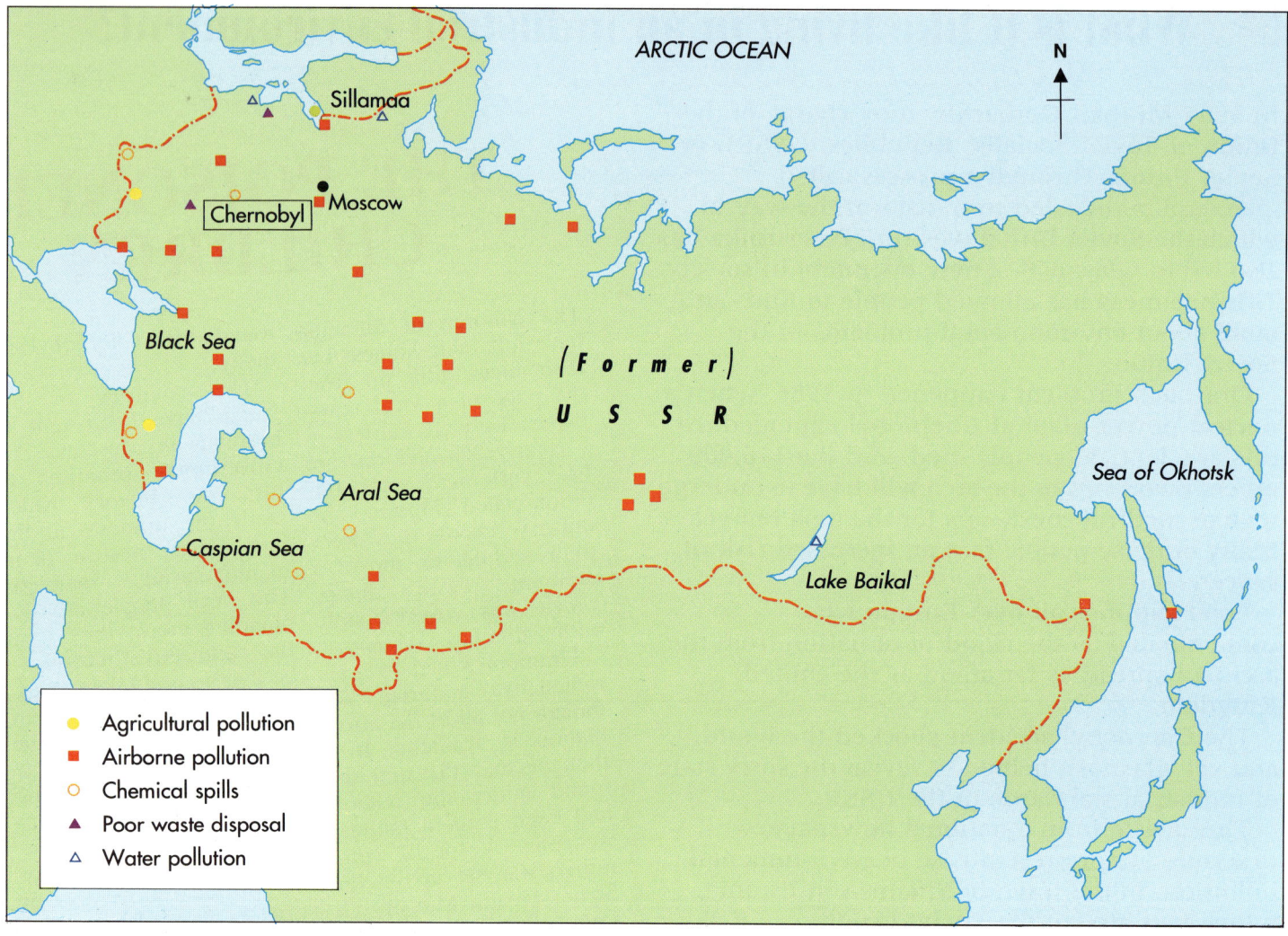

6.13 *Pollution in the former USSR.*

Read through page 107 again.

1. When did Mikhail Gorbachov come to power?

2. In your own words, explain what the word 'perestroika' means.

3. In 1986 a major accident happened at Chernobyl in the Ukraine. Make a list of the impacts on people and on the environment.

4. Describe the location of the town of Sillamaa in Estonia. Use the maps on pages 107 and 108 to help you.

5. What is the environmental problem described in the article on Sillamaa?

6. How did this problem affect the children of Sillamaa?

Look at the map above.

7. Name two places which suffer from water pollution.

8. Name two places which suffer from airborne pollution.

9. Describe the pattern of pollution in the former USSR.

10. You are a television news journalist and your speciality is reporting on the environment of Eastern Europe. You are called to film a case of environmental pollution in Sillamaa. Using *all* the evidence on pages 107–108, write the script for your two-minute report.

The following news reports A–E are about other environmental problems caused by industry in countries of the former USSR.

A

In the Soviet Union air pollution has reached critical levels in 68 industrial centres. Last January the snow turned pink as a result of a leak from a chemical factory which makes toxic dye. The chemical plant was more than a hundred years old and therefore dangerous ...

The Indy, 12 April 1990

B

In the coalfield areas of the Ukraine, death rates are so high that local people call the industrial area between the region's three main towns, 'The Bermuda Triangle'.

From a national newspaper, September 1989

C

Two years ago, a farmworker flicked his cigarette into a Ukrainian river. The river exploded and burned for five hours. Apparently a bulldozer had cracked an oil pipeline, causing a massive oil slick.

The Indy, 12 April 1990

D

The town of Nizhi Tagil in the Ural Mountains is a tired town suffocating from poisonous smoke and dust. One factory lets out 700,000 tonnes of poisonous fumes every year. This works out at about two tonnes for every person living in the town.

From a television news report

E

At midday the city of Narva is enveloped in a thick, sulphurous mist. Four power stations in and around Narva burn 23 million tonnes of oil-shale a year, letting out 380,000 tonnes of sulphur dioxide and 200,000 tonnes of poisonous ash. Women push prams as in any other city, and try not to think of the consequences ...

From a national newspaper, September 1989

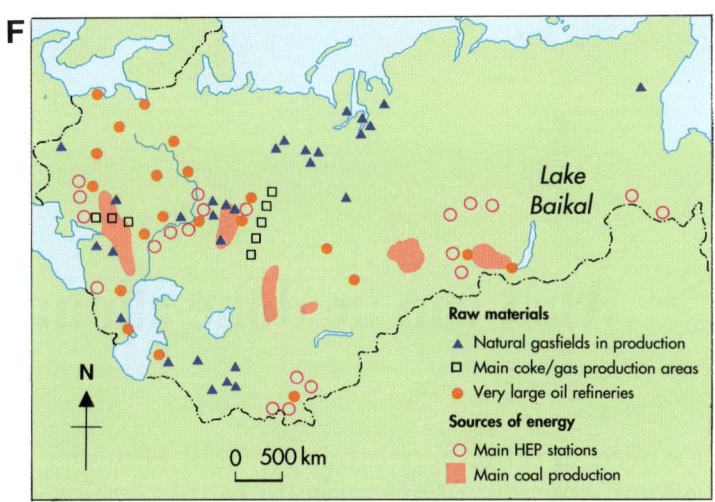

6·14 *The distribution of raw materials and energy for the plastics industry in the former USSR.*

G

6·15 *The distribution of population in the former USSR.*

UNIT 6

Place	Main cause of problem	Effects
A Cities in the former USSR	Leak from an old chemical factory	The snow turned pink

1 Complete a table like the one above for items B, C, D and E. The details for item A have been filled in for you.

Study map F on page 109.

2a How many hydro-electric power stations are there within 2,000 kilometres of Lake Baikal?

b How many large oil refineries are there in the former USSR?

c Describe the pattern of oil refineries in the former USSR.

Study map G on page 109.

3a Name three cities in the former USSR with populations of over one million.

b What is the size of the largest of the cities around Lake Baikal?

c Describe the pattern of where people live and where they do not live, in the former USSR.

4 'It is people who create industry, and industry often leads to pollution.' Referring to items C, F and G, explain whether or not you think this statement is true.

▷ What can be done about pollution?

Jim Brettel.

We need to think very carefully about how we use and abuse our environment. In this section we will see how some industries have made changes to our natural world.

In 1988 Jim Brettel was travelling on the Trans-Siberian railway on his way from Beijing in China to Moscow in Russia. At the time he had little idea that this would be the start of an environmental detective story. Jim takes up the tale.

It had been 60 hours since leaving Beijing. It was early morning and most people on the train were asleep. As we approached Lake Baikal, dawn broke, touching the water with silver and gold. The snow-clad mountains on the opposite shore seemed so close and yet they were 40 kilometres away.

6·16 *Along the shores of Lake Baikal, at different times of the year.*

The train sped on towards Moscow. A week later Jim read newspaper reports about pollution in Lake Baikal. He was surprised that this lovely lake was in danger. Jim went back to investigate.

First, he visited a local writer, Mark Tokarev. Here is what they said.

During his visit to Baikal, Jim talked to a number of local people and collected facts and ideas about the lake. Here are some pages from his notebook.

How industry in the cities pollutes Lake Baikal.

Jim: When did you first come to Lake Baikal?
Mark: I moved here with my family in 1956. My father got a job helping to build a chain of hydro-electric power stations on the Angara River, which flows into the lake. These supply power to industry.
Jim: How did this affect the environment?
Mark: Dams were built across the Angara River to trap and release water so that electricity could be made. This affected the river: for example, fish could no longer move freely up and down the river, so they were unable to breed, and fish stocks declined. Also, parts of the forest were chopped down so that power lines could be built.
Jim: How did people react to this?
Mark: At first people said that the industry was good. They thought that Lake Baikal and the forest around it would last for ever. Then people began to think again!
Jim: Why was this?
Mark: The growth of industry around the lake as well as in nearby cities caused many changes. In the lake, fish began to die, and people who drank the once pure water, became ill. Some species of birds have also vanished from the area.
Jim: So people's attitudes to the environment have changed?
Mark: Yes! Recent political changes have encouraged people to speak out about environmental problems. More people are realising that our environment needs to be looked after carefully.

- World's deepest lake at 1,620 metres.
- World's oldest lake at 250 million years.
- Area of the lake is 31,500 square kilometres.
- The lake has 1,500 species of animals and plants, 75% of which cannot be found anywhere else in the world e.g. the nerpa seal.
- The lake is surrounded by 50,000 hectares of taiga. (coniferous forest).
- 10,000 privately owned motor boats use the lake.
- 90% of eastern Siberia's population live around Lake Baikal.
- There are two huge wood-pulp mills on the lake shore, at Selenginsk and Baykal'sk. They spill their waste into the lake.
- Only July and August are suitable months for tourists. Most of the year it is cold with gales.
- 500,000 tourists visit the lake each year.
- Fuel from boat engines pollutes the lake.
- The chopping down of trees (logging) is an important industry. The logs are floated across the lake in 'rafts'.

- Chemicals from the wood and bark poison the water. Logs which have sunk to the bottom of the lake rot and pollute the lake.
- Young fish and fish eggs are easily killed off by pollution.
- Through natural causes 60,000 tonnes of soil are washed into the lake each year. Since forest has been chopped down, 400,000 tonnes of soil choke the lake each year.
- The lake is not a sea. There are no tides to wash away the pollution.
- Microscopic animals which keep the water pure are dying because of pollution.
- The nearest large cities, Irkutsk and Cherenkhovo, have many polluting industries.

6·17 Pages from Jim Brettel's notebook.

UNIT 6

1a Write a list of words which describe the photographs on page 110.
b Use some of these words to write a short paragraph on Lake Baikal for a tourist brochure.

2 What changes have taken place in and around the lake in the last 30–40 years?

3 Jim's notebook contains lots of information. Rearrange this information using these headings:

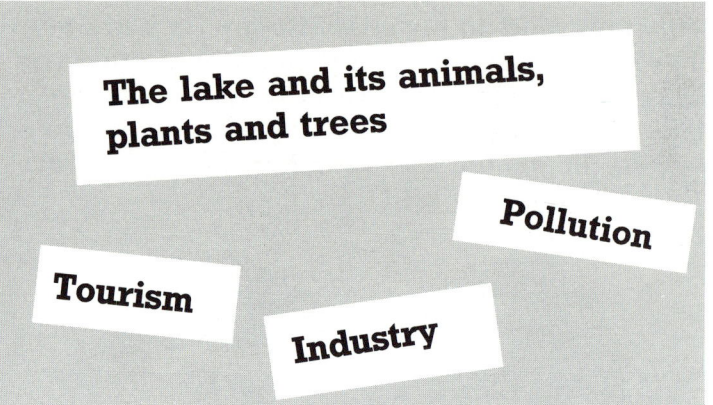

The lake and its animals, plants and trees

Pollution

Tourism

Industry

Different views on pollution

Local people are proud of Lake Baikal and are worried that it is dying. If we are to decide what should be done about pollution, we need to understand the views of local people. In this section some of them tell us their opinions.

A fisherman
We depend on the omul, a fish found in Lake Baikal, for a living. Stocks of omul were once plentiful but now have fallen. We think pollution from industry is to blame. The omul's eggs are very sensitive to pollution and if they are contaminated they do not hatch.

Those fish which are left in the lake are fewer in number and are much thinner. Without the fish the people of Baikal will lose a valuable source of food and an important industry.

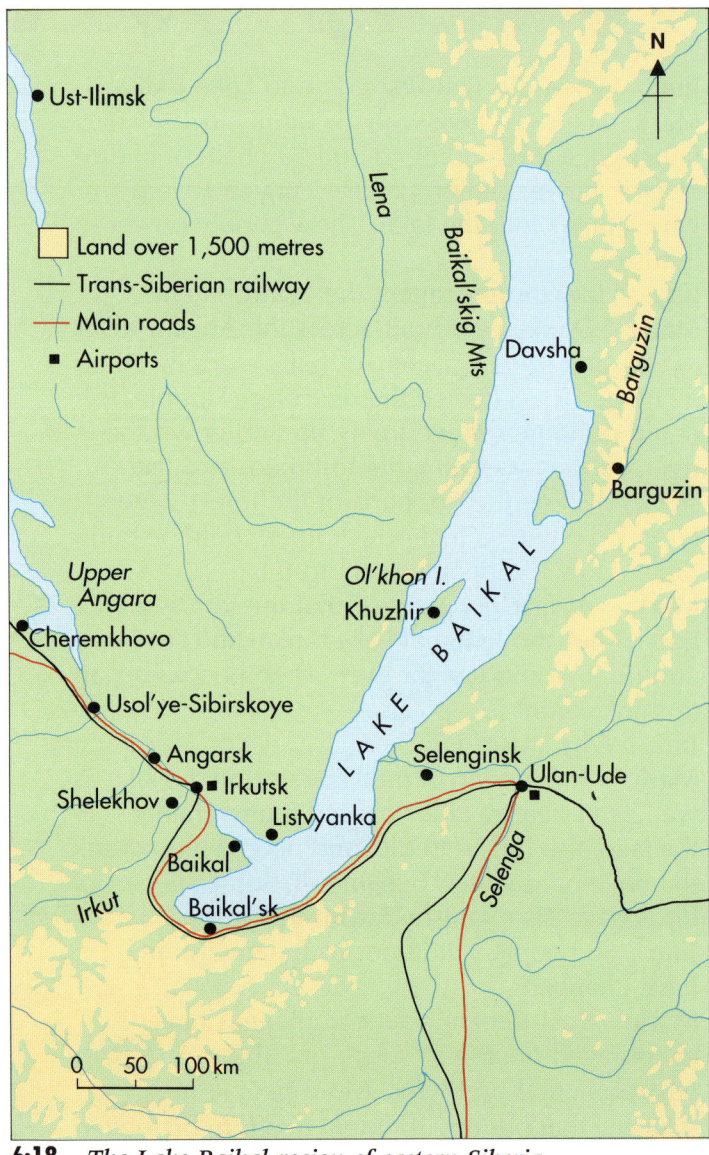

6·18 *The Lake Baikal region of eastern Siberia.*

The manager of a wood-pulp mill

The very pure water of the lake has allowed us to make high-quality products. The future for this industry is good, as more people want to buy our product. We employ lots of people. We are cutting back on the amount of pollution we release into the lake. However, it is expensive to do this and increases the cost of our products. If the price is too high we will not be able to sell enough. This could put us out of business. The country is in economic crisis, and we need to sell all we can.

A worker from Irkutsk

Despite recent political changes, life is still very difficult for most people. Under the old-style government our jobs were safe. Since 'perestroika', many jobs have been lost. I worry that I might lose my job.

There is a shortage of basic items, like shampoo, in the shops. I often have to queue for food. This winter I will need new shoes but they will probably cost two-thirds of my monthly wage. I worry about pollution and its effects on our health, but control is expensive and I need a job.

A tourist board official

There are many parts of Lake Baikal which are very beautiful. Tourism brings in a lot of money. However, there are still several sites which could be developed, such as local mineral springs. Although travelling is now easier and cheaper, we will not get more tourists unless we build more hotels and clean up the lake.

A scientist

There is only one Lake Baikal. It is the world's oldest and deepest lake. It has many unique animal and plant species. All of this is under threat because industry feeds pollution into the lake. This pollution will remain in the lake for thousands if not millions of years. At the moment, the way people are using the lake, they are killing it. If Lake Baikal is to survive, things must change.

An official from the Ministry of Timber, Paper and Woodworking

Lake Baikal's timber, water and hydro-electricity make it an ideal place for pulp mills. These mills give jobs to local people. Pollution from the mills has already been cut, but we are not the only ones to harm the lake. In winter, pollution from Irkutsk and Cheremkhovo settles on the snow around the lake, turning it black. When the snow melts in spring, the dirt sinks into the lake water.

UNIT 6

Decision-making exercise: Part 1

1a Roughly how far are the following places from the town of Baikal:
- Cheremkhovo
- Irkutsk?

b Which two cities have airports?

2 For this exercise, work in groups of six. Each person should choose one of the characters on pages 112–113, so that everyone in the group is different.

Read the statement written by 'your' character very carefully, and look back at Jim Brettel's notebook on page 111. Then write a detailed account of your character's way of life, and worries for the future. Include facts and figures in your account, which should be as detailed as possible.

What solutions are there?

Many possible solutions have been put forward to deal with the problems of Lake Baikal. These include ways of reducing pollution and protecting areas of the lake and its shore. Some of these ideas are presented here.

> Develop a tourist resort and health spa around the mineral springs at Barguzin. Roads for cars, and car parks, would need to be included in the development.

> Put limits on the amount of pollution a factory can release into the lake and rivers.

> INSTEAD OF FLOATING LOGS ON THE LAKE, TRANSPORT THEM EITHER BY ROAD OR BY SHIP.

> Convert the wood-pulp mills into factories making furniture.

> Put (expensive) purification equipment into factories which at present dump pollution into the lake and the rivers which feed it.

> Carry the waste from the pulp mills at Selenginsk and Baikal'sk into the River Irkut by pipeline. As the Irkut does not flow directly into Lake Baikal, this will reduce pollution of the lake water.

> Set up a planning committee made up of local people, industrialists, government officials and scientists, to study the area and give advice on any development plans.

6·19 *Some suggestions on how to solve problems in the Lake Baikal region.*

UNIT 6

Ban fishing in certain areas of the lake so that the omul have a chance of increasing their numbers.

Set up hatcheries to raise omul eggs.

Stop all logging within a 2-kilometre zone around the lake shore, to help prevent soil erosion.

Set up a team of scientists to check on the amount of pollution in the lake, and to discover exactly where the pollution comes from.

SET UP NATURE RESERVES WHERE NO TOURISTS AND NO INDUSTRY ARE ALLOWED.

Move the two wood-pulp mills from the lake shore to the city of Ust-Ilimsk.

Fit pollution filters on the chimneys of all electricity power stations in the Irkutsk-Cheremkhovo area to cut down on the amount of pollution entering the air.

Give out permits to private boats using the lake so that their numbers can be checked and, if necessary, restricted.

Make strict new laws on how much pollution a factory can release into the air. Factories that do not keep within the law should be fined.

Decision-making exercise: Part 2

The aim of this activity is for your group to come up with a plan for solving the problems of Lake Baikal.

1   You should again take on the role of the character you wrote about in Part 1. Discuss with the others in your group what you think are the lake's main problems.

2   Explain the *causes* of these problems. Decide which problems need to be solved in one year, and which can be solved within the next five years. Remember, solutions are expensive, so you will want to spread the cost over as many years as possible.

3   Now carefully read through the various solutions presented on pages 114–115. In your group, choose those solutions to the problems listed in (1) that you think are the best. Remember, you must think about short-term solutions (within a year) *and* long-term solutions (within five years). You will find that some problems are easier to deal with than others.

4   Finally, your group is to produce a display of your plans for Lake Baikal. You should be prepared to present your display to other members of your class. Your display should include the following:
- An outline of the main problems, their causes and when they need to be solved.
- An account of your solutions, both short- and long-term.
- Reasons why you chose the solutions you did.
- A map of the Baikal area on which you have shown the problems and solutions.
- A letter to the country's Minister for the Environment, explaining the advantages of your group's scheme.

All this information should be displayed in a clear and attractive way.

Industry produces things of value. Industry makes wealth. Making wealth is an incentive both for individuals and for nations.

Many nations place much importance on developing industry – on making wealth. They do this in slightly different ways, but all countries have to face the same question: *How do we let industry develop without harming the environment?* This unit helped us to examine this question, and presented a number of key points.

Industrialised nations

The former USSR, the USA and Japan are *different* industrialised nations. Together they produce over half the world's wealth. All have environmental problems.

It is possible that the environmental problems in the former USSR are more serious than in the USA or Japan. This is because in the past ordinary people had no direct say; there was no right to speak out. Often factories were built without any thought to their effect on ordinary people's lives.

Glasnost and perestroika

'Glasnost' means 'openness', and 'perestroika' means 'restructuring'. Mikhail Gorbachov began to modernise the USSR by giving people rights and freedoms. Industry must also change (restructure) to produce what the market – that is, people – wants to buy.

Environmental problems are now out in the open. In the old days, before glasnost, there were some terrible accidents, but the government of the USSR kept them secret.

Pollution

Many industries produce unwanted, waste products. In the past, waste products have been dumped or disposed of in the easiest way possible. This has often led to damage to the environment.

Laws and regulations can stop this. Such laws are only likely to be passed when the general public demand them. Even then, the industries will often argue: 'If you want us to dispose of waste safely and without harm to the environment, it will be more expensive. Will you pay a higher price for our goods to help us pay the cost of pollution control?'

Disaster Strikes!

UNIT 7

7·1 *Victims of oil pollution. In March 1989, 50 million litres of oil were spilt into Prince William Sound in Alaska. Eagles, sea otters, salmon, whales . . . millions of animals died. One woman working to save the animals was told: 'Cry for one animal, but let's work to save the rest.'*

UNIT 7

What do you know?

1 We have all heard people refer to 'environmental disasters'. What do *you* think an environmental disaster is? On your own, try to write down your answer in one short sentence.

2 As a class, think of as many environmental disasters as you can. Write them all down. Using an atlas, try to find the location of some of these disasters.

3 In pairs, rank all the disasters in order of the damage they do or have done to the environment. 1 is the worst disaster, 2 the next, and so on.

4 What types of disaster are your worst disasters? Write down the reasons why you think they are so bad. Compare your 'worst disasters' list with those of others in the class, and try to come up with an agreed list of the worst disasters.

5 On your own, look back to your original definition of an environmental disaster (question 1). In the light of the discussions you have had, do you now need to change your definition?

Living environments

An *environment* is an area of the Earth's surface, of any size, and usually there is some form of life.

There are many different environments around the world – the pictures on this page show just four examples. However, between environmental extremes such as these there are millions of other environments, each containing animals and plants that live together.

Life forms appear anywhere, from the deep sea floor to 6,500 metres above sea level. Each life form lives in its own *habitat*, where it finds its food and water and makes its home. Environments contain various habitats, and these differ from each other for a number of reasons.

b

c

a

d

7·2 *Some of our Earth's environments:*
a An urban area.   c Desert.
b Tropical rainforest.   d Arctic region.

Temperature

Plants need temperatures above 5°C to grow successfully, so in very cold climates as in the Arctic, where temperatures are often below this level, there is very little plant growth. Where there are few plants, there will be few animals.

Water

Plants need water to grow. Without plants or water, animals cannot survive – that is why so few creatures can live in deserts (a desert is an area which receives less than 200 mm of rainfall per year). In a desert the only organisms that can exist have to be specially adapted to the conditions. For example:
- A cactus stores its water in a succulent stem, and may protect this with spikes.
- The Mexican kangaroo rat can live without any water – it uses only the juice it extracts from the food it eats.

Sunlight

Different parts of the world have different amounts of sunlight. The area between the Tropics has most sunlight. Plants need sunlight to *photosynthesise*, to make the food they need to live and grow. Insects and animals need plants to survive, so an area with more sunlight has more plants, insects and animals.

All of these – warmth, water, sunlight – are required for life. A desert has a lot of sunlight and heat, but little water, so few plants and animals can survive here. It is because each of these three aspects, or *factors*, of life can vary so much, that no two habitats on the Earth's surface are exactly the same. For example, all areas of the tropical rainforest have similar features, but each habitat is different, in its own individual way.

Ecosystems

Within each habitat, creatures live together, or *co-exist*. The habitat, and the interaction between the plants and animals that live in that habitat, are together described as an *ecosystem*. For example, in a pond, carp fish eat pondweed. If all the carp were removed, then too much pondweed would grow, and other plants and animals would die. Similarly, herons eat carp. If all the herons were removed from the pond, then there would be too many carp, and too much pondweed would be eaten. So there would be too little plant matter left in the pond and other herbivores (plant eaters) would die. There are even waste eaters to clear up the dead and dying plants and animals. They help to release the food which is locked up in the plant and animal material. This allows new plants to grow.

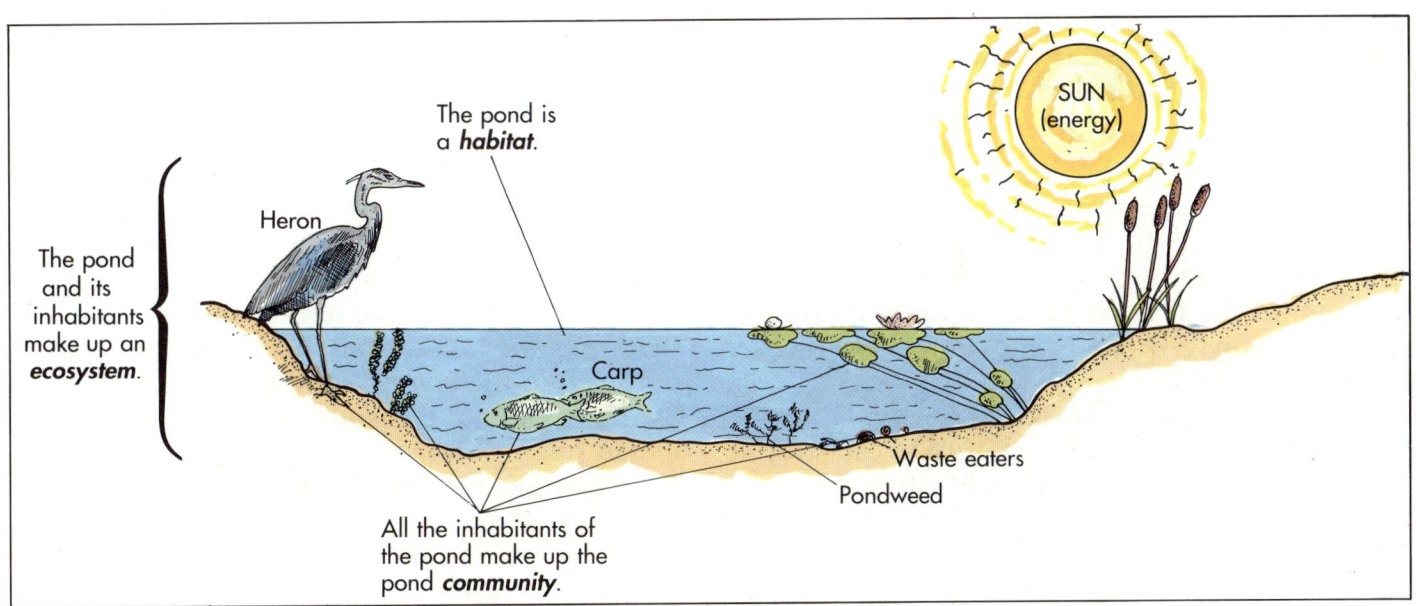

7·3 *A pond and its inhabitants – an example of an ecosystem.*

UNIT 7

Equilibrium

Different events can alter this delicate balance, or *equilibrium*. A disease, for instance, might kill all the carp, or a drought might dry up the pond. However, in most cases the pond will recover and eventually return to a new equilibrium.

People also alter the equilibrium, in lots of different ways. Some of these ways are shown in the photographs on this page. These activities all disturb the equilibrium of the environment.

7·4 *Some of the ways people change the natural environment:* **a** *By ploughing.* **b** *By logging.* **c** *By polluting. Ploughing up the land destroys the food and home of plants and animals. As there are fewer plants to hold the soil in place, it is washed down by rain into streams and rivers, where it disturbs the plants and animals living there.*

Fragile environments

Environments are not all the same. Tropical rainforest environments are home for millions of different plants and animals which grow very quickly. Polar environments have few plants and animals, and these grow only slowly. Polar environments are more *fragile*, because it can take years for damaged plants and animals to recover and grow again.

People can upset the balance of any environment. But damage can turn to catastrophe in a fragile environment. This is why most countries of the world agree that Antarctica should be protected and be made into a World Park, where risky activities such as mining will be banned (see page 158).

One such catastrophe in a fragile environment was the spilling of oil off the coast of Alaska (see pages 132–135). Spills are happening with increasing frequency around the world. For example, in just one day, 23 June 1989, there were three major spills in the USA, totalling more than 4,600 tonnes of fuel oil.

Oil must be taken from the country where it is produced to the countries where it is to be used. The international transport of oil is usually carried out by oil tankers. It is important to the oil companies to keep the cost of oil transport as low as possible. It has been discovered that the larger the tanker, the cheaper the cost of transport. So tankers are getting bigger and bigger. As tanker size increases, so does the scale of the disaster when an accident happens.

UNIT 7

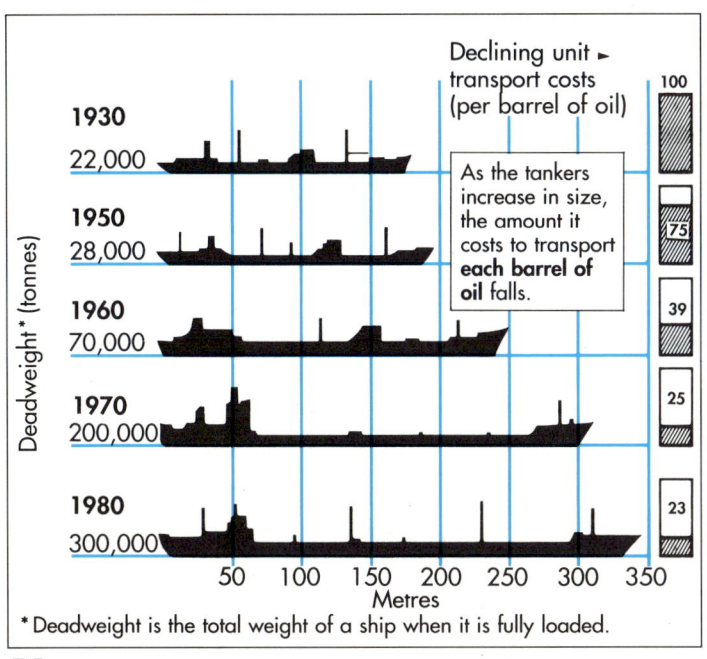

7.5 *The growing size of oil tankers and declining unit transport costs.*

The immediate, short-term impact of an oilspill is catastrophic, but the long-term effects are not yet fully understood. In this unit we look at why oil is considered so important that countries are prepared to risk major environmental disasters to obtain it in enough quantity. We then go on to analyse the impact that a major oilspill has on the environment, and what can be done to lessen the damage caused by such spills. We shall be investigating the following questions:

▷ How is oil formed, and how is it extracted?

▷ Will the search for energy beneath the land and sea ever end?

▷ Can accidents be avoided?

7.6 *A huge modern oil tanker. Today, oil tankers are the largest vessels afloat. The paint alone on the ship's hull can weigh 400 tonnes, and a walk around the deck can be a distance of up to half a mile. Yet only 30 or so crew are needed to manage the ship, because so much of the equipment is automatically controlled.*

UNIT 7

▷ How is oil formed, and how is it extracted?

Crude oil is a thick, dark, sticky liquid that is found in certain types of rocks (the word 'petroleum' literally means 'oil from rocks'). No one is quite certain exactly how oil was formed, but we do know it is a *fossil fuel*: that is, it is made from organisms that lived on the Earth many millions of years ago. These creatures died and fell to the bottom of the sea, where they formed a kind of sludge. This layer of sludge may have been slowly heated in the Earth's mantle, deep below the Earth's surface. Over many millions of years, deposits of mud and sand built up on top of the sludge. As the layer of sludge was heated and squeezed in this way, it gradually turned into oil.

Oil is a liquid. Some rocks are *impermeable* – that is, liquids cannot pass through them. Oil is found among such rocks, usually trapped in layers of *porous* rock (rock like a sponge, which has holes in it to hold liquids) beneath a layer of impermeable rock. Above the oil and also trapped in the layer of porous rock, is a layer of gas which is released by the oil during its formation. Most oil is found in *anticlines*, where the rocks are folded upwards like a dome (see the diagram), because it is only in situations like this that the oil can become trapped.

1 What does oil look and feel like?

2 Name another substance which we can also call a *fossil fuel*.

3 The diagrams on this page illustrate the formation of oil. After you have studied these diagrams, examine the labels opposite. Rearrange them into the correct order.

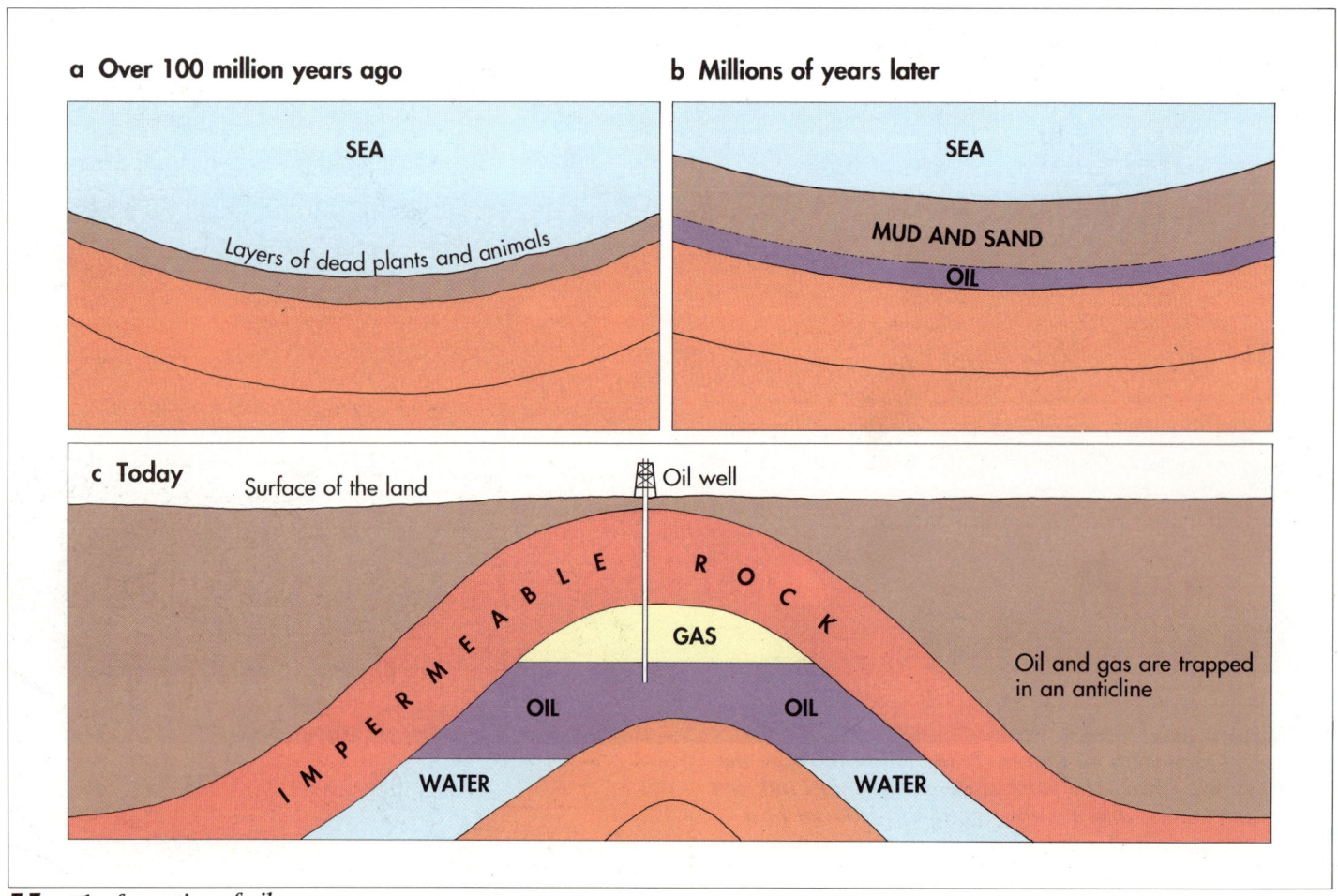

7·7 *The formation of oil.*

4 Use the labels to write the story of how oil is formed. Or use them to create your own diagram to show the formation of oil.

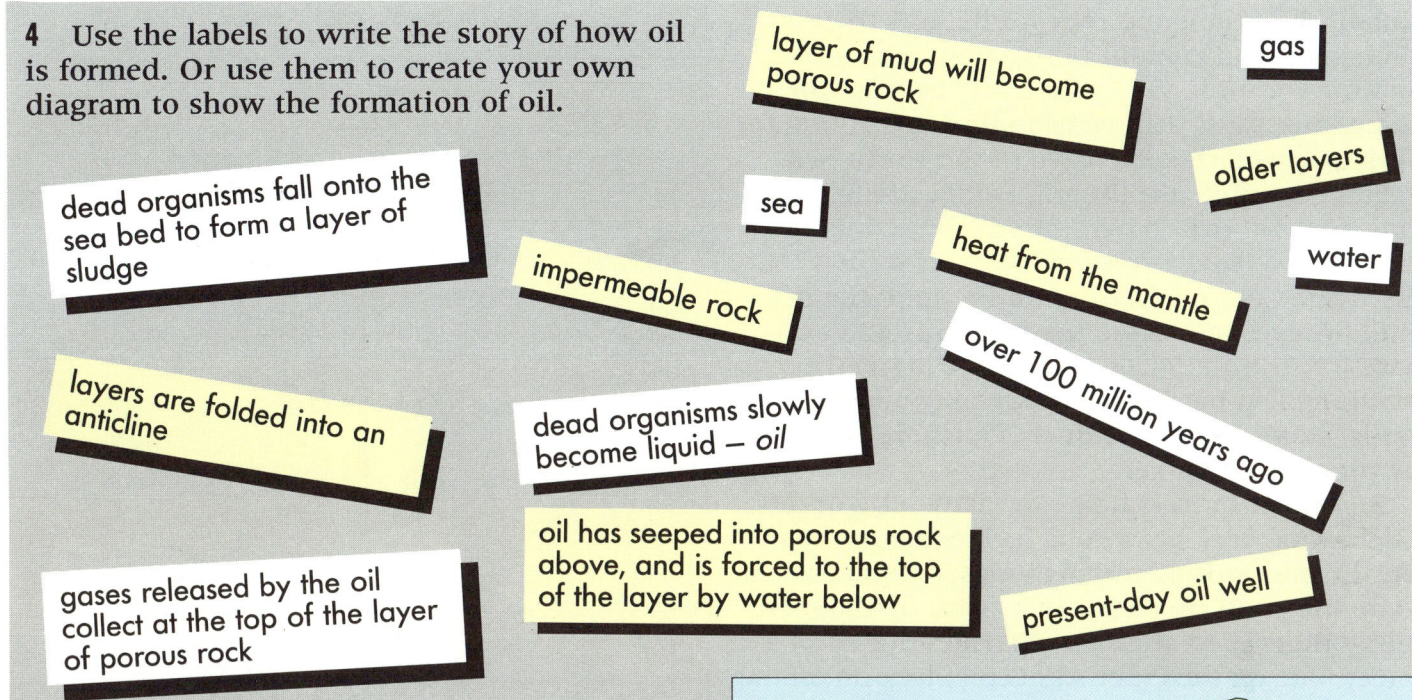

Oil is difficult to find...

How do oil companies know where to drill for oil? The answer is through a combination of past experience, of skilled technicians, modern technology, hard work – and luck!

The first clue comes from understanding how oil was formed. Geologists look for anticlines. They know that oil deposits can be found in layers of porous rock, 'trapped' below a layer of impermeable rock. To find this type of rock formation is not easy, and needs special equipment. Different types of survey may be used – seismic, magnetic or gravity surveys are just three kinds.

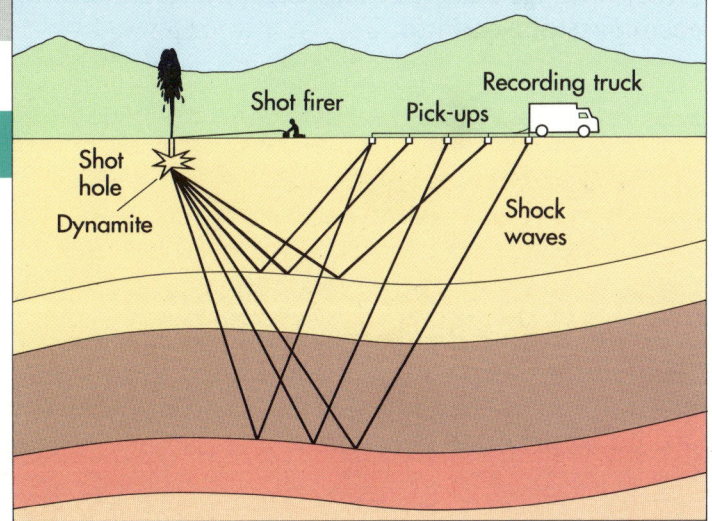

7·8 *Conducting a seismic survey.*

Oil exploration

Seismic surveys use small explosions which are set off to make shock waves. These are reflected back differently by each type of rock. Many measurements of this kind are taken to build up a full picture of the *geology* in an area, so that suitable *anticlines* may be found.

7·9 *Experts study the results of a seismic survey for oil.*

UNIT 7

Not all the promising rock formations that geologists find contain oil. The business of looking for oil is very expensive, because oil companies must drill wells to find it. Drilling for oil is particularly expensive in the North Sea.

First, a mobile drilling rig is moved out to sea, and this will drill down into the anticline, to depths of 6,000 metres and more. If oil is discovered, an oil platform is set up at the drill site, firmly fixed to the sea bed. This acts as a base for drilling for oil and extracting it. The platform also receives oil from surrounding wells, stores it, and sends it to onshore refineries by pipeline or tanker.

An oil platform is home to many oil workers. Life can be very hazardous for them. On top of the threat of storms and high seas, natural gas has to be burnt off by means of a flare. In 1988, 167 oil workers died after an explosion due to a faulty flare on the Piper Alpha oil platform off the east coast of Scotland.

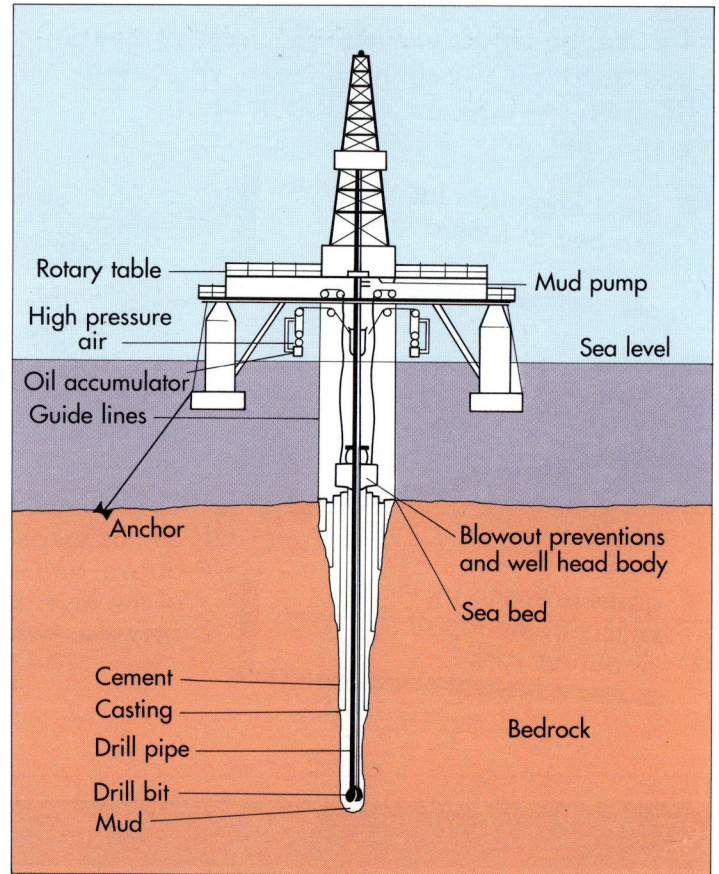

7.10 *The process of drilling for oil.*

You are a journalist working for a magazine. The editor has decided to run a special interest section called 'The Story of Oil'. You have been asked to produce two items:

1 A table, like an information box, headed 'Oil: a non-renewable resource'. The table must show *two* lists of resources:

Renewable	Non-renewable

At the bottom of the table you need to supply a two-sentence caption explaining exactly what a non-renewable resource is.

2 You must report an interview called 'The work of an oil man'. Charlie Whyte is a very experienced and skilled oil man. You have a chance to interview him. Write a transcript of your interview. You must think of, and write down, both the questions you will ask *and* the answers Charlie gives. These words and phrases may help you think of questions:

- Exploration drilling
- Oil platforms
- Helideck
- Drilling rig
- Gas flare
- Natural gas
- Seismic surveys
- Anticlines
- Oil pipelines
- Dangerous process
- Mud tank

▶ Will the search for energy beneath the land and sea ever end?

The North Sea

The graph on this page shows that the *demand* (need) for oil has increased considerably since 1955. Governments and oil companies around the world are therefore prepared to pay billions of pounds to search for new sources of oil to satisfy this increased demand.

In the 1960s oil was discovered in the Ekofisk field in the North Sea. Since then many new oilfields have been discovered in the North Sea, and Britain now produces as much oil as it needs. The oil produced here is of high quality and much of it is sold at high prices in the Rotterdam *spot market*, which is the world's largest marketplace for buying and selling oil.

Once oil is drawn from below the sea bed, it is pumped along pipelines to the nearest oil terminal. It can then be piped or sent by ship to the nearest oil refinery. Oil has to be refined to make oil products such as petrol or aircraft fuel. Most oil refineries have been built near the coast, where there is deep water (for oil tankers) and flat land. A good example is Milford Haven in South Wales (below right).

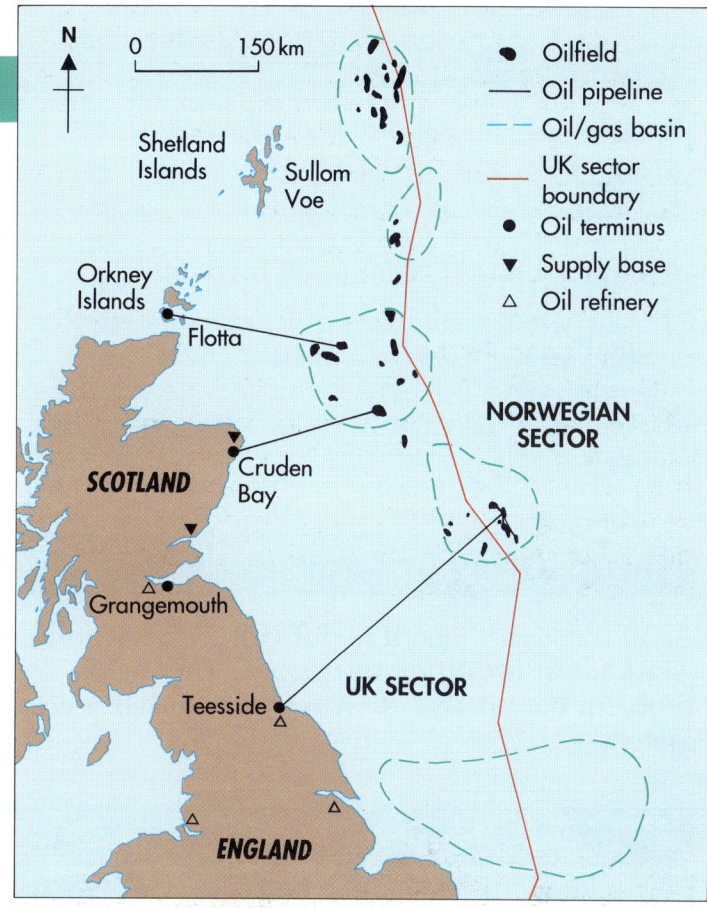

7·12 North Sea oilfields.

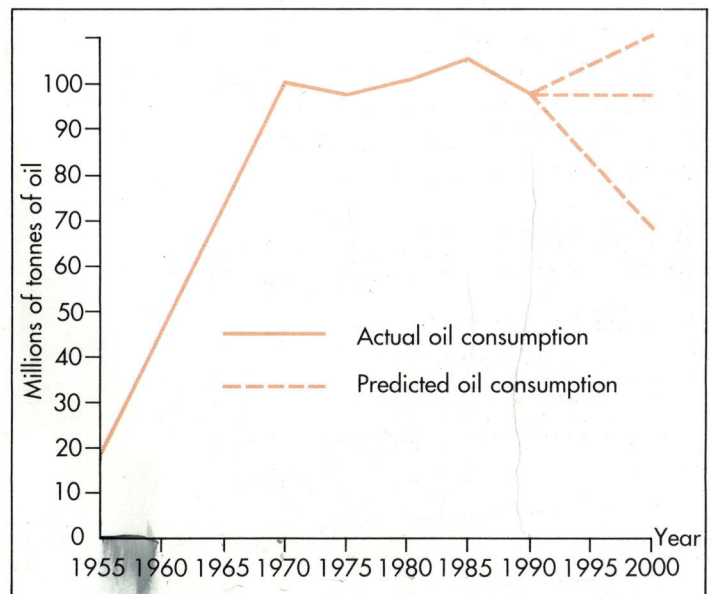

7·11 The demand for oil in Britain from 1955 to the year 2000.

7·13 An oil refinery/terminal at Milford Haven in South Wales.

UNIT 7

Discussion activity

Work in pairs for this activity.

1 Examine the graph of oil consumption in Britain on page 125. Describe to each other what the graph shows.

2 Each of you should draw a *sketch* of the graph. Divide the line into three sections:
▸ Demand for oil *rises fast*
▸ Demand for oil *flattens out*
▸ Demand for oil *begins to fall* (perhaps).

3 Discuss the predictions of oil consumption for the 1990s, and then answer these questions:

a What is a 'prediction'? How are predictions made?

b Why do you think it is possible to draw *three* different prediction lines on the graph?

c Try to imagine two different futures:
▸ a future in which oil consumption rises fast, or
▸ a future in which oil consumption falls.

Imagine you are living in one of these futures. Write a letter to your *present* self, from the future, describing what it is like. Think about these things to start you off:
▸ price of petrol
▸ the type of car you have (and how many cars you have)
▸ pollution of the air
▸ your family's way of life.

The Alaskan environment

As in the North Sea, it is difficult to extract oil in Alaska, but for different reasons. The main problem here is that the environment has a *polar climate*.

7·14 *Alaska.*

Alaska is located in the high latitudes. Much of it is within the Arctic Circle. As a result, the climate of Alaska is harsh. For long periods of the year the temperature does not rise above 0°C. This means that the ground is frozen for much of the year.

In most areas only the top metre or so (the 'active layer') thaws out in the summer. The area below this thaw area is permanently frozen and so is called *permafrost*. In this climate only a few plants and creatures can survive.

1 Climatic figures for Fairbanks in Alaska are shown below. Copy and complete the graph using these figures (the first three months have been done for you).

2 Look at the diagram showing permafrost. How does the layer of permafrost change as you travel from north to south?

3 What happens to the size of the 'active layer'? Why do you think it is called the 'active layer'?

4 Latitude, or distance from the Equator, is one important factor affecting the amount of permafrost in an area. Find out from an atlas the latitude of the northernmost point of Scotland. How many degrees of latitude to the north of Scotland does permafrost exist in Alaska?

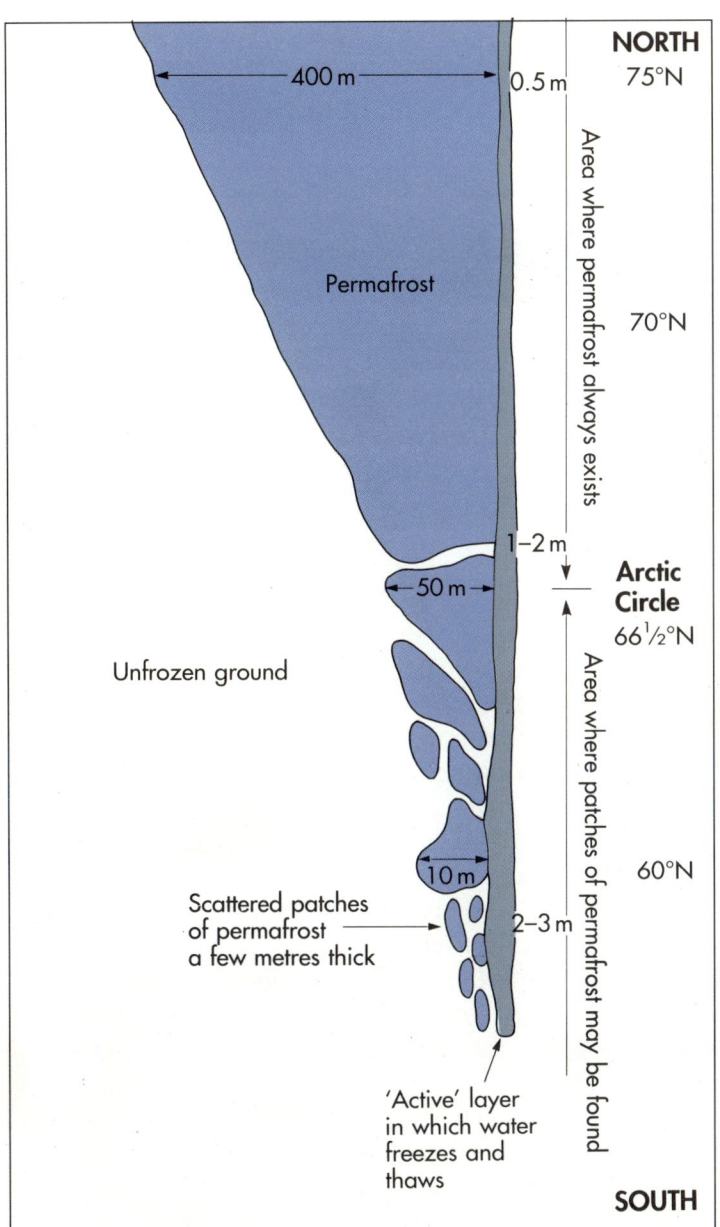

7·15 *Depth of permafrost in the high latitudes.*

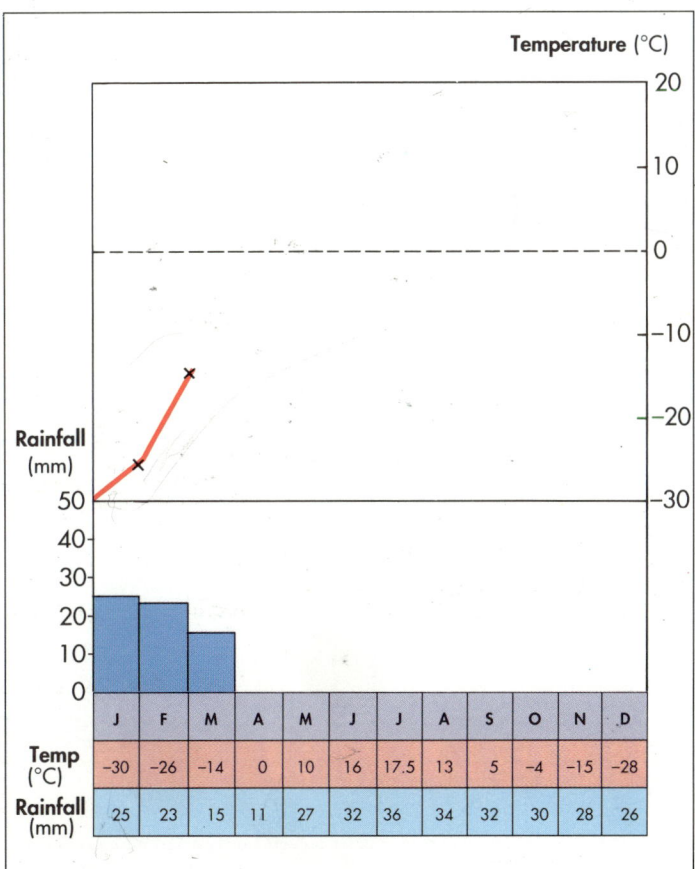

	J	F	M	A	M	J	J	A	S	O	N	D
Temp (°C)	−30	−26	−14	0	10	16	17.5	13	5	−4	−15	−28
Rainfall (mm)	25	23	15	11	27	32	36	34	32	30	28	26

7·16 *Temperature and rainfall figures for Fairbanks, Alaska, 64° 50′N 147°50′W.*

The Arctic environment is fragile. Because only a few species of plants and animals can survive in this climate, it does not take much to upset the balance of the ecosystem. There is not the wide choice of creatures and plants – the *diversity of species* – here that there is in the tropical rainforest ecosystem, for example. This means that if one species is eliminated, the 'knock-on' effect is immense.

Also, because the climate is so cold, chemical and biological breakdown of waste is much slower. There are only a few waste-eating creatures in the Arctic. Thus any waste put into the environment by people (an oilspill, for example) will remain to pollute the environment for a very, very long time.

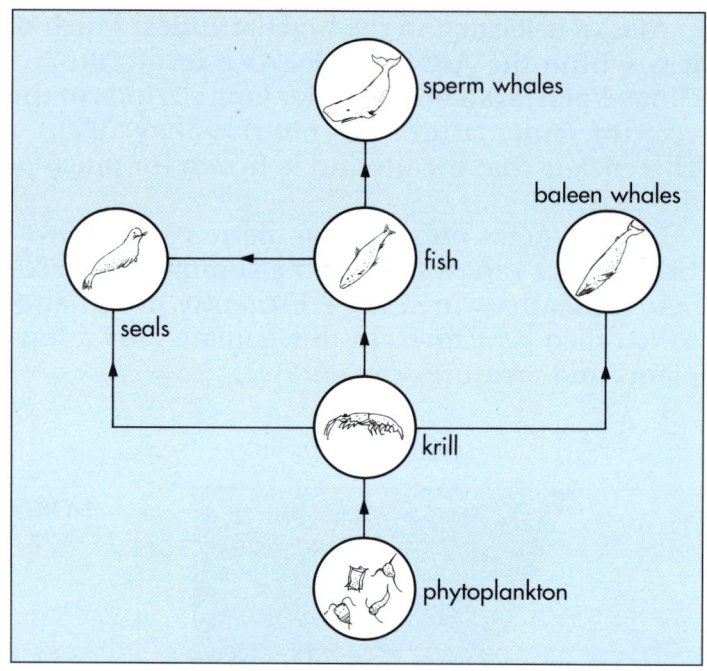

7·17 *A simple marine (sea) food web.*

Problems for the oil industry

Like many oil workers, Charlie Whyte has worked all over the world. He has worked both in the North Sea and in Alaska. We asked him to compare working conditions in the two areas.

The oil driller, Charlie Whyte, in Alaska.

There's probably more danger in the North Sea. But life in Alaska is really hard. The biggest difficulty is the transport of machinery, men and of course oil. Machinery and hoses have to be kept heated night and day. Cabins have to be kept on stilts to avoid sinking into the ground. Pipelines have to be kept heated to prevent the oil freezing up, and are raised off the ground to allow the migration of wild animals like bears and moose across the Alaskan wilderness.

Life is hard for the Alaskan oil workers. In the few warmer months the ground becomes muddy and wet, but it is covered in blossoming flowers. However, in the long winter months, snow covers the ground and there is darkness for up to six months of the year.

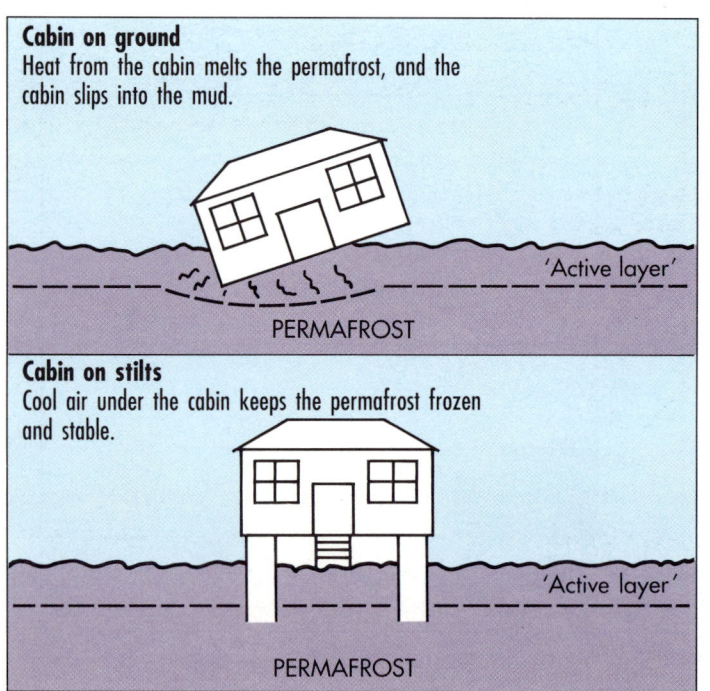

7·18 *Cabins built on stilts to avoid problems of permafrost. Ordinary houses would melt the permafrost and sink into the ground.*

1 Look at the bottom diagram on page 128. Try to explain why building houses on stilts prevents them from sinking into the ground.

2 When oil was discovered in Prudhoe Bay in northern Alaska in 1968, BP had three choices for transporting its oil to sell in the main cities in the eastern USA.
▶ To ship the oil through the Bering Strait and across the north of Canada. This is an icy, dangerous route weaving through many islands.
▶ To build a pipeline across Canada to the east coast.
▶ To build a pipeline to the south Alaskan port of Valdez and then ship the oil to the USA's west coast.

The US Government agreed on the last option. Give reasons why you think they decided this.

3 Look at the map below showing the route of the Trans-Alaska Pipeline (TAP). How long is the pipeline?

4 Examine the route followed by the pipeline. Try to give reasons
▶ why the construction of the pipeline was so expensive (it cost US$2,100 million).
▶ why many conservationists were so strongly against this development.

7·19 Scenes from life in Alaska:
a In summer the midnight sun dips towards the horizon over the Beaufort Sea, but does not set. In the winter, there are many months of darkness.
b The Trans-Alaska Pipeline snakes through the mountains of Alaska.

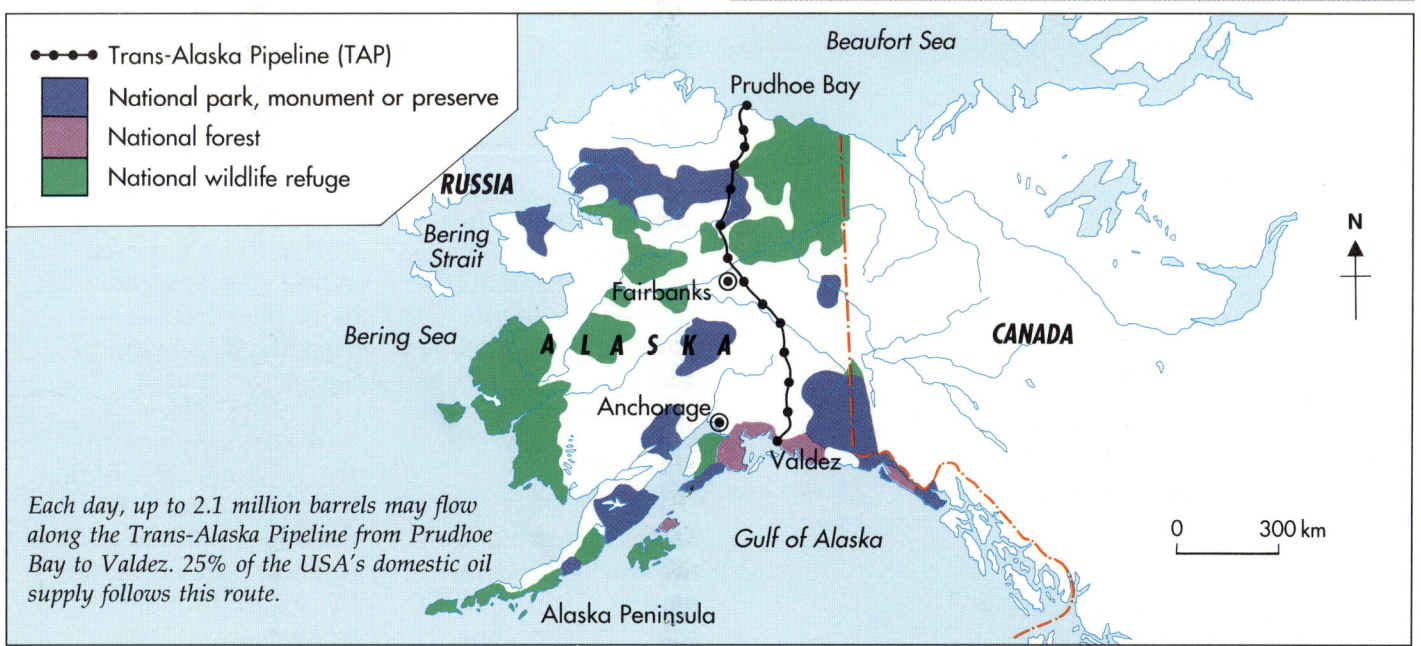

Each day, up to 2.1 million barrels may flow along the Trans-Alaska Pipeline from Prudhoe Bay to Valdez. 25% of the USA's domestic oil supply follows this route.

7·20 The Trans-Alaska Pipeline (TAP).

UNIT 7

▷ Can accidents be avoided?

This poem expresses the feelings of the poet against the horrors of oil spillages and their effects on the ocean environment. It is not a new problem: the poem was written in 1933. Oilspills occur through accidents involving oil tankers, oil terminals or oil rigs. Many oil tankers also deliberately clean out their tanks at sea as it is cheaper and quicker than using the facilities in dock.

In 1985, for example, there were 366 incidents involving the spillage of oil around Britain's coast. Four of the worst of these are described in the following table.

> I am the Sea
> The ancient moon lover calling!
> My tides grow slack and are failing,
> My whales mate no more,
> Nor the seals on my dim north shore,
> Nor my serpents in their mailing.
> I lip the Earth, and her saviour is paling,
> Her salt to my salt is tasteless and failing.
>
> O my tides, my rocks and waving flowers,
> What is your sickness?
> What hurts you, my dolphins, my seals
> In your slipping quickness?
> What oil, what poison lulls
> Your wings and webs, my cormorants and gulls?
> My fresh winds blow to the Earth
> But cannot heal her . . .
>
> *from 'The Marriage of Machines' by Stella Gibbons*

Place	Month	Problem	Oil lost
Aberdeen Harbour	January	BP terminal tank failure	400 tonnes (paraffin)
Sullom Voe	April	Leak at oil rig (BP Vision)	62 tonnes
Firth of Forth	June	Fractured pipeline	300 tonnes (of oily water)
St Ann's Head	June	*Bridgeness* ran aground	167 tonnes

The most serious oilspills around Britain in 1985.

Part of the problem comes from tanker captains choosing riskier routes. The newspaper article below explains why they might do this.

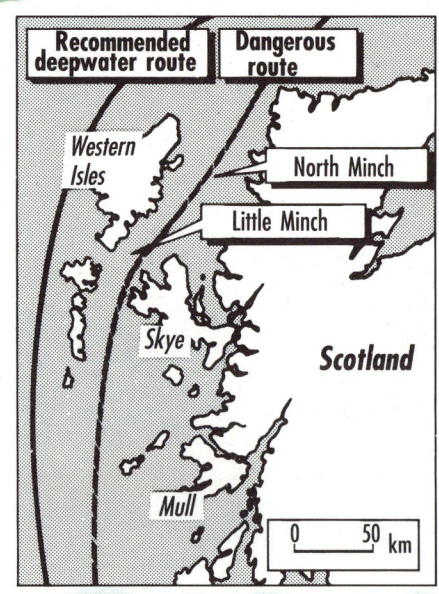

7·21 *From a national newspaper, October 1990.*

OIL THREAT TO SCOTTISH RESERVES

A recent report has concluded that 80% of oil tanker captains are choosing to ignore government guidelines and are sailing through The Minches between Skye and the Western Isles.

The Minches are one of the richest habitats in the world for seabirds, marine mammals and fish. The shoreline threatened by spillage contains five national nature reserves and more than 100 sites designated as being of Special Scientific Interest (SSSI).

A spokesperson for the government said that it was important that the tankers should be able to choose this route in the event of bad weather.

What impact does oil have on the environment?

Birds

- Birds of prey are contaminated as they scavenge oil-soaked prey.
- Seabirds preen to try to restore the shape of their feathers, but take in oil as they do so.
- Colonies of birds are very vulnerable to an oilspill when they come together to breed.
- Feathers are designed with tiny, interlocking barbs to form a watertight seal. Oiled feathers lose their shape, and are no longer able to keep the bird warm.
- Oil damages the birds' red blood cells and causes anaemia.

Marine mammals

- Animals swimming through the oil can suffer nosebleeds, and some are blinded.
- The oil causes lung disease, which makes it difficult for the animal to dive, and can be the cause of its death.
- Liver and kidneys can be damaged by the oil, often resulting in death.
- Oil-matted fur loses its insulating properties, reducing the animal's body temperature (hypothermia).
- Sea otters, the only sea mammals that do not have a thick layer of fat (blubber) just below the skin, are particularly badly affected.

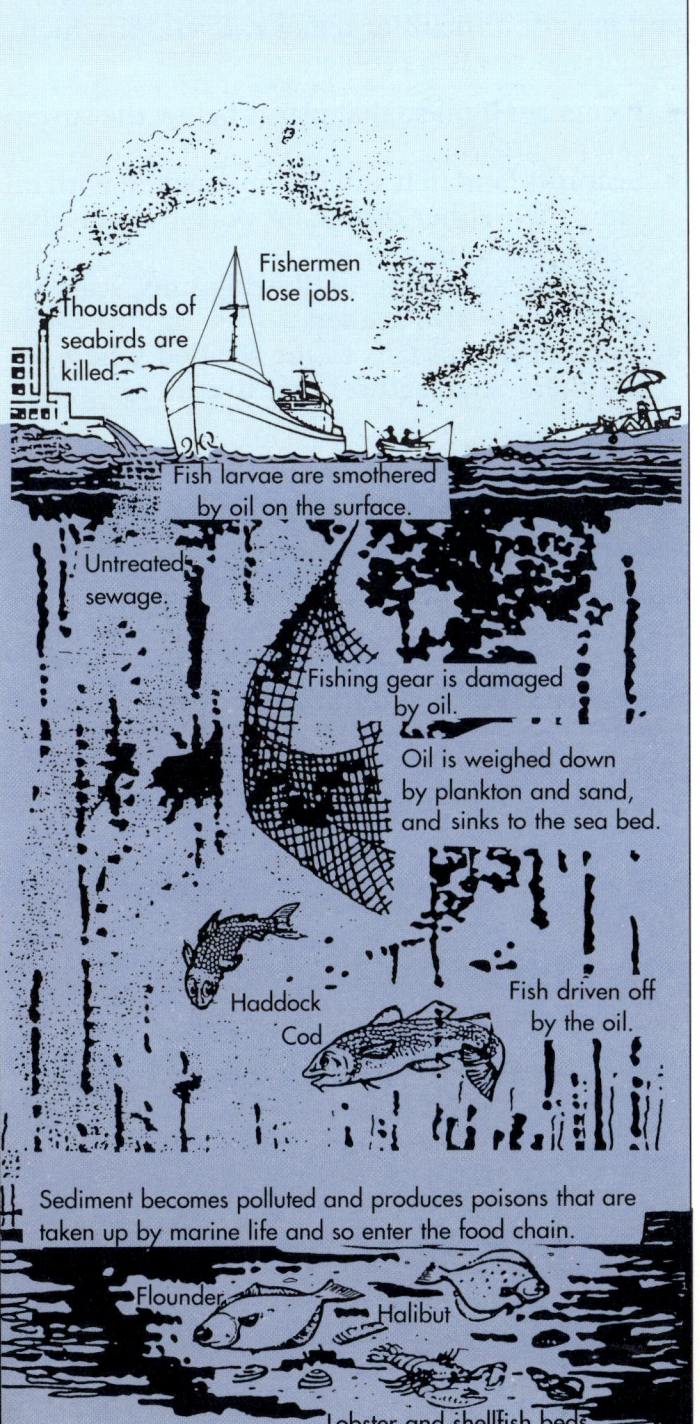

7·22 *Oil pollution on the coast.*

Cleaning up the coastline: workers cleaning a beach of oil, with sprays, spades and water hoses.

7·23 *Oil pollution at sea.*

The diagrams and photographs on pages 117 and 131 show how oil can ravage wildlife. Some oil finds its way to the shoreline, blown there by onshore winds. Once there it sticks to rocks, pebbles, seaweed and other forms of wildlife, and is very difficult to remove. Even oil which remains at sea is a problem:

- It cuts out light so that plants below the surface cannot grow.
- Seabirds land in it and become soaked with oil. They then either drown, or poison themselves when preening.
- Surfacing sea creatures like dolphins, seals and sealions are also soaked.
- Some of the oil falls to the sea bed where it smothers the creatures that live there.
- Some oil remains floating just below the surface where it clogs the gills of fish and suffocates them.

Make a list of the effects of oilspills on the environment, using a copy of this table:

Effects on underwater wildlife	Effects on surface wildlife	Effects on shore wildlife

The Alaskan oilspill, 24 March 1989

Throughout this section, imagine that you (the class) are environmental officers in charge of the area of Alaska shown on the map. There is an oilspill emergency. You have two important tasks.

The *Exxon Valdez* left the outbound shipping lane to avoid icebergs. She failed to return to her normal course, and struck Bligh Reef.

7·24 The 'Exxon Valdez' disaster.

UNIT 7

Task A To describe the scale of the environmental damage, locating and naming the affected areas.

Task B To produce a report to an agreed deadline, recommending appropriate methods of dealing with the oil slick.

Task A

At midnight on Friday, 24 March 1989, the oil supertanker *Exxon Valdez* ran aground in Prince William Sound, Alaska. The result was that some 11 million tonnes of crude oil was spilt into the sea, forming a slick 10 km in diameter.

Stage One From the point where it was spilled (marked 'X' on the map), the slick was blown west for 3½ hours at 10 km per hour.

Stage Two The slick was then blown south for 4 hours at 12 km per hour.

Stage Three The slick was finally blown south-west for 2½ hours with winds of 20 km per hour, until the last of the oil was deposited on Latouche Island.

1 On a copy of the map on page 132, use the information given above to plot the course of the oil slick on the map until it runs aground on Latouche Island. As you are plotting the course of the slick, shade in the total area affected by the oil.

2 Now copy this table (right). Use the plotted course of the slick to produce your report, showing the environmental impacts of the slick during its passage through the Sound. Part of the first stage has been completed for you.

Task B

1 This activity should be done in small groups of five. You now have to produce a report recommending appropriate methods of dealing with the slick. The methods available to you and their advantages and disadvantages are set out on the next two pages. Each person in the group is to choose one oil protection technique. Read it carefully, then take it in turns to describe your method to the others in your group.

2 Bearing in mind the cost of each method and the time each would take, decide upon your course of action. Then write your report, giving reasons for your choices as well as their advantages and disadvantages. Be prepared to present your report to the rest of the class. Some points to discuss:

▶ How might burning oil affect the environment?
▶ Where does the oil go when it has been collected with a boom?
▶ Is it better to deal with the slick at sea, or wait until it reaches the shore?

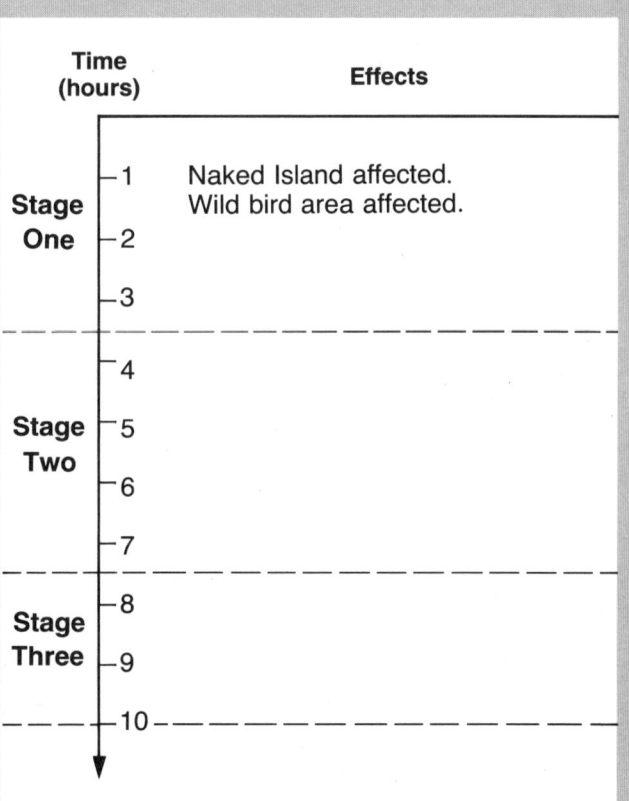

ABSORPTION

There are several materials which will absorb crude oil – straw, peat, polystyrene. These can be spread on an oil slick and mixed in. Then the oily mixture must be collected and disposed of on land, either by burning or burying.

For a 100-tonne spill:

Time required (hrs)			Total cost
Prepare and load	Travel time	Apply and recover	
2	3/4	7	£2,000

Advantages
- Actually removes oil from surface instead of merely sinking or dispersing.
- Economic.
- Works well in calm, sheltered waters.

Disadvantages
- Its lightness makes it difficult to apply in high winds and seas.
- Difficult to collect – especially in bad weather.
- Suitable dumping places for disposal on land must be found.

SINKING

Oil floating on the surface can be sunk by certain materials like specially treated chalk which floats until it is mixed with oil. It then becomes heavy and causes the oil to sink.

For a 100-tonne spill:

Time required (hrs)			Total cost
Prepare and load	Travel time	Apply	
2	3/4	2	£1,500

Advantages
- Removes oil from the surface of the sea, eliminating danger to diving birds.
- Oil can be sunk quickly.
- Economic.

Disadvantages
- Oil is removed from the surface but remains in the sea. It may affect fishing grounds and fishing gear.
- Oil can still travel with underwater currents. It may appear on shore weeks later if the oil is sunk close to land.

DISPERSANT

Dispersants help to split up oil. This allows natural forces such as waves, the wind, sun and bacteria to break it down. Dispersant is mixed with the oil after it has been sprayed on.

For a 100-tonne spill:

Time required (hrs)			Total cost
Prepare and load	Travel time	Apply	
1½	3/4	3	£3,000

Advantages
- Can be an effective, harmless method in the open sea.

Disadvantages
- Should not be used in harbours or close to shore inside estuaries.
- Should not be used close to shellfish beds for fear of contamination.
- Oil is not removed from the sea immediately.

OIL ON THE SHORE

If oil does come ashore it will in time be broken down by the action of the sun, waves and bacteria. But this may take many years in an Arctic environment.

Dispersants can be used and are sprayed along the beach before the tide comes in. Specially designed beach-cleaning vehicles are available. One large beach could take a whole week to clear. This would cost at least £4,000.

Local Task Force
This is a special team of local people armed with spades and tractors. The task force may use straw to absorb incoming pockets of oil. Any oil on the beach is removed by spraying with a low-toxic dispersant which is hosed down with sea water.

The cost of preparing such a local task force and having them stand by to deal with a small amount of oil is £1,000.

Only small quantities of oil in small local areas can be dealt with in this way. Alaska has a long coastline and few people.

7·25 *Oil protection measures, and their advantages and disadvantages.*

BOOMS

A boom is a floating barrier. Booms can be constructed from rubber, foam, wood, etc. They can only be used close to the shore. They can be used in three ways:

1 As a barrier to protect harbours, rivers and other vulnerable areas from oil.
2 To move oil from a sensitive area to a less sensitive area.
3 To move oil into calmer waters.

Lengths available	Cost per length	Time required (hrs)	
		Prepare and load	Install and anchor
20 m lengths	£50	1	2

Skimmers
When a boom has collected or moved oil, the oil can be removed from the surface of water by a mechanical device called a skimmer. This machine can collect oil at the rate of 100 tonnes per hour. It would cost about £1,000 per day.

In this unit we have taken a long look at perhaps the most useful and valuable of all the Earth's mineral resources: oil. It provides the fuel for most of the world's transport on land, sea and air. It heats our homes. It is also the basis for the petrochemical industry, which produces plastics, artificial fibres, paint, drugs . . . the list is endless. Our demand for oil has pushed the search for oil to hazardous environments, where accidents can be disastrous.

Fragile environments

An environment is a bit like a very, very complicated machine. Like a machine it works by using energy. An environment obtains its energy from the sun.

Polar environments do not receive much energy. This means they drive only slowly. Therefore, if such an environment is damaged, for example by an oilspill, it takes many years to recover. The oil decomposes very slowly. Plants and animals grow again, but slowly.

This is why polar environments are fragile. The continent of Antarctica, which lies in polar latitudes in the southern hemisphere, is to become a World Park. All mining and exploration is banned here for at least 50 years. Most countries agree with this because they want to protect it from everlasting damage. (See page 158.)

Non-renewable resources

Oil is a fossil fuel which took *millions* of years to form in sedimentary rocks. Once burned, oil has gone for ever. It is non-renewable. Some other natural resources are not consumed in a once-and-for-all way: trees can be planted as fast as they are chopped down; electricity can be made using wind, the tide or running water, which will always continue.

Supertankers

Oil rapidly became the fuel of the twentieth century, and it soon became obvious that there was a big stumbling block: the places where oil was produced (like Saudi Arabia) were not the same places as those where oil was consumed (like France and Germany). Transporting millions of gallons of oil every day of every year became a big problem to solve. It was solved partly by pipeline: but pipelines can carry only a certain amount.

Then supertankers were invented. These solved one problem but created another. Just one accident with one of these monster ships could be disastrous . . . and the *Exxon Valdez* proved the point.

Consuming the Earth's Resources

UNIT 8

8·1 This man in California is 'conspicuously wealthy'. He knows he has a way of life that is based on consumption. For example, he has his own personal jetplane, a Lamborghini car, a large house, a swimming pool, three holidays a year...

In many ways he is very fortunate. But he is beginning to get worried about the future. What do you think worries him?

UNIT 8

Brainstorm

Work through this activity in pairs.

Step One: Consumption

1 Discuss and then write down what you understand by the following:
▸ *conspicuously wealthy*
▸ *consumption*.

2 In all the more prosperous parts of the world, such as Western Europe and North America, people on average consume a lot. Choose a country in one of these continents. Now try to imagine the average family in the country you have chosen. Write down the heading *Average family consumption in* (your country – France, for example). List all the things that your imaginary family consume in a day.

Step Two: Resources

1 Discuss and then write down what you think is meant by the phrase *Earth's resources*.

2 Make a copy of the diagram below.

Try to complete the diagram by writing down two examples of the Earth's resources which are used when each of the things shown is consumed.

Step Three

The man in the picture on page 137 was very surprised when he first read this item in an American magazine article:

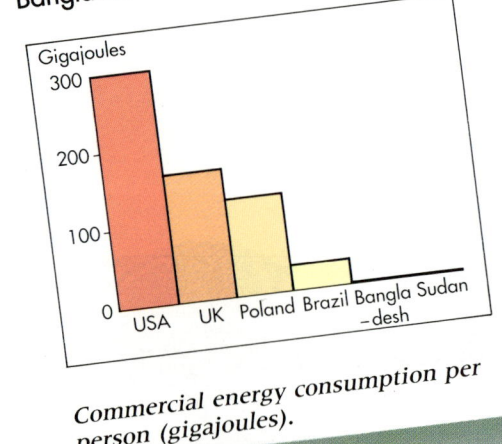

Although the USA accounts for less than 5% of the world population, it consumes around a third (33%) of the world's resources. Each American, on average, consumes twice as much electricity and gasoline (petrol) as each European, and 140 times more than someone in Bangladesh or Sudan.

Commercial energy consumption per person (gigajoules).

A gigajoule is 1,000 million (10^9) joules. A joule is a unit of energy. Energy is measured in joules.

Wealthy people with lots of money spend it on . . .	Earth's resources used up
food	
houses	
cars	
holidays	
electrical gadgets	

UNIT 8

The man in the picture started to get a bit worried about the future. 'We consume far too much,' he would say to his friends at work. 'We have to find ways to consume less energy,' he argued with his family.

1 Discuss this with your partner. Why exactly do you think this Californian man is worried? You might think of a number of different reasons.

2 Do you think *your* family could consume less energy? How?

Energy

- Energy is what makes things work. It comes from fuel.
- The human body needs energy and for people the fuel is food.
- Machines need energy. Some, like cars, get their energy from burning fuel directly. They use oil (in the form of petrol). Some get their energy from electricity which has to be made in power stations, usually by burning a fuel such as coal or oil.
- Energy is measured in joules. A human body needs between 600 and 700 joules per day.
- People in prosperous countries buy large amounts of energy so that they can run their homes and drive their cars.

Setting the scene

Using the Earth's riches

The Earth is a large planet, with a circumference of about 39,000 kilometres at the Equator. It is mostly solid rock, weighing in at about 6,000,000,000,000,000,000,000 – i.e. ($6,000 \times 10^{18}$) tonnes. People can only reach a very small amount of this rock – really only the rock in the Earth's crust – but there are still billions of tonnes of useful rocks and minerals within our reach.

Ever since people first began to live on Earth they have used its resources. Plants, animals, soil, water and rock: it was all there to be used, and people were inventive, finding more and more *uses* for the Earth's rock and minerals. For example, a black sticky substance in Pennsylvania (USA) was of limited use until in 1859 someone developed a way to refine it. This is when the *oil industry* started. If you owned land and found oil under it, you could become very rich indeed – after 1859!

As the consumption of the Earth's resources grows, big companies, like British Petroleum or Exxon, spend vast sums of money on better ways to find new resources in the Earth. In the future, even the deep ocean beds could be scraped clean of valuable rocks and minerals.

The Earth is not a 'bottomless pit'

Now, for the first time ever, it looks as if there could be a problem in the way people use the Earth's resources, especially oil. For example:

- Big companies are no longer finding *new* reserves of oil fast enough to keep up with the growing consumption of oil.
  and
- New supplies might only be found in fragile, remote places like Antarctica. Antarctica would be badly damaged if any oil were spilt there (see Unit 7).
  and
- The rich countries of the world now consume so much that they have caused another serious problem: pollution and waste disposal.

UNIT 8

The price of power

It is wonderful to have electricity for our televisions, washing machines, street lights and radiators. But to decide how to produce electricity in the future is not an easy decision to take. It is particularly difficult to decide whether or not to build more *nuclear* power stations which are able to produce huge amounts of electricity from just a small quantity of nuclear fuel. This article discusses why.

Blinded by Science? by Julian Coleman

The price of power

In a special report Julian Coleman investigates the cost of energy

THE MEDIA has been full of people saying that the nuclear industry is too dangerous and that nuclear plants ought to be shut down immediately. Unfortunately it is not that simple.

This is because if we shut down our nuclear power stations we would have to burn more coal and oil. And that would damage our health and the environment.

So long as we want to turn our heating on, drive our cars, cook meals or listen to the stereo we will also have to accept that some people will get sick or even die delivering the energy we want.

In fact the nuclear industry has a good safety record.

Radiation

And according to Health and Safety Executive figures only one person has died working in the nuclear industry. They point out that each of us is exposed to much more radiation from other sources. Most of this is natural radiation coming from rocks and from the sun. The other big contribution comes from medicine – X-rays for example.

Of course the big worry over nuclear power is that there could be an accident like the one at Chernobyl in Russia. That spread radiation over a wide area leaving it too contaminated to live on and killing maybe thousands of people.

The other big worry is what to do with the nuclear waste. Some of it will be radioactive and dangerous for many thousands of years. So far we have no way of getting rid of it safely.

Of course the dangers of nuclear power are worrying but there should be equal concern for the numbers of people killed mining coal and extracting oil.

According to figures from the Health and Safety Executive, in the same period as just one person died working on nuclear power, 63 people were killed working in coal mines and another 20 died in the oil and gas industry.

Piper Alpha

But then in 1988 there was also the Piper Alpha disaster. The Piper Alpha oil platform in the North Sea exploded killing 167 people.

And the story gets worse. Burning coal and oil in our power stations and cars has very serious effects on our health. A World Health Organisation (WHO) study in the United States showed that as many as 40,000 deaths per year could be saved if the US turned off all its coal and oil fired stations and switched to nuclear power.

The problem is that when fossil fuels (coal, oil and gas) are burned they create gases that pollute our air. Those gases can also cause smog. And it's those waste gases that make people ill.

The WHO also pointed out how damaging coal and oil are to our environment. A big problem is acid rain. Acid rain is made when waste gases from coal and oil power stations mix with water in the atmosphere and make it acid.

Acid rain damages trees, rivers and lakes and also makes our drinking water more dangerous. This is because there are chemicals in the soil (like aluminium) that ordinary rain just leaves behind. But acid rain can dissolve them and so the water that eventually reaches our taps is less pure.

To repair the damage that acid rain does is very expensive indeed. Damaged forests simply can't be repaired. The only solution is to stop creating acid rain and let nature repair the damage itself.

Cleaning up cars

But perhaps the best solution to cutting the health risks and pollution caused by power generation is to find ways of reducing how much energy we use altogether. We should use our cars less and use public transport instead. And we should insulate our homes better so as not to use as much energy. We could even learn to turn our heating down.

British nuclear power stations like this one at Calder Hall have a good safety record but is nuclear power really worth the risk?

Picture: British Nuclear Fuels

8·2 *From the 'Early Times', 22–28 March 1990.*

Are the oceans choking to death?

A traveller and explorer describes some of his recent memories like this:

The North Atlantic Ocean is like a basin of water that a child has played with, causing it to move in a clockwise flow. If the child drops a sweet wrapper into the water it will be the start of a grand cruise around the basin. The same happens to a piece of plastic dropped into the Atlantic. It will still be travelling long after we are forgotten.

Recently I sat becalmed on the deck of a schooner 1,300 kilometres west of the Azores, about as near to the middle of the Atlantic as you can get. I was surprised by the amount of plastic floating by. I have seen exactly the same in the high Arctic.

Plastic dropped in Britain's waters can first be taken south where, off the bulge of Africa, it will slide west to the Caribbean. Once there it turns north to join up with the Gulf Stream and moves back towards the British Isles at a rate of 20 kilometres a day.

On its way it may choke dolphins and seals but is not itself destroyed. Some of it will be pushed north past Norway and into the Arctic Ocean.

On the west coast of the island of Novaya Zemlya, one sunlit summer night, my experience of the wild natural beauty was tainted by the beaches. They were awash with the bright, brazen colours of plastic. It is here that the Atlantic finally dumps its waste. I picked up a washing-up liquid container and could still make out the print. It had been made in Newcastle upon Tyne.

© The Guardian

Extract from an article by R. Fannin in *Guardian Environment*, 28 September 1990

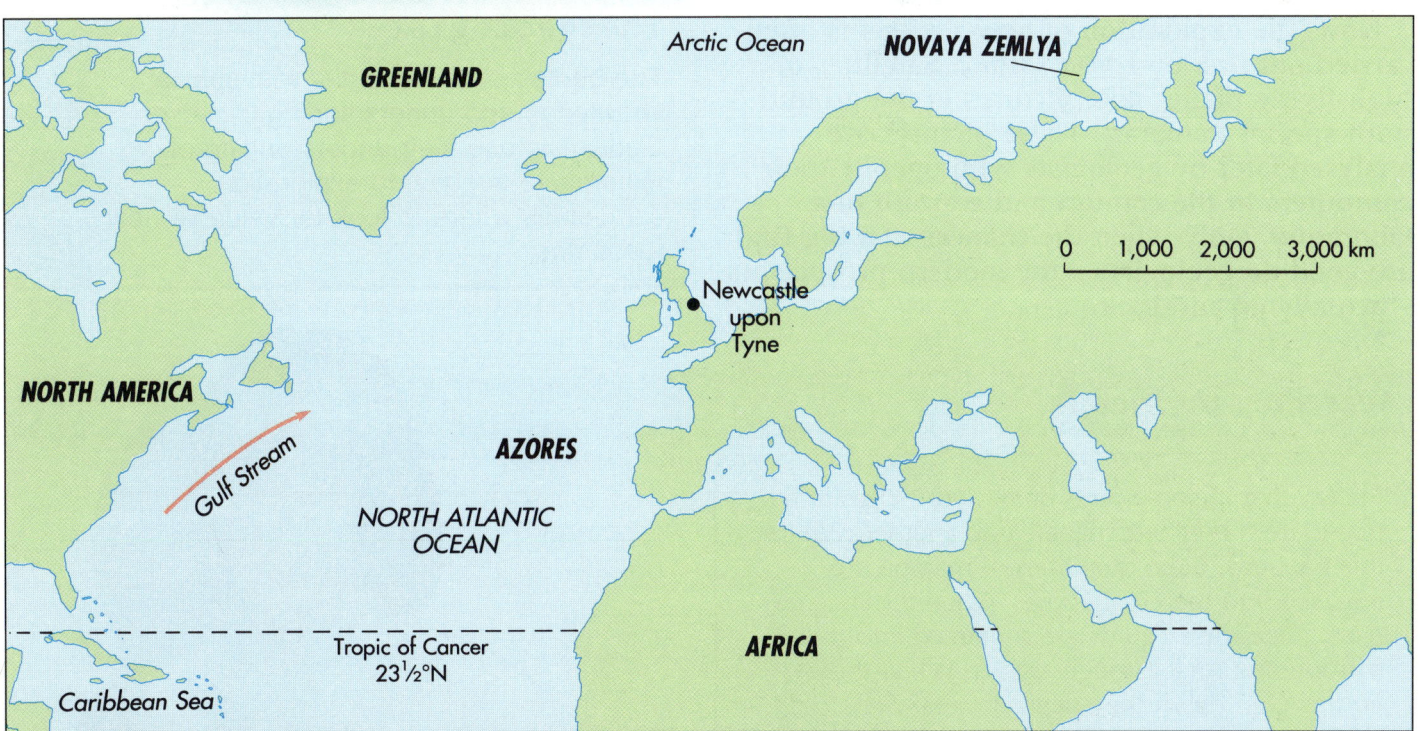

This unit is concerned with some very important matters – matters that affect the future of us all: can people find ways to use the Earth's resources more carefully? Can the Earth's resources be used less wastefully? Can the land, the sea and the air be protected from waste and pollution?

To help us investigate these things we have three key questions to answer:

▷ How does technology assist in mineral exploration?

▷ What are the hazards of burning fossil fuels?

▷ What is a sustainable way of life?

UNIT 8

▷ How does technology assist in mineral exploration?

These days, hundreds of millions of pounds are spent every year by companies searching for new sources of valuable rocks and minerals. Long gone are the days when a lone prospector would explore remote regions depending on his nose and luck as much as on his skills and understanding of geology.

Now, the exploration of new regions is often carried out first by *remote sensing*. Satellites or high-flying planes take pictures of the ground with special 'cameras'. These pictures are analysed later by geologists who operate their computers in the comfort and warmth of a laboratory. Only when the chances of a big find are good do geologists – the modern prospectors – actually go and look.

8·4 *A geologist using a computer in the search for minerals.*

> **The geologist**
>
> The geologist is a scientist with special knowledge and understanding of rocks. Geologists use their understanding of minerals to suggest to exploration companies where to look for valuable new resources.

Searching for metals

> I know that in some parts of the world the Earth's plates are subducted beneath one another. Where this happens, huge quantities of magma are released into the crust above. When the magma rises, metal-rich liquids are squeezed into the surrounding rock through cracks. When these liquids cool down they deposit metal-rich minerals in the cracks. For some rare metals only very small amounts collect in this way, but still they can be worth mining or quarrying – molybdenum, for example, can be worth mining when the rocks contain only 0.015% of the metal.
>
> I can tell where there might be minerals worth quarrying by examining satellite images. These pictures can show parts of the crust which have been altered by the heat of magma in the past.

Dr Ruth Stein.

> These areas are called *alteration zones*, and they show up in different colours on the satellite images.
>
> It's rather like being a detective, and the colours are my first clue. Opposite are some diagrams to show what alteration zones are.

UNIT 8

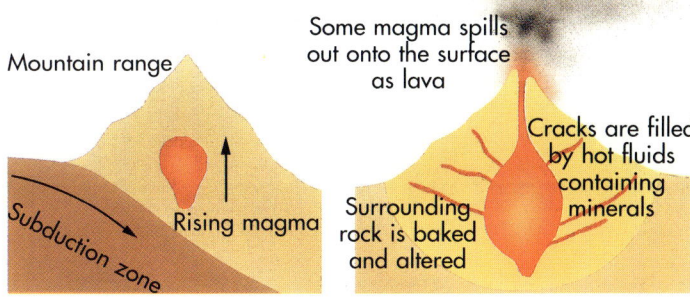

1 The story begins about 100 million years ago. Two plates collide, and one plate is forced below the other (subducted). Hot molten rock rises through the crust.

2 At the surface some magma may erupt forming a volcano. Rocks near the magma are heated and changed.

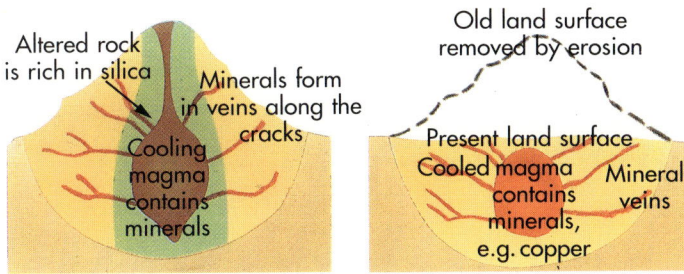

3 As the magma cools, minerals solidify in veins and in the magma body.

4 In time, the land surface is worn down. The centre of the mineral-bearing rock is near the surface.

Because these mineral deposits are near the surface, they can be mined by opencast methods. These kinds of deposits vary in size but they can provide 140–2,000 million tonnes of ore. For example, in a copper deposit, only 0.5% of this may be copper.

5 After mining.

8·5 *The formation of an alteration zone.*

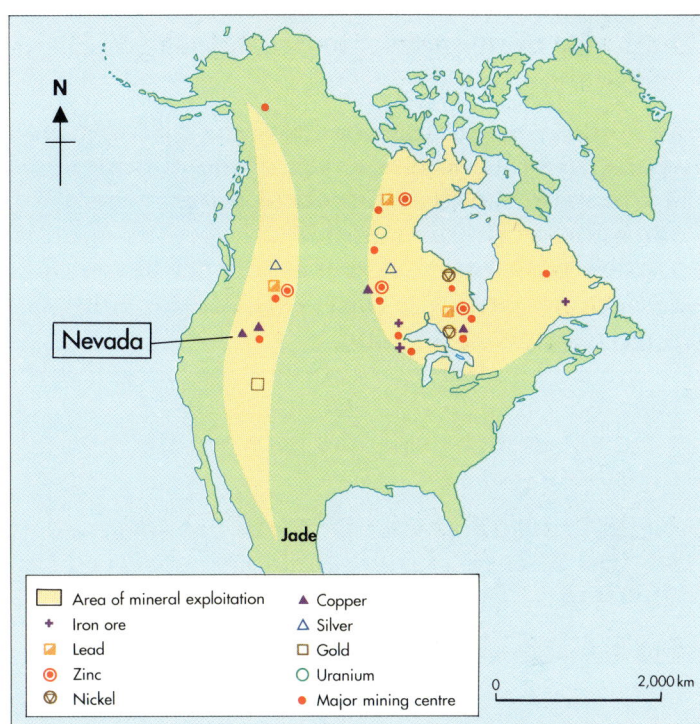

8·6 *Searching for copper in Nevada, USA. Here, large amounts of copper have been taken from the ground using a method called 'opencast mining'. This is the cheapest way to remove millions of tonnes of rock, which is then crushed and the copper taken out using a refining process. Often, a large ugly hole is left behind.*

Is there a use to which holes like this can be put? Or is this a permanent scar on the face of the Earth?

UNIT 8

You may need an atlas to help you with questions 1 and 2.

1a Find a world map to show the distribution (pattern) of known reserves of metal minerals.
b Compare the distribution of these minerals with the world distribution of
i areas which have had volcanic activity – either now or in the past – which therefore have igneous rocks, and
ii areas of sedimentary rocks with no volcanic activity.
c Do you notice any links between the distributions?

2 After reading what Dr Stein has to say, suggest a reason for the links you observed in question 1.

3 Look at this list of metals. Try to find out how these metals are used by people. Copy the table and write your answers in the second column.

Metal	Some uses
Gold	
Silver	
Molybdenum	
Copper	
Tungsten	
Uranium	

Looking at the evidence

The next page show two kinds of photographic evidence. These give us our first clues. Where would you start looking in the hope of finding a new copper deposit?

Class activity

Work in pairs for this activity. You will need a base map of the area and a piece of tracing paper. Your teacher will give you these items.
First, read this out loud to each other:

The two photographs opposite are images of the same piece of the Earth's surface, but they have been processed in different ways:

The *satellite picture* reproduces what the naked eye would see from a satellite or aircraft at a great height.

In the *false colour image* the area has been scanned by a special 'camera' and the information processed in order to see the colour image on the photograph. Different colours mean different things:

Using your tracing paper, your base map and referring to the false colour photograph, try the following exercise. You might need to read again what Dr Ruth Stein said on page 142.

- Unaltered volcanic rocks (basalts and tuffs) are shown as *blue to black* in colour.
- Altered rocks which are very rich in silica and other minerals are shown as *red-brown* in colour.
- Altered rock is shown in *magenta (deep red) to yellow* colours.
- *Green* areas are rocks which are rich in iron.

This is called a 'false colour image' because the ground is not really this colour!

UNIT 8

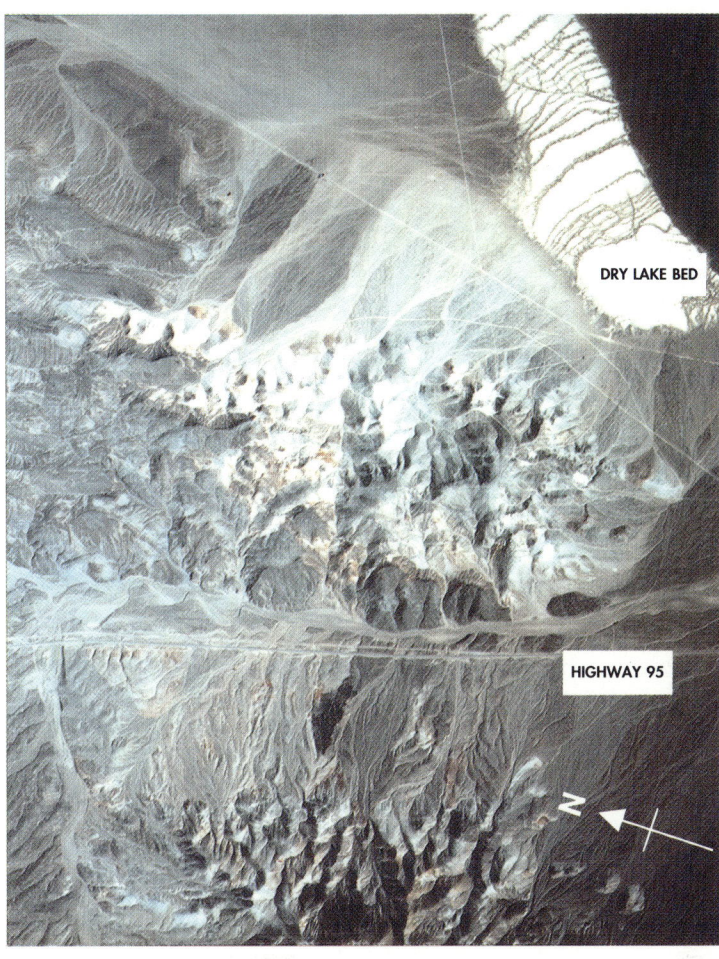

8·7 *A satellite picture of the copper deposit in Nevada, USA.*

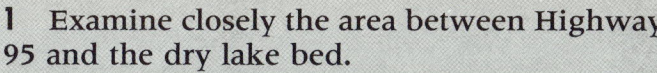

A false colour image of the same area. ▶

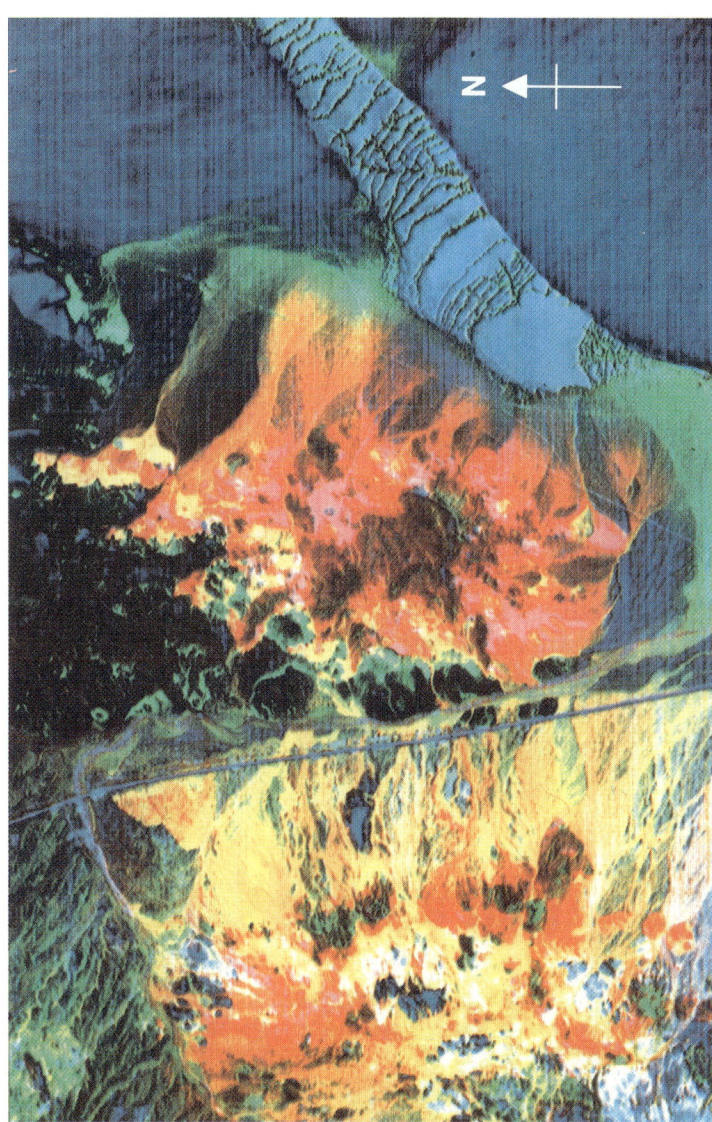

1 Examine closely the area between Highway 95 and the dry lake bed.

2 Look at the false colour image and refer to the key given in the notes you have just read on page 144. On your outline of the area, use coloured pencils to shade in four zones. Leave the other areas blank. You now have a simplified geological interpretation of the area. But what does it mean?

3 Working in pairs, you should decide on an area of 4 square kilometres which you would recommend for further exploration. Mark this on your base map.
Remember: 4 square km is a box with sides of 2 km each.

4 Let us assume that the area you have marked is chosen for development. If a company wants to carry out mining, it would need the following:
- Offices and services (e.g. canteens and showers)
- Access roads from the main highway.
- Crushing plant (a tall building, 250 m² in area)
- Concentrating plant (a lower building but 750 m² in area).

Mark and label these on your map, using a simple key.

5 Give a simple summary of how the landscape will change if the development goes ahead.

6 Modern methods of exploring the Earth make it harder for the Earth to hide its riches. People are able to take more and more from the Earth. Discuss what David Bellamy – a well-known scientist and *conservationist* – said about this.

a Do you agree with David Bellamy?
b Do you think it is possible for people to consume less of resources like copper? If so, how?

> Until now, most atlases have advertised the Earth as *real estate*, open to ownership and exploitation. Any 'unexplored' areas are there to be tamed, exploited, settled, made productive. This idea has become part of our 'civilisation'. All this we claim in the name of progress . . . resources are things to be grabbed while there are still some left. But there is now a lot of evidence to show that these activities are destroying the Earth. We need to use resources more wisely and remember that they are part of a living whole.
>
> Adapted from *The Gaia Atlas of Planet Management*, N. Myers (ed.), 1985

David Bellamy.

▷ What are the hazards of burning fossil fuels?

Who uses the world's energy?

The demand for energy – to heat homes, to run factories and for transport – is increasing all around the world. Some scientists think that the demand for some of the *fuels* we need, especially oil, is greater than the rate at which the oil companies can find new supplies.

Oil, like coal, is a *fossil fuel*. These fuels formed from the remains of plants and animals over millions of years. Once burnt, they cannot be replaced; they are *non-renewable* (see Unit 7).

All countries use fossil fuels, but some use much more than others. More than ten years ago an international group of experts produced this report.

> The use of energy in the world is grossly unbalanced . . . One American uses as much commercial energy as 2 Germans or Australians, 3 Swiss or Japanese, 6 Yugoslavs, 9 Mexicans or Cubans, 16 Chinese, 19 Malaysians, 53 Indians or Indonesians, 109 Sri Lankans, 438 Malians or 1,072 Nepalese.
>
> *North–South: A Programme for Survival*, The Brandt Report, 1980

Today, the gap between the rich and poor countries of the world is even wider. Willy Brandt, the author of the report, divided the world into the 'North' and the 'South'. The broken line on this map shows the boundary between the rich world and the poor world. The table of figures shows the amount of energy consumed in these parts of the world, and a prediction about the future.

World energy production, 1970–2020.

1970	1985	2000	2020
6.3	10.8	17.8	26.7

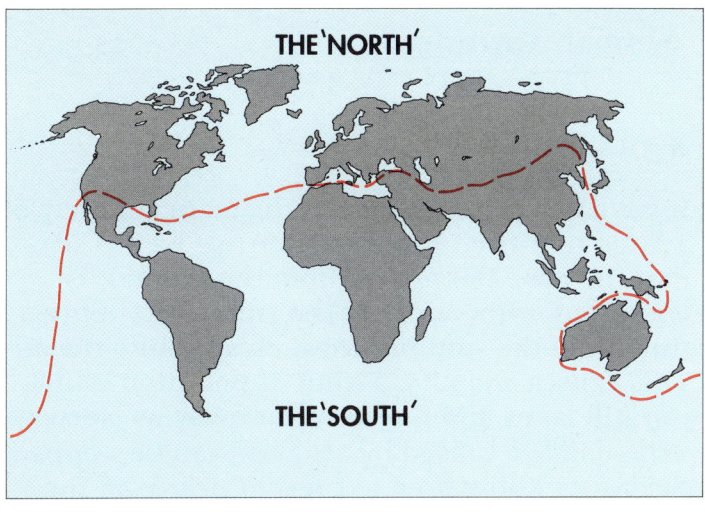

8·8 *The North–South divide.*

World energy demand, 1970–2020.

Part of the world	1970	1985	2000	2020
The North: countries in Europe, North America, former USSR, Japan, Australia	5.4	7.9	13.3	24.0
The South: countries in Africa, South America and most of Asia	0.8	1.2	2.4	6.0

Note: All these figures are in billions of tonnes of 'oil equivalent'.

Energy

Energy *predictions* are very difficult to make. The amount of energy people use depends on how much it costs, how easy it is to conserve (save), and technology (how efficiently fuels can be used, e.g. car engines are becoming more 'fuel efficient').

Energy *use* can be measured in two ways:
1 Directly: the units are *joules*. You may have used joules in science lessons. The amount of energy in different foods is also measured in joules. (See page 138.)
2 Indirectly: the units are usually *tonnes of fuel*. Different fuels have different amounts of energy in them (just like different foods). So scientists often use computers to adjust the figures for different fuels so that we can imagine they are the same: this is what 'tonnes of oil equivalent' means.

1 Construct a line graph which shows clearly the changes in world energy demand and production between the years 1970 and 2020. Your graph should show the growing gap in energy demand between the North and the South, and the time when demand may outstrip supply.

2 On a copy of the map above, locate and label each of the countries listed in the Brandt report (page 146).

3 Use the figures from the Brandt report, your map and graph, and any other materials or ideas which you may have, to design a large poster under the heading, 'Energy Futures: North and South'.

You must decide *why* you think there is an energy problem now or in the future. You must say what the problem is, and whose responsibility you think it is. What solutions may be possible? Your poster should show *what you really think*.

UNIT 8

Global warnings

Acid rain

If we had a close-up look at the main chimney of a large coal-fired power station we would see that the rim, 260 metres from the ground, is encrusted with sulphur. The rim collects only a tiny bit of the sulphur. Most escapes into the air. This causes *acid rain*, a kind of pollution which can kill lakes and forests as far away as Norway.

The damage caused by acid rain can be stopped. Scientists know how to prevent nearly all the sulphur escaping into the air. By 1996, the Drax power station will have desulphurisation equipment which will cut 90 per cent of sulphur emissions.

8·9 *Dilution: the solution to pollution? Coal-fired power stations in northern England.*

The man is repairing the chimney. The chimney is very high so that the pollution can be spread thinly over a large area. Notice the two cooling towers – these put only steam into the air. This power station is at Drax in Yorkshire. It uses coal that is mined nearby.

1 Imagine you have to explain to a younger sister or brother the causes and consequences of acid rain. Write down what you would say. Use the information opposite to help you.

2 To stop acid rain, everyone will have to pay a bit more for their electricity. Explain why this is so.

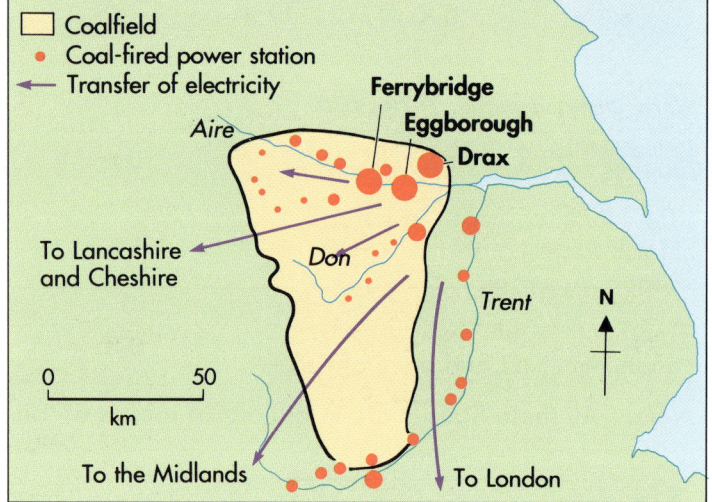

Acid rain – the facts

This page gives you some information on the causes of acid rain and its consequences.

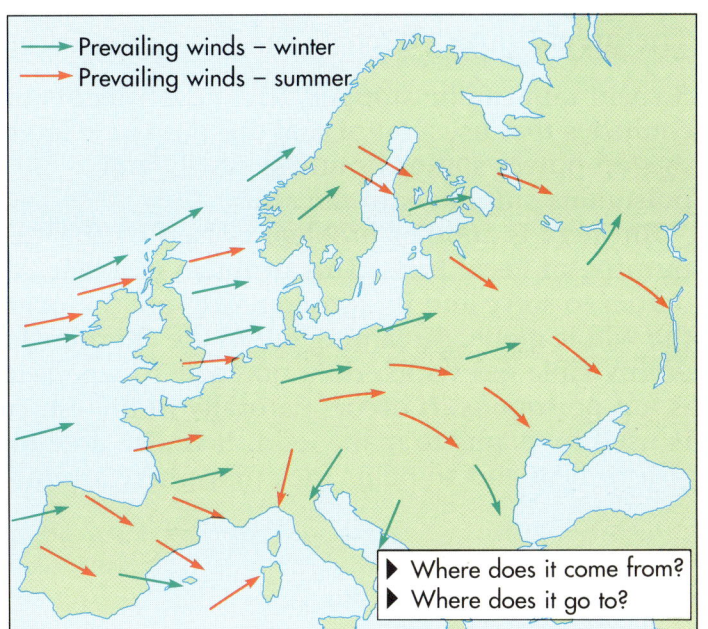

- → Prevailing winds – winter
- → Prevailing winds – summer

▸ Where does it come from?
▸ Where does it go to?

The effects of acid rain on forest trees.

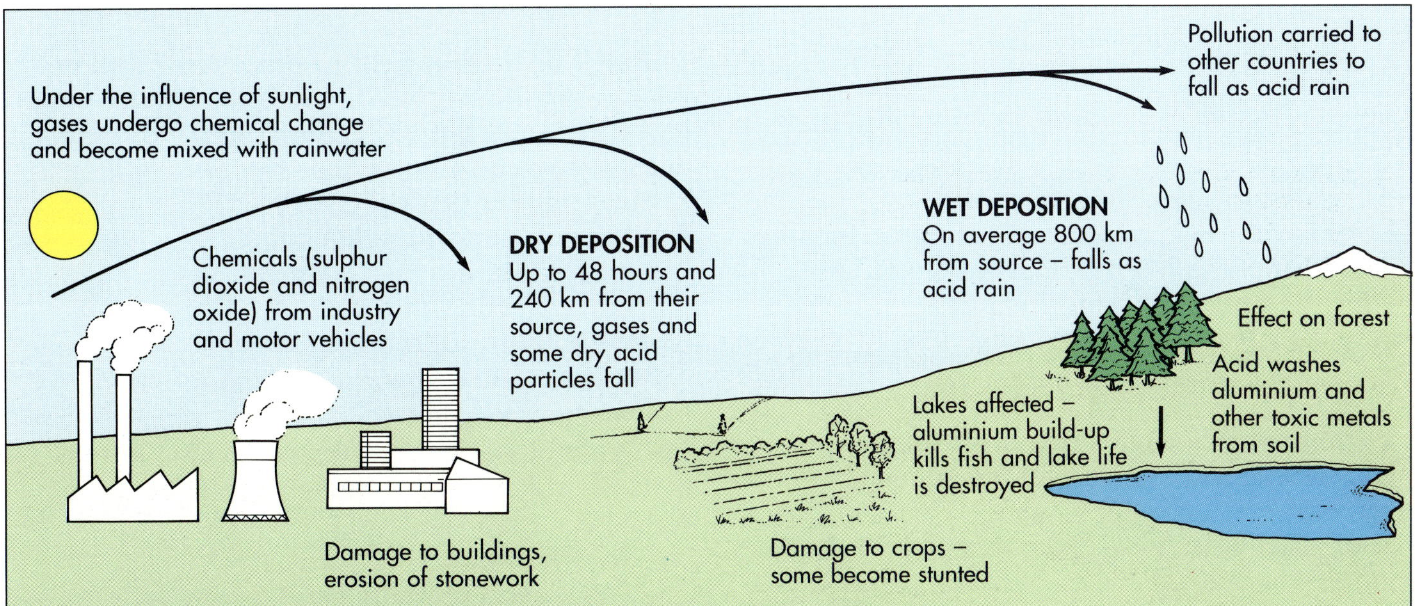

Under the influence of sunlight, gases undergo chemical change and become mixed with rainwater

Chemicals (sulphur dioxide and nitrogen oxide) from industry and motor vehicles

DRY DEPOSITION
Up to 48 hours and 240 km from their source, gases and some dry acid particles fall

Pollution carried to other countries to fall as acid rain

WET DEPOSITION
On average 800 km from source – falls as acid rain

Effect on forest
Acid washes aluminium and other toxic metals from soil

Lakes affected – aluminium build-up kills fish and lake life is destroyed

Damage to buildings, erosion of stonework

Damage to crops – some become stunted

The pH scale

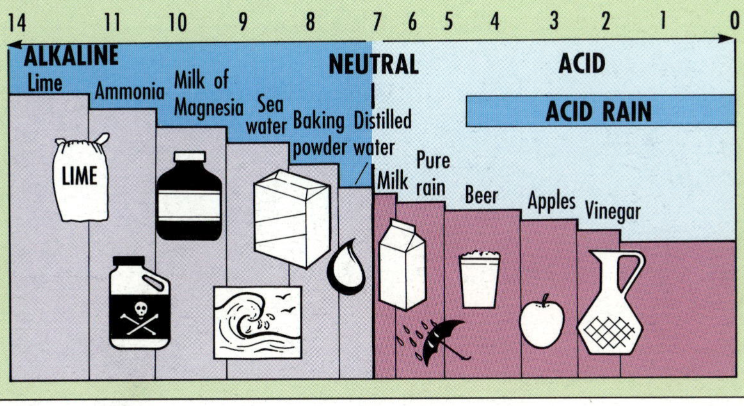

| 14 | 11 | 10 | 9 | 8 | 7 | 6 | 5 | 4 | 3 | 2 | 1 | 0 |

ALKALINE — NEUTRAL — ACID — ACID RAIN

Lime, Ammonia, Milk of Magnesia, Sea water, Baking powder, Distilled water, Milk, Pure rain, Beer, Apples, Vinegar

The pH scale is used to measure whether a substance is acid or alkaline. Each step from 7 to 0 means that the substance is 10 times more acid. So pH 6 is ten times more acid than pH 7 and pH 5 is 100 times more acid than pH 7. Normal pure rainwater is slightly acidic at around 5.6. On 10 April 1974, the rain at Pitlochry in Scotland was recorded at pH 2.4.

8·10 *Acid rain.*

UNIT 8

The greenhouse effect

So acid rain can be stopped. The governments of countries that use a lot of coal can pass new laws to stop power stations putting smelly and poisonous sulphur into the air.

But here is another problem caused by the burning of fossil fuels. This problem is much harder to solve and its consequences are felt over the whole globe. Streaming out of the chimney is an invisible gas which does not taste or smell. It is not poisonous. It occurs naturally in the air. It is used by plants to make food. It is also able to absorb heat and so helps the atmosphere around the Earth to act like a huge blanket, stopping warmth from escaping to outer space.

This mystery gas is carbon dioxide (CO_2). It is a very important 'greenhouse gas', which we have already discussed (see Unit 3, page 56–58). When coal is burnt in a power station, or gas is burnt in a kitchen cooker, or petrol is burnt in a car engine, a little bit more carbon dioxide is put into the air. There is no way to stop this from happening. More of the sun's heat will be absorbed by the air. The atmosphere will gradually become warmer.

Class activity

For this activity you need to be in groups of four.

A Quizzing the information

1 On your own, make sure you can remember everything you learnt about the greenhouse effect in Unit 3, and on this page.

2 In *pairs*, decide on five quiz questions about the subject of the greenhouse effect.

3 With another pair, take it in turns to ask your questions. Which pair answered the most correctly?
Your teacher may organise this activity into a whole class quiz.

B Looking back from the future

The aim of this activity is to write a letter from the future to someone living in the 1990s. Your letter should describe life in the year 2030, and explain to the person in the 1990s how *their* lifestyles will affect the future.

Looking into the future is very difficult. But imagine you are living in the year 2030. Assume that all the predictions stated on pages 151–52 prove to be correct.

It will be a great help to discuss all this in your groups to begin with, and then write your letter. Think about *all* of these questions before deciding what to write:
▶ How old will you be?
▶ What will your lifestyle be like?
  – Will you live with a partner?
  – Will you have children?
  – What will your job be?
  – How will you spend your leisure time?
  – Where will you live?
  – What possessions will you have?
▶ In what ways might life be very different in the year 2030?
  – Your house?
  – Transport, especially cars?
  – The price of electricity?
  – The price of food?
  – The weather?
▶ What problems will have resulted from the effects of global warming?
  – Flooding?
  – Drought?
  – Refugees?
▶ What *choices* could people living in the 1990s make which could reduce some of these problems?

Here some scientists give you information on the greenhouse effect, often described as 'global warming', and its possible consequences.

Greenhouse gases

In 1800 there were 280 parts per millions (ppm) of CO_2 in the air. Now there are 350 ppm. In the year 2030 there could be 560 ppm. There are other greenhouse gases too: chlorofluorocarbons (CFCs), methane, and nitrous oxide (N_2O). But CO_2 is the most important. This graph shows the proportion of the greenhouse effect that is caused by each of the gases.

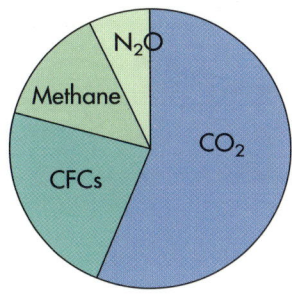

8·11 *Proportion of different greenhouse gases.*

Temperatures

Scientists believe that by the year 2030 the temperature of the globe may have increased by more than 1°C on average. But the temperature increase will not be exactly the same in all parts of the globe. For example, the Tropics may stay about the same, but the Poles could heat up by more than 10°C.

Sea levels

Huge glaciers and ice sheets in the Arctic or Antarctica would melt if the temperature increased.

Also, as water warms it expands. The oceans of the world will become deeper because they are warmer.

All in all, scientists believe that the sea level could rise by over 1 metre by the year 2030.

People at risk

Many people live on low river plains or deltas, where the soil is fertile. A good example is the Ganges Delta in India and Bangladesh, which already suffers occasional flooding from the sea. If the sea rises by 1 metre, most of this land would be destroyed. Around the world, 200 million people live in danger of losing their homes and livelihood by flooding.

8·12 *Victims of the 1991 floods in Bangladesh.*

UNIT 8

Global flooding in the next century

RISING SEA levels and creeping deserts will engulf the homes of more than 30 million people by the year 2100 unless the emission of greenhouse gases is controlled.

☐ **Christian Smith**

This is predicted in the latest report by United Nations scientists. They believe that if governments worldwide do not impose curbs on the offending gases, sea levels will rise by a metre. Small islands are particularly at risk. Eight to 10 million people live within one metre of high tide in Bangladesh, Egypt and Vietnam. Entire nations, such as the Maldives (in the Indian Ocean) and Tuvalu and Kiribati (both in the Pacific Ocean) would simply disappear.

Advancing deserts would ruin the agriculture of some of the poorest regions in the world. This is particularly the case in north Africa, where the Sahara is expected to become larger.

William Tegart, vice-chairman of the UN research team, said they were now looking for a political response. But, he added: 'There are clearly countries that are not wishing to proceed rapidly for a number of reasons.' Now that the Prime Minister has finally pledged to curb carbon dioxide emissions by the year 2005, America and Japan are the only leading industrial nations not to have made some commitment.

- **America emits 5.5 tonnes of carbon dioxide per head each year, Japan 2.2 tonnes and Britain 3 tonnes.**

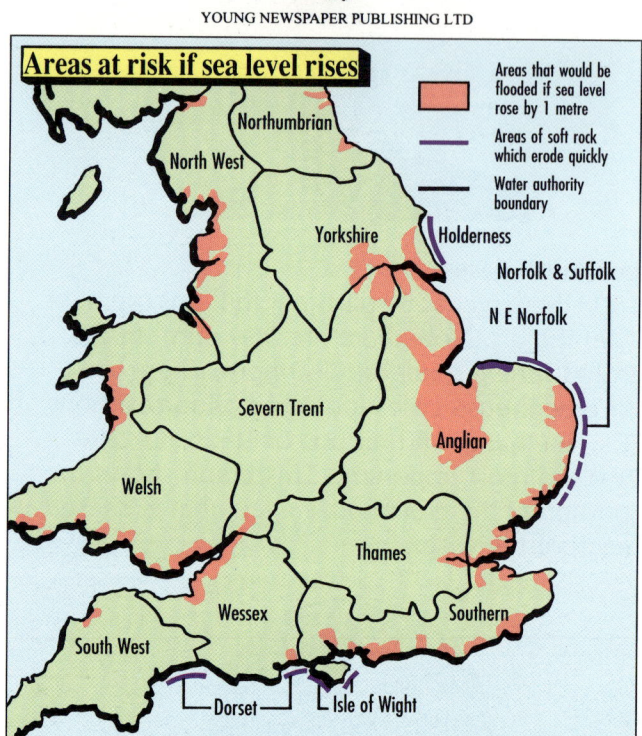

From 'The Indy', 7 June 1990.

Famine peril from warming spelt out

By Tom Wilkie
Science Editor

GLOBAL WARMING could cause widespread famines as warmer, dryer conditions cut production in the "bread-baskets of the world."

World grain production could fall by nearly a third within the next 40 years if carbon dioxide emissions continue at present levels, Professor Martin Parry, told a press conference in London yesterday. The "bread-baskets of the world" – regions such as the Great Plains of North America, the Ukraine and northern central Europe – would see smaller yields of all major crops. US exports of agricultural products could fall by as much as 70 per cent, and that country could lose £33bn a year.

Professor Parry warned that arid and semi-arid regions "could see their situation change dramatically for the worse. The human suffering that could result from famines (and) mass migrations is a problem for the whole world". Among such regions were Central America, South-east Asia, western Africa, and the Horn of Africa.

These warnings are based on predictions that mean global temperatures would increase by 1.1°C by about 2030. Professor Parry emphasised that his conclusions were projections of what could happen if no action was taken. But world leaders should not think in terms of "winners and losers" from global warming. There would be winners and losers even within one country, he said.

In the UK, the best estimate is a temperature rise of about 1°C by 2030. That would shift the limits of cereal production north by about 300km (200 miles).

Professor Parry said upland dairy farmers could suffer as pasture land is converted to arable use. Sunflowers and maize could be grown commercially in South-east England while the areas that grow malting barley – a major cash crop – would shift north and west.

It would be possible to grow vines over a larger area of the UK and Professor Parry, who is in the Geography Department at Birmingham University, noted that a 1°C increase would bring Birmingham's mean annual temperature up to that now enjoyed by Bordeaux.

From 'The Independent', 25 October 1990.

8·13 *Some possible effects of global warming.*

▷ What is a sustainable way of life?

A sustainable way of life is one that conserves the environment so that it can continue to support life. If the environment is damaged, and cannot be repaired, people must change what they do – or destroy the world in which they live!

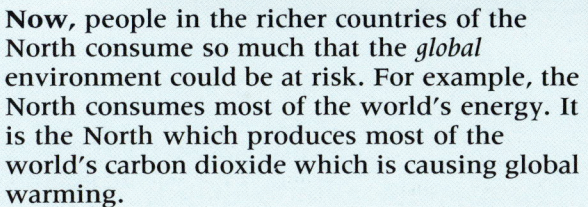
Bitterfeld.

In the past, people have destroyed *local* environments. At Aberfan in South Wales, for example, the waste from the coal mines was just dumped in a huge pile. One day in 1966, after heavy rain, the pile collapsed killing 144 people. And at Bitterfeld in Germany, the pollution from factories in the 1980s was so bad that trees and rivers died and people, especially the children, suffered from various illnesses.

Now, people in the richer countries of the North consume so much that the *global* environment could be at risk. For example, the North consumes most of the world's energy. It is the North which produces most of the world's carbon dioxide which is causing global warming.

Aberfan.

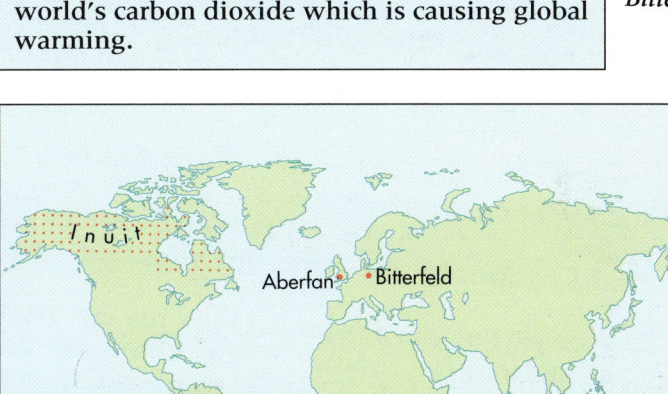

In the past, people could live in a sustainable way in local environments. In the 1990s some traditional communities still try to do this. For example, the Yanomami Indians know how to farm the tropical forest without destroying it. Inuit people in northern Canada know how to fish and to hunt without destroying their source of food.

Now, the global environment could be at risk. The modern way of life depends upon fossil fuels which are being burnt too quickly.

▸ Do people all over the world, but especially in the North, need to find a way to live that is sustainable *for the globe*?

▸ Do people all over the world, but especially in the North, need to find more sustainable ways of using the Earth's resources, and especially *energy*?

These questions lead to many more questions about *energy choices*. The following activity makes you examine some of these choices for Britain.

Yanomami.

8·14 *Disaster . . . or a sustainable way of life?*

Class activity

1 The challenge

This activity should be discussed in pairs first. Then individuals need to write a letter. You are Charlie Green, the Chair of a special committee appointed by the Prime Minister called the Energy Futures Committee. The Committee has two other members, Professor Geraldine Mann and Mr Bradwell Kraft MP. You need to advise the Prime Minister, and time is running out. Your meeting with the Prime Minister is soon and you must have an answer to the main question in the letter.

Dear Charlie

As you know, the Prime Minister has been very concerned over recent months about the Government's energy policy. We have some important decisions coming up which will affect future generations, and we must get these right.

This is why we want you to convene the Energy Futures Committee. This is a small committee which will, we hope, come to a rapid and clear decision. We want you to examine all aspects of *energy choices*. We want to know:

- Should we spend billions of pounds on tidal barrages?
- Should we spend more than we do at present on wind power?
- Should we build up nuclear power?

But our *main* question is about fossil fuel:

- Should this country burn less fossil fuel for electricity generation?

Of course, whether you answer 'yes' or 'no', we shall want you to advise us of your reasons and the consequences of your response.

The Prime Minister is looking forward to meeting you with your answer in one month's time, and thanks you for agreeing to this difficult and important task.

Yours sincerely

Bernard Wilson

Bernard Wilson
Private Secretary to the Prime Minister

2 The information

In pairs, discuss the Prime Minister's questions using the briefing sheets that follow on pages 156–157, and any extra information you can find. At the moment electricity in the UK is produced using fuels in the proportions shown in this pie graph.

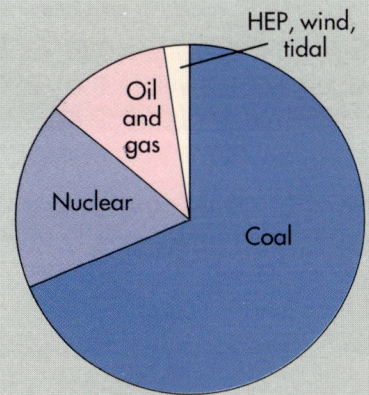

Sources of electricity in the UK.

3 The dilemma

During the final meeting of the committee, you ask the other members for their decisions. This is what they have decided:

Any cut in the amount of coal burnt in power stations in this country would have serious consequences:
- Thousands of miners would be made unemployed.
- The cost of electricity would go up.
- Factories which use a lot of electricity might have to close down.

Modern power stations can produce more electricity for less fuel because they are more efficient. These days, power stations are also clean.

I say, let us use the resources we have. In the UK we have huge supplies of coal. We should not keep it buried under the ground just because of unproven scare stories about global warming.

Professor Mann

Now, you must decide what *you* think. Will you go with Geraldine Mann or Bradwell Kraft?

Electricity is our most important gift: without it, industry, schools, hospitals – everything – grinds to a halt. But we must not make it from dirty fossil fuels any more. There are alternatives:
- *Nuclear* power is *clean* and does not depend upon fossil fuels. It does not produce CO_2. It is *reliable*, as the fuel (uranium) will not run out for at least 5,000 years. It is *safe* – over a year, more people die in mines or on oil rigs than in nuclear power stations!
- *Renewable* sources of energy are largely untapped and we should use these more, especially the huge reserves of tidal power and wind power which we have in this country.

I say, we must burn less fossil fuel. We can do so without reducing our electricity consumption. Let's leave the coal underground where it belongs and make a safer future.

Bradwell Kraft MP

4

Write a detailed letter to the Prime Minister with your final judgement. This should include
- your *answer* to the questions,
- the *reasons* for your answers, and
- the *consequences* of the choices you decide.

UNIT 8

Nuclear Power Briefing Sheet

Nuclear power in Britain
Britain has 19 nuclear power stations. The first to be built was at Sellafield in 1955. The 20th will be at Sizewell in the 1990s. Together they make about 20% of Britain's electricity.

Nuclear power in other countries
France takes 70% of its electricity from nuclear power stations.
Belgium takes 60%.
Finland, Spain, Sweden, Switzerland, all about 30%.

On the other hand:
The *USA* has not built a new nuclear power station since 1974.
Sweden has decided to stop all nuclear power production by the year 2010.
Italy voted to shut all its nuclear power stations in 1988.
Australia, New Zealand, Luxemburg, Denmark, Iceland, Ireland, Portugal and *Norway* have all decided not to have nuclear power stations.

Why are people worried about nuclear power?
- Nuclear power stations do *not* produce gases which cause acid rain.
- Nuclear power stations do *not* produce greenhouse gases.

In these ways, nuclear power stations are clean.
But people have always been concerned about safety. (What is it about the locations chosen for nuclear power stations which shows this concern?)
The concern is about radioactivity which can kill and can cause cancer.
These questions need to be asked:
- Can radioactivity escape from nuclear power stations?
- How can radioactive waste be disposed of safely?
- What would happen if a nuclear power station broke down or had an accident?

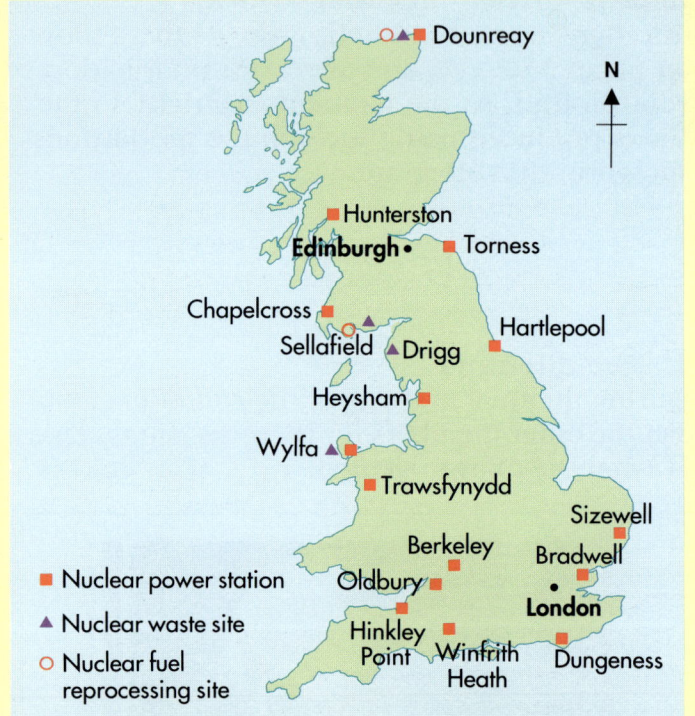

Nuclear sites in Britain.

The Chernobyl disaster
In 1986 there was a fire at the nuclear power station in Chernobyl, Ukraine. These maps show how radioactivity spread quickly to affect much of Europe. But the fact remains that in 1990, 96 new nuclear power stations were being built around the world.

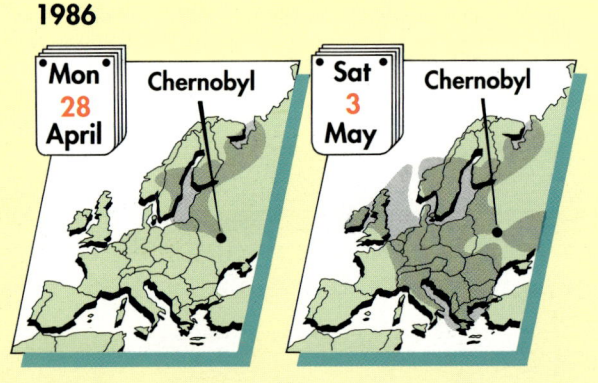

Renewable Energy Briefing Sheet

Tidal barrages

When the tide goes in or out, some strong currents can be caused, especially in fairly narrow estuaries like the Mersey or Severn. If the estuary is dammed, the currents can be squeezed through turbines to generate electricity. Some of these currents are very powerful: the tidal range in the Mersey estuary, for example, is more than 10 metres – that is, the water level changes by 10 metres about twice a day.

The newspaper report here is on the prospect of a Mersey tide barrage.

*From the 'Early Times',
30 November–6 December 1989.*

Wind power

Turbines can be turned to produce electricity by one of nature's 'free gifts': the wind. The wind is renewable – it will never run out. Britain is a windy country. So why don't we make more electricity from the wind?

The attraction of wind power

- Wind is plentiful and renewable.
- Capturing wind energy costs about the same as generating electricity from fossil fuels (and about half the cost of nuclear power).
- 20 per cent of Britain's electricity could be produced from 40,000 wind turbines.
- There is no pollution or waste disposal problem. Wind turbines are safe for animals and the land around can be farmed.

A wind farm.

Blinded by Science?

Mersey tide project

by Julian Coleman

A GROUP of large companies will tomorrow announce their plans to build a tidal barrage across the Mersey river estuary in Liverpool.

The barrage will harness the power of the tides to provide electricity. A barrage is really a dam across the river. As the tide flows in, gates in the barrage let the water flow upstream freely. But at high tide, the gates are shut holding the water back.

When the tide has gone part way out, the water trapped behind the barrage will be at a higher level than the water on the seaward side. Then the water is let out through turbines that generate electricity.

The idea isn't new. There are several old tide mills in this country — where tide power is used to drive a flour mill. There are also some big modern tidal schemes around the world. The biggest is at La Rance in France.

Many people find the idea of tidal power very attractive because it doesn't burn coal or oil and so does not create pollution or contribute to the greenhouse effect. Unfortunately it's not that simple. Friends of the Earth objected strongly to the proposed Severn Barrage because of the damage it would do to the ecology of the Severn Estuary — an area famed for its birdlife.

They told me they have an open mind about the Mersey project at the moment as they have not had time to study the scheme. But their worries are that the scheme would affect the amount of pollution in the river and that it might badly affect the birdlife too.

Affect the river

A spokesman for the Mersey Barrage company told me that they are spending a lot of money in order to discover how the scheme would affect the river and its wildlife.

He says they have found that the effects will not all be bad. The scheme should actually lead to an increase in the amount of fish in the estuary, for example. They are confident the benefits will outweigh the possible losses.

The main benefit, of course, would be clean electricity for many years, cutting greenhouse emissions and saving precious fossil fuels.

An artist's impression of one of the two proposed schemes for the Mersey tidal barrage

But do we want it?

- Modern wind turbines are not attractive to look at, especially when there are lots of them in a 'wind farm'.
- They could be built out of sight at sea, but this would make the electricity much more expensive.
- In October 1990, a plan for a wind farm in Powys in Wales, which could supply electricity to 6,500 homes, was opposed by conservation groups. The farm would cover 3 hectares of land. Each turbine would be 25 m high and 32 m in diameter. There would be 24 turbines in all, each producing 7 megawatts of electricity*. The Countryside Commission and the Council for the Protection of Rural Wales said that the farm would spoil views across Snowdonia National Park.

* 1 megawatt = 1,000 kilowatts. 1 megawatt can provide enough electricity to switch on 10,000 100-watt light bulbs.

Antarctica

The continent of Antarctica covers one-tenth of the world's surface. It is bigger than the USA. Nobody lives here permanently, and it is often called 'the last wilderness on Earth'. Many people believe that it should be made into a World Park in which any large building or mining developments would be completely banned.

Minerals

There are probably considerable reserves of oil and coal in Antarctica and the surrounding oceans. There may also be other valuable minerals here, like uranium, iron ore, copper and chromium. At present these minerals would be very expensive to mine, so actual mining is unlikely. However, many countries want to search for these resources. The effects of such activity on the Antarctic environment would be devastating.

The Antarctic Treaty

The Antarctic Treaty was proposed in 1959 as an attempt to control claims on Antarctic territory and to restrict developments such as mining in the continent. The Treaty came into force in 1961. It was reviewed thirty years later, in 1991, and a further 50-year ban on further development was imposed.

Today, five countries have major shares of Antarctic territory: Britain, Australia, Norway, France and New Zealand. Twenty-five countries have voting rights, including twelve countries that are signatory members. Other countries have made claims, and conduct research in the continent.

▶ What do you feel should be the future of this great unspoilt land?

The British Faraday Research Station on the Antarctic Peninsula.

This unit tries to help us look into the future and to imagine alternatives and choices that each of us may need to think about.

Sustainable lifestyles

Sustain means 'to continue'. Some aspects of modern life are very wasteful and damaging to the environment. Such aspects of modern life cannot continue for ever, they are not sustainable.

Conservationists are people who want to protect the natural environment against destruction. Conservationists are *not* people who are against progress. But they are against developments that are not sustainable.

Resources

Resources are materials used by people. Energy resources are particularly important because we need energy to keep warm, to run farms and factories, to transport goods and people – for nearly all aspects of our lives. Some resources are *renewable* – they replenish or regenerate.

Other resources are *non-renewable*. For example, fossil fuels are found in layers in sedimentary rocks. They are formed over millions of years from dead plant and animal matter. These deposits burn because they contain lots of carbon. They include coal, oil and natural gas. Once burnt, they are gone for ever.

Consumption

From the moment we are born we all begin to consume large quantities of the Earth's resources. To consume too much might not be sustainable. People (especially those in the richer North) could try to consume less or try to waste less. (You could discuss in class how you could begin to do this.) People in the poorer South – the economically developing countries – will probably want to consume much more in the future.

Global warming

One result of burning oil fuels is the production of carbon dioxide (CO_2). This is an important greenhouse gas. The more CO_2 there is in the air, the more the atmosphere absorbs heat. The atmosphere around the whole globe will warm up.

Global warming will have a number of consequences, but it is impossible to predict these with certainty.

Mineralisation

When rocks are forming, hot liquids and gases can cause concentrations of minerals (like metals, for example) to accumulate as the rocks cool down. Geologists (people who study rocks) are becoming better and better at tracking down areas of mineralisation. Planet Earth seems at the mercy of the exploration industries using the latest techniques, such as *remote sensing*, which allows surveying of the land from a distance. Not a square kilometre of the Earth escapes the remote eye of a satellite.

INDEX

acid rain 148–49
air mass 51–52
air pressure 53
Alaska 126–29
alteration zone 142–43
Antarctica 159
anticlines 122, 123
Aral Sea 96–99

Bangladesh 59
Bellamy, D. 145
Big Green 88
Brandt Report 147

California 86–95
carbon dioxide 56
carbon dioxide exchange 57
chalk rock 72
Chernobyl 107, 156
climate 46, 60
climate change 55, 60
climate patterns (UK) 47–49
clouds 50
coal 148
coffee 15–16
commercial farming 9, 10–11, 22
Common Agricultural Policy (CAP) 27, 28, 30
Commonwealth of Independent States (CIS) 105
condensation 50
consumption 137–38, 158
convectional rainfall 51

deficiency disease 25

ecosystem 119
electricity (UK) 148, 155
energy
    choices of 153–57
    consumption of 138
    cost of 140
    definition of 139
    in the USSR 109
    measures of 147
    renewable forms 157
    world demand for 147
environmental catastrophe 95–99
environmental disaster 117–18
equilibrium 120
Estonia 107
evaporation 67, 71
Exmoor 73–77
Exxon Valdez 132–33

false colour image 144–45
farming
    and climate 37
    and relief 33
    and soil 37
farming system 32
farming types 24
    high tech 38
    organic 41
food imports and exports 27
food surplus and shortages 29–31
fossil fuel 122, 146, 154

fragile environment 120, 128, 136
frontal rain 52
fronts 52
Frost Fair 44

geologist 123, 142
Gibbons, S. 130
glasnost 107, 116
global warming 58, 60, 152, 158
Gorbachov, M. 107, 116
greenhouse effect 56, 150–52
grocery shopping 26
groundwater 71, 72

habitat 118
high pressure 53

Ifuago 6
igneous rock 142–44
India 8–17
industry, types of 105

Kazakhstan 96
Kielder Reservoir 70

Lake Baikal 110–15
life expectancy 106
limestone rock 72
low pressure 53

Madapura (South India) 13–16
Maldive Islands 58
mineral resources (USA) 143
mineralisation 158
    see also alteration zone
monsoon 8, 45, 51
Moscow 102

Naipaul, V.S. 17
nuclear power 140, 156

oil
    demand for 125
    exploration for 123
    formation of 122–23
    in the North Sea 125
    transport of 121
oil drilling 124
oil pollution 131–32
oil protection measures 134–35
oil spills 120, 130–35
oil spot market 125

perestroika 107, 116
permafrost 127, 128
permeable rock 72, 122
Philippines 5–7
photosynthesis 119
polar climate 126–27
pollution 107–109, 110–15, 116, 131–32, 141
population density 104
population distribution
    former USSR 108
    UK 69
    world 104
population growth 104
porous rock 122
precipitation (world) 83

rainfall map (UK) 49
relief map (UK) 49
relief rainfall 50
remote sensing 142
resources
    consumption of 138, 158
    definition of 139, 158
    non-renewable 124, 136, 146
    renewable 124, 157
river channel 73, 75
River Colorado 90–92
river confluence 75
river delta 64
river floods 79, 80
river landscapes 78
river meanders 75, 76–77, 80
River Mississippi 63
River Ouse 65–67
rivers
    deposition by 80
    erosion by 76–77, 80
    transport by 64–65, 76
river sediment 64–65
river source 73, 75
River Thames 61
river valley 75

San Diego–Tijuana 93
sanitation 83
seismic survey 123
set-aside 31
soil erosion 17–21
soil humus 37
soil nutrients 37
Soviet Union (former) 101–16
subsistence farming 9, 11–12, 22
supertanker 136
sustainable lifestyles 153, 158
Swift, G. 65–67

Tees–Exe line 69
temperature maps (UK) 49
terraces 5, 6, 21
Tokyo 103
Trans-Alaska Pipeline (TAP) 129
Twain, M. 63–64

Uzbekistan 96

Vermuyden 65
volcanic activity 142–44

Washington DC 103
water
    consumption of 84–85, 100
    control of 79, 100
    pollution of 84, 93–94, 100
water cycle 67, 67–71, 80, 82
water projects 95
water supply 70, 88, 100
water table 71
water vapour 50
watershed 73
weather 46, 60
weather forecasts 53–54, 60